The Bill of Rights
A History in Documents

Congress OF THE United States,

begun and held at the City of New York, on

Wednesday, the fourth of March, one thousand seven hundred and eighty nine.

THE Conventions of a number of the States having, at the time of their adopting the Constitution, expressed a desire, in order to prevent misconstruction or abuse of its powers, that further declaratory and restrictive clauses should be added: And as extending the ground of public confidence in the Government, will best ensure the beneficent ends of its institution.

RESOLVED, by the Senate and House of Representatives of the United States of America, in Congress assembled, two thirds of both Houses concurring, That the following Articles be proposed to the Legislatures of the several States, as amendments to the Constitution of the United States; all, or any of which articles, when ratified by three fourths of the said Legislatures, to be valid to all intents and purposes, as part of the said Constitution; viz.

ARTICLES in addition to, and amendment of the Constitution of the United States of America, proposed by Congress, and ratified by the Legislatures of the several States, pursuant to the fifth Article of the original Constitution.

Article the first..... After the first enumeration required by the first Article of the Constitution, there shall be one Representative for every thirty thousand, until the number shall amount to one hundred, after which, the proportion shall be so regulated by Congress, that there shall be not less than one hundred Representatives, nor less than one Representative for every forty thousand persons, until the number of Representatives shall amount to two hundred, after which the proportion shall be so regulated by Congress, that there shall not be less than two hundred Representatives, nor more than one Representative for every fifty thousand persons.

Article the second..... No law, varying the compensation for the services of the Senators and Representatives, shall take effect, until an election of Representatives shall have intervened.

Article the third..... Congress shall make no law respecting an establishment of religion, or prohibiting the free exercise thereof; or abridging the freedom of speech, or of the press; or the right of the people peaceably to assemble, and to petition the Government for a redress of grievances.

Article the fourth..... A well regulated Militia, being necessary to the security of a free State, the right of the people to keep and bear Arms, shall not be infringed.

Article the fifth..... No Soldier shall, in time of peace, be quartered in any house, without the consent of the owner, nor in time of war, but in a manner to be prescribed by law.

Article the sixth..... The right of the people to be secure in their persons, houses, papers, and effects, against unreasonable searches and seizures, shall not be violated, and no Warrants shall issue, but upon probable cause, supported by oath or affirmation, and particularly describing the place to be searched, and the persons or things to be seized.

Article the seventh..... No person shall be held to answer for a capital, or otherwise infamous crime, unless on a presentment or indictment of a grand jury, except in cases arising in the land or naval forces, or in the Militia, when in actual service in time of War or public danger; nor shall any person be subject for the same offence to be twice put in jeopardy of life or limb; nor shall be compelled in any criminal case, to be a witness against himself; nor be deprived of life, liberty, or property, without due process of law; nor shall private property be taken for public use, without just compensation.

Article the eighth..... In all criminal prosecutions, the accused shall enjoy the right to a speedy and public trial, by an impartial jury of the State and district wherein the crime shall have been committed, which district shall have been previously ascertained by law, and to be informed of the nature and cause of the accusation; to be confronted with the witnesses against him; to have compulsory process for obtaining witnesses in his favor, and to have the assistance of counsel for his defence.

Article the ninth..... In suits at common law, where the value in controversy shall exceed twenty dollars, the right of trial by jury shall be preserved, and no fact, tried by a jury, shall be otherwise re-examined in any Court of the United States, than according to the rules of the common law.

Article the tenth..... Excessive bail shall not be required, nor excessive fines imposed, nor cruel and unusual punishments inflicted.

Article the eleventh. The enumeration in the Constitution, of certain rights, shall not be construed to deny or disparage others retained by the people.

Article the twelfth. The powers not delegated to the United States by the Constitution, nor prohibited by it to the States, are reserved to the States respectively, or to the people.

Frederick Augustus Muhlenberg, Speaker of the House of Representatives.

John Adams, Vice-President of the United States, and President of the Senate.

ATTEST,

John Beckley, Clerk of the House of Representatives.

Sam. A. Otis, Secretary of the Senate.

The Bill of Rights
A History in Documents

John J. Patrick

OXFORD
UNIVERSITY PRESS

This book is dedicated to my wife, Patricia,
our daughters, Rebecca and Barbara, and our
granddaughters, Rachel and Abigail.

OXFORD
UNIVERSITY PRESS

Oxford New York

Auckland Bangkok Buenos Aires Cape Town
Chennai Dar es Salaam Delhi Hong Kong Istanbul Karachi
Kolkata Kuala Lumpur Madrid Melbourne Mexico City Mumbai
Nairobi São Paulo Shanghai Singapore Taipei Tokyo Toronto

Copyright © 2003 by John J. Patrick

Design: Sandy Kaufman
Layout: Loraine Machlin
Picture Research: Lisa Barnett

Published by Oxford University Press, Inc.
198 Madison Avenue, New York, New York 10016
www.oup.com

Library of Congress Cataloging-in-Publication Data
Patrick, John J.
The American Bill of Rights : a history in documents / John J. Patrick.
p. cm. — (Pages from history)
Summary: Uses contemporary documents to explore the history of
the first ten amendments to the U.S. Constitution, the British traditions
on which they were based, and their impact on American society.
Includes bibliographical references and index.
ISBN-13 978-0-19-510354-0 (alk. paper)

1. United States. Constitution. 1st–10th Amendments—History—
Juvenile literature. 2. Civil rights—United States—History—Juvenile
literature. [1. United States. Constitution. 1st–10th Amendments. 2.
Civil rights. 3. Constitutional amendments.] I. Title. II. Series.
KF4750 .P274 2002
342.73'085—dc21
2002006294

Printed in the United States of America on acid-free paper

5 6 7 8 9 10

Cover: *People enter the U.S. Supreme Court
on December 11, 2000, to hear arguments before
the Court about the constitutionality of the
recount of Florida votes in the 2000 Presidential
election. The recount was ordered by the Florida
Supreme Court on December 8.*

Frontispiece: *A handwritten copy of the Bill
of Rights*

Title page: *An etching of the Supreme Court
building in Washington, D.C.*

Contents

6   WHAT IS A DOCUMENT
8   HOW TO READ A DOCUMENT
11   INTRODUCTION

Chapter One
15   THE ROOTS OF
       AMERICAN RIGHTS
20   Transporting Rights to the
       American Colonies
24   New Charters of Rights
30   A New Philosophy of Rights

Chapter Two
35   RIGHTS AND REVOLUTION
       IN AMERICA
41   American Protests
45   Resolutions in Defense of Rights
47   The Declaration of Independence

Chapter Three
53   THE BIRTH OF THE
       BILL OF RIGHTS
58   Rights in the New American States
63   Rights in the U.S. Constitution
67   Constitutional Amendments

Chapter Four
73   THE BILL OF RIGHTS
       MARGINALIZED
80   The Sedition Act Controversy
82   Landmark Opinions of
       Chief Justice Marshall
84   Contradiction of Ideals
91   The Dred Scott Case

Chapter Five
97   RIGHTS RENEWED AND DENIED
101   Rights Proclaimed and Restricted
106   Rights Denied to Women
110   Rights Denied to African Americans

Chapter Six
117   A RESURGENCE OF RIGHTS
123   Freedom and National Security
       during World War I
126   The Incorporation Doctrine
134   Issues of Freedom during World War II

Chapter Seven
141   NATIONALIZATION OF
       THE BILL OF RIGHTS
148   Standards for Using the
       Incorporation Doctrine
153   Equal Protection of the Laws
155   National Standards on Rights
       of the Accused

Chapter Eight: Picture Essay
161   POLITICAL CARTOONS ON THE
       RIGHT TO BEAR ARMS

Chapter Nine
171   CONSENSUS AND
       CONTROVERSY
177   The Rights to Privacy and Abortion
182   Limits to Freedom of Expression
186   The Government and Religion
192   An American Heritage

194   TIMELINE
197   FURTHER READING
198   TEXT CREDITS
200   PICTURE CREDITS
201   INDEX

What Is a Document?

To the historian, a document is, quite simply, any sort of historical evidence. It is a primary source, the raw material of history. A document may be more than the expected government paperwork, such as a treaty or passport. It is also a letter, diary, will, grocery list, newspaper article, recipe, memoir, oral history, school yearbook, map, chart, architectural plan, poster, musical score, play script, novel, political cartoon, painting, photograph—even an object.

Using primary sources allows us not just to read *about* history, but to read history itself. It allows us to immerse ourselves in the look and feel of an era gone by, to understand its people and their language, whether verbal or visual. And it allows us to take an active, hands-on role in (re)constructing history.

Using primary sources requires us to use our powers of detection to ferret out the relevant facts and to draw conclusions from them; just as Agatha Christie uses the scores in a bridge game to determine the identity of a murderer, the historian uses facts from a variety of sources—some, perhaps, seemingly inconsequential—to build a historical case.

The poet W. H. Auden wrote that history was the study of questions. Primary sources force us to ask questions—and then, by answering them, to construct a narrative or an argument that makes sense to us. Moreover, as we draw on the many sources from "the dust-bin of history," we can endow that narrative with character, personality, and texture—all the elements that make history so endlessly intriguing.

Cartoon
This political cartoon addresses the issue of church and state. It illustrates the Supreme Court's role in balancing the demands of the 1st Amendment of the Constitution and the desires of the religious population.

Illustration
Illustrations from children's books, such as this alphabet from the New England Primer, tell us how children were educated, and also what the religious and moral values of the time were.

In *Adam's* Fall
We Sinned all.

Thy Life to Mend
This *Book* Attend.

The *Cat* doth play
And after slay.

A *Dog* will bite
A Thief at night.

An *Eagles* flight
Is out of sight.

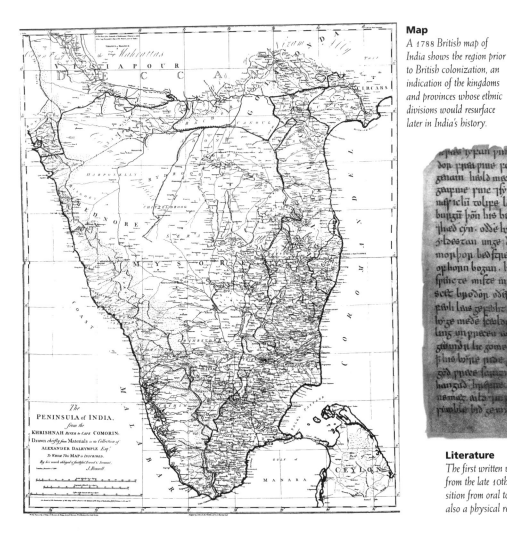

Treaty

A government document such as this 1805 treaty can reveal not only the details of government policy, but information about the people who signed it. Here, the Indians' names were written in English transliteration by U.S. officials; the Indians added pictographs to the right of their names.

Map

A 1788 British map of India shows the region prior to British colonization, an indication of the kingdoms and provinces whose ethnic divisions would resurface later in India's history.

Literature

The first written version of the Old English epic Beowulf, from the late 10th century, is physical evidence of the transition from oral to written history. Charred by fire, it is also a physical record of the wear and tear of history.

How to Read a Document

Historians read and interpret documents to find evidence about people, places, and events of the past. What one learns from a document, however, depends upon how carefully and systematically one examines it. Historians ask questions to determine what the document does or does not reveal.

It is necessary to identify the authorship, source, purposes, and subject of the document. So one asks: Who was the author or creator of the document? When and where was it created? Why was it created? Who was the intended audience? What was the author's message? What was he or she trying to say, to whom, and for what purpose or effect?

When reading and interpreting a document, it is important to examine the context in which it was created. So one asks: What is the period or era of history in which this document was created? What events, persons, and ideas of the period are related to the document? How do these relationships enhance our interpretation and understanding of the document? How can this document be related to other documents of the era to yield a broader and deeper understanding of particular people, places, and events? Why is the document significant or important to an inquiry about a particular period of history?

In order to detect subtle biases or other nuances, one must read a document creatively. Historians try to read "between the lines" of a written document or "beyond the images" in a picture in order to discern clues and messages that are not stated or depicted directly. They must also refrain from reading their own biases into an interpretation of a document in order to avoid gross distortions of the author's intentions or message.

Caricature

Political cartoonists often use caricature or exaggeration in their portrayal of people or events to emphasize or highlight their message. This political cartoon, for example, is a caricature of a fight in the U.S. House of Representatives. The fight started after Roger Griswold, Federalist Party representative from Connecticut, insulted Matthew Lyon, Republican Party representative from Vermont. In this cartoon, Griswold wields a cane and kicks Lyon, who grabs Griswold's arm and threatens to hit him with fireplace tongs.

Context

By placing the Griswold-Lyon fight in the context of the birth of American political parties in the 1790s, the Federalists and Republicans, we can read and interpret this political cartoon more meaningfully. In 1798, there was a Federalist majority in Congress and a Federalist, John Adams, was President. The Republicans criticized the Federalist Party leaders severely and relentlessly. The Federalists responded by passing a law, the Sedition Act of 1798, to limit criticism of the government in the interest of national security. Matthew Lyon was one of several Republicans arrested and convicted under terms of the Sedition Act.

Text

The text in this political cartoon, which appears below the picture, identifies the participants in the fight: "He in a trice struck Lyon thrice/Upon his head, enrag'd sir,/Who seiz'd the tongs to ease his wrongs,/And Griswold thus engag'd, sir." At the bottom right side are these words: "Congress Hall, in Philada. [Philadelphia, Pennsylvania] Feb. 15. 1798," which provide the date and place of the confrontation.

Subject

A photographer's subject is chosen to convey a particular message or point of view. In this picture, the message is patriotism. These public school students in a New York City classroom express loyalty to the United States of America. They ceremoniously stand at attention, salute the flag, and seem to be reciting the pledge of allegiance. The photographer's image is a solemn and respectful portrayal of traditional civic behavior.

Source

The source of a photograph may reveal the purposes and intended audience of the photographer. This picture, for example, was made in January 1943 for the Office of War Information of the United States Government. It apparently was used to convey an image of patriotism and national loyalty during a time of national crisis, World War II, in which the United States had been involved since December 1941.

Context

This photograph can be interpreted more insightfully if the context is examined. This photograph was not only taken during the U.S. involvement in World War II, it was also taken during a Supreme Court controversy about flag-saluting ceremonies. In *Minersville School District* v. *Gobitis* (1940), the U.S. Supreme Court upheld a school district regulation requiring children to participate in flag-salute ceremonies despite the claims from a religious group that the requirement violated 1st Amendment rights. Three years later, in *West Virginia Board of Education* v. *Barnette* (1943), the Court overruled the *Gobitis* decision. This photograph may have been intended to influence public opinion about such ceremonies in public schools at a time when they were at issue in federal courts.

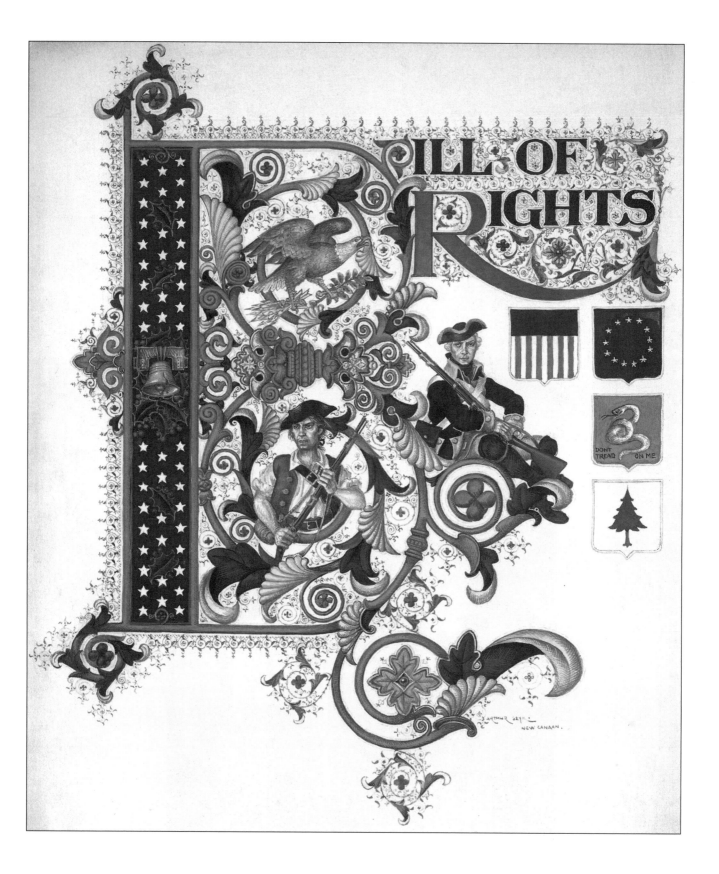

ILL OF RIGHTS

Introduction

An Introduction to the Bill of Rights

From their founding era until today, Americans have believed that the highest purpose of government is protection of the rights of the people to whom it is accountable. Commitment to ideals about rights to liberty and equality is the foundation of an American national identity. These ideals are the core by which unity is sustained among the extraordinarily diverse people of the United States of America.

The first government of the United States, under the Articles of Confederation, was so weak and ineffective that the rights of the people were at risk. The government seemed too weak to protect the people's safety and security against enemies from foreign countries or lawbreakers within the United States. Americans realized they needed a government strong enough to protect them against threats to their rights to life, liberty, and property.

In 1787–88, in response to their crisis of government under the Articles of Confederation, Americans made and ratified a new constitution and government, which most thought would be sufficiently strong to guarantee their rights, but not strong enough to violate them. If the government under the 1787 Constitution could be simultaneously empowered and limited by law, Americans believed it would "secure the Blessings of Liberty" for them and their descendants.

In 1791, citizens of the newly independent nation ratified a Bill of Rights, Amendments 1–10 of their Constitution, which specified certain rights that the government is supposed to protect and never to

This drawing by artist Arthur Szyk shows the Bill of Rights in concert with various symbols of freedom in United States history.

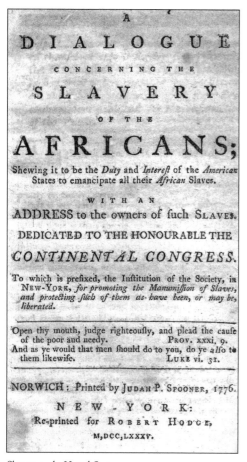

Slavery in the United States was a gross contradiction of the ideals about freedom and equality put forth in the new nation's founding documents. This title page of a widely distributed 1776 publication asserts that it is the "duty and interest of the American states to emancipate all their African slaves."

abuse. Among these constitutionally guaranteed rights are freedom of speech, free exercise of religion, freedom to own and use property, freedom of assembly, and due process of law. These examples are only a few of the many rights to freedom, equality, and justice anchored in the Constitution and Bill of Rights that Americans claim as their heritage.

By our standards today the rights of people in the founding era seem stunted and flawed. Slavery, for example, was a cruel contradiction of the Bill of Rights, which afflicted the founding of the republic and its subsequent development. Further, the proportion of Americans who enjoyed fully the rights to freedom of the founding era was a small minority of the country's population. The constitutional rights guaranteed to most adult white males were not equally applicable to women, African Americans, and various indigenous peoples.

Nonetheless, the proportion of Americans with the right to vote or otherwise participate in their governance was unparalleled in the world of the 1780s. And constitutional guarantees of rights we take for granted today—such as freedom of conscience and speech, security against unwarranted seizures of property or invasion of privacy, and fair legal procedures for persons accused of crimes—were rare or nonexistent outside the United States in the world of the 18th century. Thus, by the world standards of their own times, the founders of the United States had broken new ground and planted new seeds for an exceptional growth and development of individual rights during the next two centuries.

The ideas about rights in the founding documents of the United States have been the standards to which unjustly treated persons and groups have appealed for redress of their grievances. From the founding of the republic until today, Americans with justified grievances about unfair treatment have pointed to statements about rights in the Declaration of Independence and the Bill of Rights and demanded that the U. S. government and citizens be true to the country's highest standards. These demands often sparked controversy and conflict. Individuals and groups unjustly denied their constitutional rights often had to confront and overcome resistance to their claims for justice. And public controversy about rights has continued. But so has progress toward narrowing the gap between America's grand ideals and its sometimes disappointing realities.

To understand the sources of this strong American concern about rights one must first look back to England in the 13th through the 17th centuries, where the origins of the American tradition on rights began. Next one must turn to North America's colonial era. During the 17th and 18th centuries the English tradition on rights, planted by founders of 13 colonies along the Atlantic coast from Massachusetts to Georgia, was maintained, modified, and in some ways superseded. Thus, the birth of the United States in 1776 and the founding of its federal and constitutional republic laid the foundations for the development of rights during the next two centuries.

From 1776 to the present, Americans have generated and responded to public issues about constitutional rights. Debates about the Bill of Rights were a very prominent part of the public agenda during most of the 20th century. A consequence of these constitutional controversies has been a great expansion of the range and reach of the Bill of Rights in the lives of Americans.

The documents that follow provide various accounts of the origins and development of rights in the United States. The voices and perspectives of diverse individuals and groups are presented in responses to the controversies and conflicts—the provocative public issues and debates—that have marked the development of constitutional rights in the United States. Through an examination of alternative viewpoints and diverse ideas in these primary sources, one may gain a larger understanding and appreciation of the centrality of rights and the Bill of Rights in the American civic and political tradition.

Leaders of the August 28, 1963, March on Washington demanded an end to unjust discrimination against African Americans. They pointed to violations of the Bill of Rights and the nation's highest ideals and urged that civil rights and liberties should be enjoyed equally by all Americans.

Chapter One

The Roots of American Rights

S ettlers from the British Isles brought to America their heritage of rights under law. When the English founded their colonies along the Atlantic coast of North America, they established governments to secure the rights they had possessed in their old country. A number of 17th- and 18th-century English philosophers and writers also contributed significantly to the development of American ideas and institutions on rights. "Let an Englishman go where he will, he carries as much of law and liberty with him as the nature of things will bear. " These words of Richard West, counsel to England's Board of Trade, expressed a common view of 17th-century settlers of England's American colonies.

In time, the Americans developed rights under law far beyond their English inheritance, which led them in 1776 to declare independence from the mother country. However, the Bill of Rights in the Constitution of the United States of America has English roots to which it is connected inextricably. Three English charters of liberty are centrally important in the development of English and American rights under law: (1) the 1215 Magna Carta, (2) the 1628 Petition of Right, and (3) the 1689 Bill of Rights. These three charters were legal limitations on the power of the English monarchy that eventually tilted the balance of power in government toward the Parliament, the representatives of the people. Limits on the monarch's power were accompanied by recognition of the Parliament's power and the people's rights in written documents. These rights of Englishmen were carried to North America in colonial charters issued by the Crown.

The story of American rights begins with a dramatic event in England on June 15, 1215. King John faced an angry band of barons and clergy at Runnymede, a flat meadow along the Thames River. They argued that the king had abused his power and violated long-standing traditions of his realm. They placed their demands for reform in writing before the king and threatened to fight him unless he agreed with them. King John did not want to give in to his opponents. His misrule, however, had cost him the allegiance of most English subjects, particularly leaders among the nobility, the church, and the townspeople. So King John signed the document, known as the Magna Carta—the Great Charter.

The Magna Carta and the legal tradition associated with it came to North America in 1607, when the first permanent English colony was planted along the James River in Virginia, several miles inland from Chesapeake Bay. This settlement was called Jamestown in honor of King James I of England and Scotland, who had issued the colonial charter for this venture. The First Charter of Virginia set forth the legal terms of this colony by which a government was to be established, laws made and enforced, and the rights of individuals secured.

After Jamestown in Virginia, the next permanent English settlement in North America was at Plymouth on the coast of Massachusetts. On September 6, 1620, 102 emigrants—the people we call the Pilgrims—crowded aboard the *Mayflower* in Plymouth, England, and set sail for North America. They arrived off the shores of New England on November 11. Prominent among the *Mayflower* passengers were Separatists, followers of the religious ideas of John Calvin, who had separated from the Church of England. The English government persecuted the Separatists for trying to practice their religion, so they looked for a new place to live where they could set up their own church and practice their religion freely.

Part of the Pilgrims' dream was to govern themselves. To this end, they drafted a remarkable document, the *Mayflower Compact* signed November 11, 1620, to proclaim their need to elect leaders and obey laws made for the good of the community. This was the first of many similar compacts made by English settlers and their descendants to establish the rule of law, based on popular sovereignty (the consent of the governed), in the American colonies.

From the time of Magna Carta until the 1600s, the rising power of Parliament had gradually limited the king of England's power. For example, the king was not supposed to tax his subjects without the consent of Parliament, which was made up of representatives of the nobility and the common people. However, in

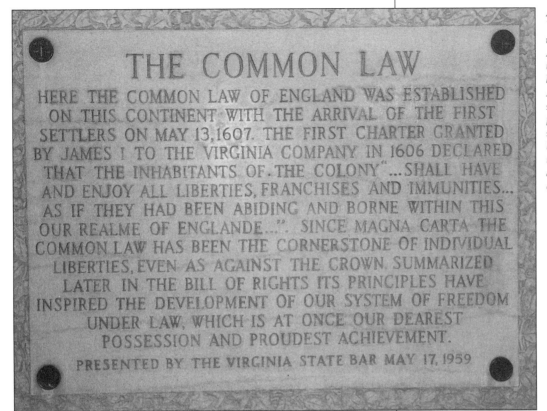

THE COMMON LAW

HERE THE COMMON LAW OF ENGLAND WAS ESTABLISHED ON THIS CONTINENT WITH THE ARRIVAL OF THE FIRST SETTLERS ON MAY 13, 1607. THE FIRST CHARTER GRANTED BY JAMES I TO THE VIRGINIA COMPANY IN 1606 DECLARED THAT THE INHABITANTS OF THE COLONY "...SHALL HAVE AND ENJOY ALL LIBERTIES, FRANCHISES AND IMMUNITIES... AS IF THEY HAD BEEN ABIDING AND BORNE WITHIN THIS OUR REALME OF ENGLANDE...". SINCE MAGNA CARTA THE COMMON LAW HAS BEEN THE CORNERSTONE OF INDIVIDUAL LIBERTIES, EVEN AS AGAINST THE CROWN. SUMMARIZED LATER IN THE BILL OF RIGHTS ITS PRINCIPLES HAVE INSPIRED THE DEVELOPMENT OF OUR SYSTEM OF FREEDOM UNDER LAW, WHICH IS AT ONCE OUR DEAREST POSSESSION AND PROUDEST ACHIEVEMENT.

PRESENTED BY THE VIRGINIA STATE BAR MAY 17, 1959

A plaque at Jamestown, Virginia, the first permanent English settlement in America, recognizes the tradition of common law brought from England to America by the early settlers. The plaque was presented by the Virginia state bar to honor the legal foundation of the individual liberties that are expressed in the Bill of Rights.

1626 King Charles I brought on a critical conflict with Parliament. He wanted money to pay for military expenses related to wars in Europe and defense against enemies at home. The Parliament, however, would not agree to support the king's military ventures and refused to help him raise taxes. So King Charles made his subjects grant him loans or otherwise give him resources. He forced people with little or no money to permit the king's soldiers to live in their homes. He coerced others to give money. When some people refused, the king sent them to prison.

A storm of public protest swept the land because King Charles had acted against the law. If he could get away with it this time, they reasoned, then their rights to liberty, based on faithful observance of the Magna Carta and other laws, would forever be at risk. At this moment of crisis, champions of English rights under law rose to challenge the king. Most prominent among these protesters was an elderly lawyer, scholar, and public servant, Sir Edward Coke.

Coke believed that English common law was the bedrock of the people's rights, and he was determined to defend common law against all threats to it. The common law of England, in

Algernon Sidney, Martyr in the Cause of Liberty

An English contemporary of John Locke, Algernon Sidney, like Locke, believed passionately in the people's rights to liberty and government by consent of the governed. Sidney spoke out against the king's usurpation of power and plotted his overthrow, and the king's agents arrested him and charged him with treason. At Sidney's trial, pages from his as yet unpublished *Discourses* were used to prove that he wanted England to be a republic, not a monarchy, and that he advocated the people's right to revolution to overthrow the king. He was convicted and sentenced to death.

Sidney was executed on December 7, 1683. His ideas, however, lived on. His book against absolute monarchy, and for liberty and popular government, was published in 1698. It greatly influenced the thoughts and actions of Americans in their revolution against King George III's government in the 1770s and their founding of a constitutional republic.

I had from my youth endeavored to uphold the common rights of mankind . . . and I now willingly lay down my life for the same.

—Algernon Sidney, *Apology on the Day of His Death*, 1683

Coke's time and today, is a body of laws based on traditions and court decisions, as opposed to a written legal code. Coke wrote, "[T]he King cannot change any part of the common law . . . without Parliament."

In 1628 Coke influenced Parliament to enact the Petition of Right, which expressed four rights also found in American colonial documents. The 1641 Massachusetts Body of Liberties, the first fully developed example of an American bill of rights, is the primary ancestor of the 1791 American Bill of Rights and includes most of the rights found in the 1791 document. Both American documents go far beyond their English antecedents. Further, it is remarkable that the Massachusetts Body of Liberties, written 48 years before the English Bill of Rights, was more expansive and detailed than its English counterpart in guarantees of individual rights.

Other American colonies followed the example of Massachusetts in their documents on individual rights that, while connected to English traditions, exceeded by far the development of rights in the mother country. Other colonial documents that built a strong American tradition on rights were the Laws and Liberties of Massachusetts (1648), the Maryland Toleration Act (1649), the Charter of Rhode Island and Providence Plantations (1663), the General Laws and Liberties of Connecticut (1672), the Laws and Liberties of New Hampshire (1682), the Pennsylvania Frame of Government and Charter of Liberties (1682), the New York Charter of Liberties and Privileges (1683), and the Pennsylvania Charter of Liberties (1701).

These colonial American documents guaranteed the rights of individuals through limitations on all branches of the government. By contrast, the 17th-century English documents on rights expressed limitations only against the monarchy on behalf of Parliament. While colonists in America protected their rights under law, people in England struggled against tyranny. King Charles, for example, was determined to nullify, or at least minimize, the 1628 Petition of Right. In 1629, he dissolved Parliament, imprisoned troublesome opponents, and began a period of tyrannical rule from 1629 to 1640 that led to public resistance, rebellion, and eventually in 1649 to revolution. King Charles I was overthrown and beheaded. The monarchy was abandoned temporarily, and a brief experiment in republican government was begun under the leadership of Oliver Cromwell.

The English monarchy was restored in 1660, and Charles II reigned until his death in 1685, when his younger brother

James II replaced him. King James II, however, quickly aroused discontent and hostility, so Parliament, with support from masses of English people, forced him to abdicate in 1688 and leave England forever.

In 1689, Parliament invited a daughter of James II, Mary, and her husband, William of Orange, to become the new king and queen of England. Parliament, however, attached strict conditions to its invitation. In exchange for the crown, the new royal family had to submit to Parliament and recognize strict limitations on their power to rule. The English Bill of Rights, enacted by Parliament in 1689, declared that certain rights of the people could not be taken away by the monarch. Thus, the power of the monarchy was limited by law. This basic change in England's government was hailed as the Glorious Revolution.

As English legal traditions and charters of liberty traveled westward to North America with settlers from England, so did a sense of rights to liberty nurtured by English and Scottish philosophers, such as James Harrington, John Locke, Algernon Sidney, David Hume, John Trenchard, and Thomas Gordon. They wrote brilliant books, letters, and essays about how to establish and maintain free governments and to secure individual rights to life, liberty, and property.

Perhaps the brightest and most celebrated of the political thinkers of 17th- and 18th-century Britain was John Locke. In the second of his *Two Treatises of Government*, Locke boldly set forth the central ideas for a revolution of the future with claims to individual rights and assumptions about society and government that went far beyond the conditions of England after the Glorious Revolution of 1688 and 1689. Instead of merely looking backward to the historically secured rights of Englishmen, Locke developed a forward-looking theory about the natural rights of individuals, a theory that could be applied to humankind, not just to the English. He claimed that *all* human beings possess certain rights to life, liberty, and property, which belong to us equally by virtue of our common membership in the human race. He held that human beings join together in civil society to establish government with one overriding purpose, which is to safeguard and sustain our natural rights, which come from God.

Humans, said Locke, bring natural rights into their social and governmental institutions. These rights cannot be granted to us by our government and the government cannot legitimately take them away. Rather, we agree among ourselves to obey certain

The English philosopher John Locke supported the Glorious Revolution of 1688 and promoted the natural rights of individuals. In 1772, his doctrine was described by the Boston Evening Post as "the doctrine of reason and truth . . . the unvarnished doctrine of Americans."

Throughout the document it is implied that here is a law which is above the King and which even he must not break. This reaffirmation of law and its expression in a general charter is the great work of Magna Carta; and this alone justifies the respect in which men have held it.

—Winston S. Churchill, *The Birth of Britain*, 1958

rules and laws of our civil society and government because we reason that our natural rights are more likely to be safe and secure under the authority of a government by consent of the governed.

Our ability to reason leads us, said Locke, to the conclusion that our rights cannot be secure in the "state of nature" that exists in the absence of civil society and government. And, said Locke, experience has taught that those who would rule us without our consent, and without legal limits on their power, will more likely violate our rights than protect them. So there are two keys to securing our natural rights. One is to create a government that has sufficient power to maintain law and order against anyone who would threaten our rights. The second key is to erect legal limitations on our government's power to prevent our rulers from threatening our rights. Thus, we might enjoy the conditions of ordered liberty in which our rights to life, liberty, and property are secured by the rule of law.

As people in England expanded their rights under law, Americans did the same and more. The Quakers, an offshoot of the Puritan religion, were a religious community founded in England. They strongly believed in equality and considered ministers, such as Puritan clergymen, to be unnecessary, seeking instead direct communication with God. Furthermore, they would not wage war under any circumstances. Their "peculiar" beliefs brought the Quakers into conflict with the Puritans, the Church of England, and other established churches and subjected them to persecution in every American colony except Rhode Island. English Quaker William Penn had long hoped to found a settlement in North America, where people might have freedom to worship as they pleased. His vision came to life in 1681, when King Charles II granted Penn a charter to establish the colony of Pennsylvania. This venture would come to represent the fullest expression in the American colonies of constitutional government for the protection of rights, which were rooted in the Magna Carta.

Transporting Rights to the American Colonies

Most of the 63 short chapters or clauses of the Magna Carta address complaints that pertained only to 13th-century England. A few chapters, however, are pregnant with meaning and generated claims to rights among later generations. This was an achievement beyond the expectations of its authors

King John I of England, shown riding in his royal forest land, tightened the laws governing the English forest in order to raise funds for his depleted treasury. This unpopular move was one source of the discontent with his rule that spurred his barons to draft the Magna Carta.

and the limitations of their culture. The barons at Runnymede, in a few phrases, did better than they knew.

The root principle of the Magna Carta, emphatically expressed in Chapter 39, is the rule of law; that is, the law, to which all consent, is supreme and equally binds all persons of the realm, even the king. No one is above the law, and all must abide by it. To the extent that the rule of law replaces the arbitrary will of rulers, then there may be security for life, liberty, and property. In the generations that followed the confrontation at Runnymede, English kings several times reaffirmed the Magna Carta. Thus it became a fundamental part of English law. In time, the English people came to accept the Magna Carta as a law above other laws that should neither be violated by the king nor the parliament, the people's representatives in government with power to enact laws.

The Magna Carta at Lincoln Cathedral, England

Four original copies of the Magna Carta have survived and can be seen today. Two copies are in the British Museum at London. One is in the cathedral at Salisbury, England. And one is in the cathedral at Lincoln, England, about 135 miles north of London. The copy at Lincoln—18 1/4 inches long by 17 3/4 inches wide—is the best preserved. In 1215, the year of the Magna Carta's birth, Lincoln was the third-largest city of England, and its cathedral was the country's largest and most splendid, as it is today. So, it was one of several prominent places in England to which copies of the Magna Carta were sent during the two to three weeks after its approval by King John and the barons at Runnymede. In this way the people of England were informed of the momentous agreement between the king and the barons, which set the course of English legal history. After its arrival at Lincoln Cathedral, the Magna Carta was displayed so that the people of the vicinity could see it. It remains there today, an ancient symbol of the everlasting principle of liberty under law.

Although the barons and their allies were concerned only with their own complaints against King John, they referred again and again to "all the free men of Our kingdom" and asserted at the end of their document, "[A]ll men in Our kingdom shall have and hold all the aforesaid liberties, rights, and concessions. . . ." These phrases were used again and again by other men of later times to widen the circle of those who could have fundamental rights to liberty, property, and equal protection of the laws. In Chapter 12, there is the seed of an idea that flowered fully in 18th-century America: no taxation without consent by elected representatives of the people. And in chapters 38, 39, and 40, we see a foundation for due process, the standard procedures by which everyone could seek equal justice before the law.

1. We have . . . granted to all the free men of Our kingdom, for Us and Our heirs forever, all the liberties underwritten, to have and to hold to them and their heirs of Us and Our heirs. . . .

12. No scutage [a tax paid in place of military service] or aid shall be imposed in Our kingdom unless by common counsel. . . .

38. In the future no bailiff shall open his own unsupported accusation put any man to trial without producing credible witnesses to the truth of the accusation.

39. No free man shall be taken, imprisoned, disseised [deprived], outlawed, banished, or in any way destroyed, nor will We proceed against or prosecute him, except by the lawful judgment of his peers and by the law of the land.

40. To no one will We sell, to none will We deny or delay, right or justice. . . .

63. Wherefore We will, and firmly charge . . . that all men in Our kingdom shall have and hold all the aforesaid liberties, rights, and concessions, well and peaceably, freely, quietly, fully, and wholly, to them and their heirs, of Us and Our heirs, in all things and places forever, as is aforesaid . . . . Given by Our hand in the meadow which is called Runnymede, between Windsor and Staines, on the fifteenth day of June in the seventeenth year of Our reign.

The 1606 Charter of Virginia was the first of a series of documents that guaranteed settlers of the English colonies all the rights of people in England. The same legal protection for rights, for example, was included in the 1629 Charter of Massachusetts Bay, the 1632 Charter of Maryland, the 1662

Charter of Connecticut, the 1663 Charter of Rhode Island, the 1663 Charter of Carolina, and the 1732 Charter of Georgia. By these colonial charters, a precedent was established that settlers of the English colonies in America would have the same rights to liberty under law, rooted in the Magna Carta of 1215, possessed by the king's subjects in England. Thus, legal seeds were planted at Jamestown in 1607 and subsequently in other English colonies from Massachusetts to Georgia. From these colonial seedbeds grew the roots and branches of an American liberty tree that bore in 1791 an American Bill of Rights.

JAMES, BY THE GRACE OF GOD, King of England, Scotland, France, and Ireland, Defender of the Faith, etc.: Whereas our loving and well-disposed subjects . . . have been humble suitors unto Us, that We would vouchsafe unto them Our license, to make habitation, plantation, and to deduce a colony of sundry of Our people into that part of America commonly called Virginia. . . .

And We do also ordain, establish, and agree, for Us, Our Heirs, and Successors, that each of the said colonies shall have a council, which shall govern and order all matters and causes, which shall arise, grow, or happen, to or within the same several colonies, according to such laws, ordinances, and instructions, as shall be, in that behalf, given and signed with Our hand or sign manual, and pass under the privy seal of Our Realm of England; Each of which councils shall consist of thirteen persons, to be ordained, made, and removed, from time to time, according as shall be directed and comprised in the same instructions. . . .

Also We do, for Us, Our Heirs, and Successors, declare, by these presents, that all and every of the persons being Our subjects, which shall dwell and inhabit within every or any of the said several colonies and plantations, and every of their children, which shall happen to be born within any of the limits and precincts of the said several colonies and plantations, shall have and enjoy all liberties, franchises, and immunities, within any of our other dominions, to all intents and purposes, as if they had been abiding and born, within this Our Realm of England, or any of Our said Dominions. . . .

IN the Name of God, Amen. We whose Names are under-written, the Loyal Subjects of our dread Soveraign Lord King *James*, by the grace of God of *Great Britain, France and Ireland*, King, *Defendor of the Faith*, etc. Having undertaken for the glory of God, and advancement of the Christian Faith, and the Honour of our King

This damaged copy of the 1215 Magna Carta was sent on loan from England to the National Archives in Washington, D.C., where it was exhibited for several weeks.

and Countrey, a Voyage to plant the first Colony in the Northern parts of Virginia; Do by these Presents, solemnly and mutually, in the presence of God and one another, Covenant and Combine ourselves together into a Civil Body Politick, for our better ordering and preservation, and furtherance of the ends aforesaid: and by virtue hereof do enact, constitute, and frame, such just and equal Laws, Ordinances, Acts, Constitutions and Officers, from time to time, as shall be thought most meet and convenient for the general good of the Colony; unto which we promise all due submission and obedience. In witness whereof we have hereunto subscribed our Names at Cape Cod, the eleventh of November, in the Reign of our Soveraign Lord King James, of England, France and Ireland the eighteenth, and of Scotland the fifty fourth, Anno Dom. 1620.

New Charters of Rights

Sir Edward Coke won election to the House of Commons in Parliament with votes from those opposed to King Charles's actions against common law. He rallied a majority in Parliament to his side and together, on March 17, 1628, they passed a law, the Petition of Right, that declared the fundamental rights in England; it was rooted in the Magna Carta and common law. They told the king that Parliament would grant him funds he desperately wanted for the wars in Europe on condition of his acceptance of their petition that affirmed longstanding rights of the common law of England.

The king reluctantly and half-heartedly agreed, and the political crisis momentarily passed. He gained the money he wanted to pay for military and other expenses. Parliament, on behalf of the people, secured traditional English rights established in the Magna Carta and common law, which one day would flourish in North America.

The 1628 Petition of Right included four main points. There should be (1) no taxes without the consent of Parliament; (2) no imprisonment of persons without just cause; (3) no quartering of soldiers in the private homes of individuals, and (4) no martial law in time of peace.

The petition exhibited to his majesty by the lords spiritual and temporal, and commons in this present parliament assembled, concerning divers rights and liberties of the subjects. . . .

[I]t is declared and enacted that from thenceforth no person should be compelled to make any loans to the king against his will. . . . [Y]our subjects have inherited this freedom, that they should not be compelled to contribute to any tax, tallage, aid, or other like charge not set by common consent in parliament. . . .

And where also, by the statute called the Great Charter of the Liberties of England [Magna Carta], it is declared and enacted that no freeman may be taken or imprisoned, or be disseised [deprived] of his freehold or liberties or his free customs, or be outlawed or exiled or in any manner destroyed, but by the lawful judgment of his peers or by the law of the land; and in the eight-and-twentieth year of the reign of King Edward III it was declared and enacted by authority of parliament that no man, of what estate or condition that he be, should be put out of his land or tenements, nor taken, nor imprisoned, nor disherited, nor put to death, without being brought to answer by due process of law. . . .

And whereas of late great companies of soldiers and mariners have been dispersed into divers counties of the realm, and the inhabitants against their wills have been compelled to receive them into their houses, and there to suffer them to sojourn, against the laws and customs of this realm, and to the great griev-ance and vexation of the people. . . .

They do therefore humbly pray your most excellent majesty that . . . the foresaid commissions for proceeding by martial law may be revoked and annulled; and that hereafter no commis-sions of like nature may issue forth to any person or persons whatsoever. . . .

[A]nd that your majesty would be also graciously pleased, for the further comfort and safety of your people, to declare your royal will and pleasure that in the things aforesaid all your officers and ministers shall serve you according to the laws and statutes of this realm, as they tender the honour of your majesty and the prosperity of this kingdom.

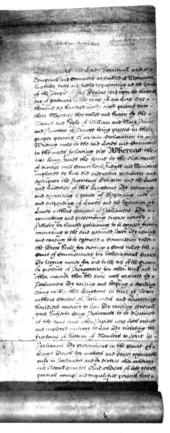

Enacted by Parliament in 1689, the English Bill of Rights contains several provisions that were includ-ed in the U.S. Bill of Rights in 1791.

The first American document to list in detail the rights of the people was the Massachusetts Body of Liberties, enacted December 10, 1641. It was approved only after widespread review, discussion, and revision of the document by the magis-trates and eligible voters of the towns of colonial Massachu-setts. This document was intended to be a fundamental law that in the name of the people would limit the power of gov-ernment in order to guarantee particular rights of individuals.

The free fruition of such liberties Immunities and priviledges as humanitie, Civilitie, and Christianitie call for as due to every man in his place and proportion; without impeachment and Infringement hath ever bene and ever will be the tranquilitie and Stabilitie of Churches and Commonwealths. And the deniall or deprivall thereof, the disturbance if not the ruine of both. . . .

Wee doe, therefore this day religiously and unanimously decree and confirme these following Rites, liberties, and priviledges concerneing our Churches, and Civill State to be respectively impartialle, and inviolably enjoyed and observed throughout our Jurisdiction for ever.

1. No mans life shall be taken away; no mans honour or good name shall be stayned; no mans person shall be arested, restrayned, banished, dismembred, nor any wayes punished; no man shall be deprived of his wife or children, no mans goods or estaite shall be taken away from him, nor any way indammaged under Coulor of law, or Countenance of Authoritie, unlesse it be by virtue or equitie of some expresse law of the country warranting the same, established by a generall Court and sufficiently published. . . .

2. Every person within [this] Jurisdiction, whether Inhabitant or forreiner, shall enjoy the same justice and laws that is generall for the plantation, which we constitute and execute one towards another without partialitie or delay . . .

5. No man shall be compelled to any publique work or service unlesse the presse be grounded upon some act of the generall Court, and have reasonable allowance therefore . . .

8. No mans cattell or goods of what kinde soever shall be pressed or taken for any publique use or service, unlesse it be by warrant grounded upon some act of the generall Court, nor without such reasonable prices and hire as the ordinarie rates of the Countrie do afford. And if his Cattle and goods shall perish or suffer damage in such service, the owners shall be suffitiently recompenced.

12. Every man whether Inhabitant or forreiner free or not free shall have libertie to come to any publique Court, Councell, or Towne meeting, and, either by speech or writeing, to move any lawful, seasonable, and materiall question, or to present any necessary motion, complaint, petition, Bill, or information, whereof that meeting hath proper cognizance, so it be done in convenient time, due order, and respective manner . . .

17. Every man of or with this Jurisdiction shall have free libertie, not with standing any Civill power to remove both himselfe,

Roger Williams and Freedom of Religion

Roger Williams was a Puritan minister in Massachusetts who objected to the heavy-handed suppression of the right to religious liberty in the Massachusetts Colony. The Puritan leaders charged Williams with heresy, or unlawful dissent from established beliefs. In 1635, the authorities tried Williams in a court of law, found him guilty, and banished him from Massachusetts. So Williams took his followers in 1636 to a nearby territory, Rhode Island, where they founded the settlement of Providence.

Williams made toleration of religious beliefs the central principle of his new settlement. This was an American invention, achieved first by settlers of Rhode Island and copied by the founders of New Jersey, Pennsylvania, and Delaware.

[N]o person within the said colony, at any time hereafter, shall be any wise molested, punished, disquieted, or called in question, for any difference in opinion in matters of religion, and do not actually disturb the civil peace of our said colony; but that all and every person and persons may, from time to time, and at all times hereafter, freely and fully have and enjoy his and their own judgments and consciences, in matters of religious concernments.

—Charter of Rhode Island and Providence Plantations, 1663

and his familie at their pleasure out of the same, provided there be no legall impediment to the contrarie . . .

26. Every man that find himselfe unfit to plead his owne cause in any Court shall have Libertie to imploy any man against whom the Court doth not except, to helpe him. . . .

29. In all Actions at law it shall be the libertie of the plaintife and defendant by mutual consent to choose whether they will be tryed by the Bench or by a Jurie, unlesse it be where the law upon just reason hath otherwise determined. The like libertie shall be granted to all persons in Criminall cases.

30. It shall be in the libertie both of plaintife and defendant, and likewise every delinquent (to be judged by a Jurie), to challenge any of the Jurors. And if his challenge be found just and reasonable by the Bench, or the rest of the Jurie, as the challenger shall choose it shall be allowed him, and tales de circumstantibus [alternate jurors] impaneled in their room [stead]. . .

42. No man shall be twise sentenced by Civill Justice for one and the same Crime, offence, or Trespasse.

43. No man shall be beaten with above 40 stripes, nor shall any true gentleman, nor any man equall to a gentleman be punished with whipping, unless his crime be very shamefull and his course of life vitious and profligate . . .

45. No man shall be forced by Torture to confesse any Crime against himselfe nor any other unlesse it be in some Capitall case, where he is first fullie convicted by cleare and suffitient evidence to be guilty, After which if the cause be of that nature, That it is very apparent there be other conspirators or confederates with him, Then he may be tortured, yet not with such Tortures as be Barbarous and inhumane.

46. For bodilie punishments we allow amongst us none that are inhumane Barbarous or cruell.

In 1689, the English Parliament passed a Bill of Rights to enact into law the conditions whereby William and Mary accepted the Crown. Enactment of this English Bill of Rights was the culmination, the ultimate achievement, of the Glorious Revolution. Above all, this English Bill of Rights established the supremacy of Parliament over the king and queen. From this time on, the monarchs of England would reign but not rule, and they would do it at the pleasure of Parliament. After 1689, no king could legally violate provisions of the Bill of Rights. There was no power but the will of the eligible voters that could restrain Parliament.

The Massachusetts Body of Liberties, enacted in 1641, was the first detailed charter of rights in America.

The English Bill of Rights declared legal limitations on the powers of the king or queen. For example, the monarchs could not suspend acts of Parliament; tax the people without consent of Parliament; maintain a standing military force in peacetime; interfere with the free election of representatives to the House of Commons; inflict cruel and unusual punishments upon prisoners or people accused of crimes; require excessive or unreasonable bail of accused criminals in exchange for their release from prison; or deny the right of petition.

An act declaring the rights and liberties of the subject and settling the succession of the crown. . . .

And whereas the said late King James II having abdicated the government, and the throne being thereby vacant. . . .

[T]he said lords spiritual and temporal and commons, pursuant to their respective letters and elections being now assembled in a full and free representative of this nation . . . do in the first place (as their ancestors in like case have usually done) for the vindicating and asserting their ancient rights and liberties, declare

that the pretended power of suspending of laws or the execution of laws by regal authority without consent of parliament is illegal;

that the pretended power of dispensing with laws or the execution of laws by regal authority, as it hath been assumed and exercised of late, is illegal;

that the commission for erecting the late court of commissioners for ecclesiastical causes and all other commissions and courts of like nature are illegal and pernicious;

that levying money for or to the use of the crown by pretense of prerogative without grant of parliament, for longer time or in other manner than the same is or shall be granted, is illegal;

that it is the right of the subjects to petition the king, and all commitments and prosecutions for such petitioning are illegal;

that the raising or keeping a standing army within the kingdom in time of peace, unless it be with consent of parliament, is against law;

that the subjects which are Protestants may have arms for their defence suitable to their conditions and as allowed by law;

that election of members of parliament ought to be free;

that the freedom of speech and debates or proceedings in parliament ought not to be impeached or questioned in any court or place out of parliament;

that excessive bail ought not to be required, nor excessive fines imposed, nor cruel and unusual punishments inflicted;

that jurors ought to be duly impanelled and returned, and jurors which pass upon men in trials for high treason ought to be freeholders;

that all grants and promises of fines and forfeitures of particular persons before conviction are illegal and void;

and that, for redress of all grievances and for the amending, strengthening, and preserving of the laws, parliaments ought to be held frequently. . . .

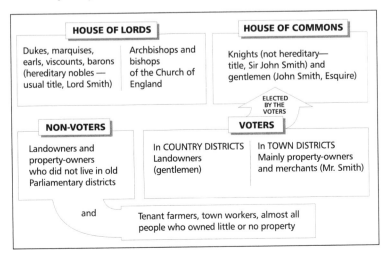

The English Parliament

By the 17th century, the king shared power with the parliament, including a House of Lords and a House of Commons. The House of Lords consisted of hereditary nobles and leaders of the church. The House of Commons was made up of prominent people who were not hereditary nobles. This is why they were called "commoners." By today's standards, they were not common folk, but gentlemen, property owners, and knights. Members of the House of Commons were elected by eligible voters, a minority of the populace. The majority of the English people did not satisfy the requirements for voting, a right reserved for the well-to-do persons of the realm.

The United Kingdom

In 1707, the crowns of England and Scotland were united. From this time, England officially is part of the United Kingdom of Great Britain. Hence, the term British becomes a comprehensive term for the people of the United Kingdom, which today includes England, Scotland, Wales, and Northern Ireland.

To which demands of their rights they are particularly encouraged . . . that . . . the prince of Orange will . . . preserve them from the violation of their rights which they have here asserted. . . . [T]he said lords spiritual and temporal and commons assembled at Westminster do resolve that William and Mary . . . be declared king and queen of England.

A New Philosophy of Rights

The ideas of John Locke justified England's Glorious Revolution of 1688. They also inspired the American Revolution of 1776. Americans selected and mixed the ideas of English politician Algernon Sidney, Locke, and others to make a revolution and establish their republic. Locke emphasized that the first object of a government created by consent of the governed is to protect the right to property. His definition of property, however, was very broad. It included not only land and goods but also our qualities as human beings, including our natural rights to life and liberty. If our government fails to protect our property—our natural rights—then we have the right to withdraw our consent and change it. This right to revolution, said Locke, should not be undertaken casually or frivolously, but only following deliberations in response to continuous abuses of our natural and God-given rights.

The flavor of Locke's ideas is given through brief selections from various parts of his _Second Treatise of Government._

3. _Political Power_ then I take to be a _Right_ of making Laws with Penalties of Death, and consequently all less Penalties, for the Regulating and Preserving of Property, and of employing the force of the Community, in the Execution of such Laws, and in the defence of the Common-wealth from Foreign Injury, and all this only for the Publick Good. . . .

95. Men being, as has been said, by Nature, all free, equal and independent, no one can be put out of this Estate, and subjected to the Political Power of another, without his own _Consent_. . . . When any number of Men have so _consented to make one Community_ or Government, they are thereby presently incorporated, and make _one Body Politick_, wherein the _Majority_ have a Right to act and conclude the rest. . . .

97. And thus every Man, by consenting with others to make one Body Politick under one Government, puts himself under an

Obligation to every one of that Society, to submit to the determination of the *majority*. . . .

123. If Man in the State of Nature be so free, as has been said; If he be absolute Lord of his own Person and Possessions, equal to the greatest, and subject to no Body, why will he part with his Freedom? Why will he give up this Empire, and subject himself to the Dominion and Controul of any other Power? To which 'tis obvious to Answer, that though in the state of Nature he hath such a right, yet the Enjoyment of it is very uncertain, and constantly exposed to the Invasion of others. . . . [T]he enjoyment of the property he has in this state is very unsafe, very unsecure. This makes him willing to quit this Condition, which however free, is full of fears and continual dangers: And 'tis not without reason, that he seeks out, and is willing to joyn in Society with others who are already united, or have a mind to unite for the mutual *Preservation* of their Lives, Liberties, and Estates, which I call by the general Name, *Property*. . . .

202. *Where-ever Law ends, Tyranny begins*, if the Law be transgressed to another's harm. And whosoever in Authority exceeds the Power given him by the Law, and makes use of the Force he has under his Command, to compass that upon the Subject, which the Law allows not, ceases in that to be a Magistrate, and acting without Authority, may be opposed, as any other Man, who by force invades the Right of another. . . .

225. . . . *Revolutions happen* not upon every little mismanagement in publick affairs. *Great mistakes* in the ruling part, many wrong and inconvenient Laws, and all the *slips* of humane frailty will be *born by the People*, without mutiny or murmur. But if a long train of Abuses, Prevarications, and Artifices, all tending the same way, make the design visible to the People, and they cannot but feel, what they lie under, and see, whither they are going; 'tis not to be wonder'd, that they should then rouze themselves, and endeavour to put the rule into such hands, which may secure to them the ends of which Government was at first erected; and without which, ancient Names, and specious Forms, are so far from being better, that they are much worse, than the state of Nature, or pure Anarchy; the inconveniences being all as great and as near, but the remedy farther off and more difficult.

After acquiring title to his colony, William Penn drafted in 1682 the Frame of Government of Pennsylvania, the first constitution or supreme law of this territory. This document was

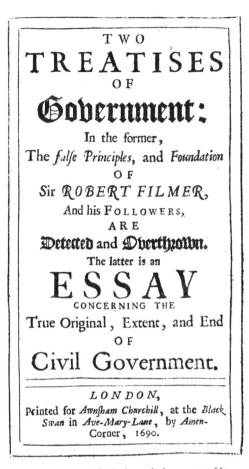

John Locke, in the first treatise of his Two Treatises of Government, refuted the authoritarian ideas of Sir Robert Filmer, who was a supporter of absolute monarchy. In his "Second Treatise," Locke discussed the characteristics of civil government, the true purpose of which should be the protection of the individual's natural rights to life, liberty, and property.

William Penn, in this drawing, wears the simple attire prescribed by the Quaker faith. Penn was trained as a lawyer and became a Quaker when he was in Ireland attending to the titles of his father's Irish land.

revised in 1683, 1696, and 1701, when the Pennsylvania Charter of Liberties was enacted. The 1701 document was retained until 1776, when Pennsylvania, a newly sovereign state of the United States of America, adopted a new constitution.

Penn's constitutions were exemplars of limited government and the rule of law for the purpose of protecting certain rights of individuals. Penn believed that government should be based on the consent of the people under it, and that the law should prevail so long as it protected the rights of the people. In particular, the 1701 Pennsylvania Charter of Liberties highlights the strong belief of William Penn and his followers in the right to freedom of religion, which they placed first in the series of rights to be secured by their constitutional government. In line with English political philosophers like Sidney and Locke, Penn and his followers believed that the natural rights of individuals came from God and not from the government. The primary purpose of government was to protect the natural rights of individuals.

The Pennsylvania Charter of Liberties enacted October 28, 1701, was the last and most fully developed constitutional document of the American colonial era. Taken together, these colonial charters, frames of government, and statements of rights were sources for the development of constitutional rights during the American Revolution. The Pennsylvania Charter of Liberties provides for limited government and rights.

WILLIAM PENN, Proprietary and Governor of the Province of Pennsylvania and Territories thereunto belonging, To all to whom these Presents shall come, sendeth Greeting. . . .

KNOW YE THEREFORE, That for the further Well-being and good Government of the said Province, and territories; and in Pursuance of the Rights and Powers before-mentioned, I the said *William Penn* do declare, grant and confirm, unto all the Freemen, Planters and Adventurers, and other Inhabitants of this Province and Territories, these following Liberties, Franchises and Privileges. . . .

I

BECAUSE no People can be truly happy, though under the greatest Enjoyment of Civil Liberties, if abridged of the Freedom of their Consciences, as to their Religious Profession and Worship: And Almighty God being the only Lord of Conscience, Father of

Without freedom of Thought, there can be no such thing as Wisdom; and no such Thing as Publick Liberty, Without Freedom of Speech: Which is the Right of every Man, as far as by it he does not hurt and control the Right of another; and this is the only Check which it ought to suffer, the only Bounds which it ought to know. This sacred Privilege is so essential to free government, that the Security of Property; and the Freedom of Speech, always go together; and in those wretched Countries where a Man cannot call his Tongue his own, he can scarce call any Thing else his own. Whoever would overthrow the Liberty of the Nation, must begin by subduing the Freedom of Speech.

—John Trenchard and Thomas Gordon, *Cato's Letters,* number 15, February 4, 1720

Light and Spirits; and the Author as well as Object of all divine Knowledge, Faith and Worship, who only doth enlighten the Minds, and persuade and convince the Understandings of People, I do hereby grant and declare, That no Person or Persons, inhabiting in this Province or Territories, who shall confess and acknowledge *One* almighty God, the Creator, Upholder and Ruler of the World; and profess him or themselves obliged to live quietly under the Civil Government, shall be in any Case molested or prejudiced, in his or their Person or Estate, because of his or their conscientious Persuasion or Practice, nor be compelled to frequent or maintain any religious Worship, Place or Ministry, contrary to his or their Mind, or to do or suffer any other Act or Thing, contrary to their religious Persuasion. . . .

V

THAT all Criminals shall have the same Privileges of Witnesses and Council as their Prosecutors. . . .

VI

THAT no Person or Persons shall or may, at any Time hereafter, be obliged to answer any Complaint, Matter or Thing whatsoever, relating to Property, before the Governor and Council, or in any other Place, but in ordinary Course of Justice, unless Appeals thereunto shall be hereafter by Law appointed. . . .

VIII

And lastly, I, the said William Penn, Proprietary and Governor of the province of Pennsylvania and territories thereunto belonging, for myself, my heirs and assigns, have solemnly declared, granted, and confirmed, and do hereby solemnly declare, grant, and confirm, that neither I, my heirs or assigns, shall procure to do anything or things whereby the liberties in this charter contained and expressed, nor any part thereof, shall be infringed or broken. And if anything shall be procured or done by any person or persons contrary to these presents, it shall be held of no force or effect.

Cato's Letters

John Trenchard and Thomas Gordon were popular defenders in the 1700s of political, civic, and legal ideas associated with England's Glorious Revolution of 1688. From 1720 to 1723 they cooperated to write 138 papers, known as Cato's Letters, published originally in a widely read English newspaper, *The London Journal*, and later as a two-volume book. Trenchard and Gordon chose the pen name Cato, a defender of the ancient Roman republic against Julius Caesar's ambitions, to symbolize their commitment to liberty, civic virtue, limited government, and the rule of law.

Trenchard and Gordon advocated government by consent of the governed, inalienable rights to life, liberty, and property possessed equally by all persons, obligations of governments and rulers to guarantee justly the rights of individuals, responsibilities of citizens to hold government accountable to them, and government limited by the rule of law. Trenchard and Gordon assumed the people's right to revolution against an unjust or inept government and rulers unwilling or unable to secure their safety and rights.

"Cato's" literary career in England ended in 1723 with the untimely death of John Trenchard, who suffered a fatal kidney disease. "Cato's" ideas, however, lived and traveled to the American colonies, where they strongly influenced the thoughts and actions of leaders who made a revolution against the British Crown and founded the United States of America.

THE REPEAL

OR THE FUNERAL OF MISS AME=STAMP

All of a Stamp

Chapter Two

Rights and Revolution in America

By the 1700s, the American colonists had developed their own institutions of constitutional government and conceptions of individual rights. But underneath the appearance of self-government, there was a reality of British sovereignty symbolized by the Crown and exercised by Parliament. According to the British view, the king and Parliament could, if they wanted to, nullify or modify any of the colonial charters of rights and frames of government. Many American settlers, nevertheless, began to believe they governed themselves in all local matters. Even though they acknowledged an allegiance to the Crown, many Americans rejected the authority of Parliament to tax them or otherwise control their local affairs, because they were not represented directly in that institution of government. This difference of views on political authority was a harbinger of critical conflicts about rights.

For much of the colonial era in North America, Great Britain had let the local governments manage their own affairs. By the middle of the 1700s, however, the British government started to interfere. In particular, British officials began to tighten regulations on trade. They strictly enforced laws that enabled them to collect taxes on commerce between the colonies and other countries.

The British government needed revenue from American taxes to pay for the costs of its long war against France. Britain won the war, and because it drove French military forces out of Canada and the Ohio River Valley, which benefited the American colonies, the British thought it fair to expect Americans to help pay the huge debt. This victory over the French, achieved in 1763, more than doubled the size of the British government's debt.

Many colonists resisted laws that, in their view, unfairly taxed and regulated their commercial and personal activities. American leaders

This political cartoon, "The Repeal, or the Funeral Procession of Miss Ame-Stamp" was printed in 1766 to celebrate the repeal of the Stamp Act by Parliament. The British prime minister, George Grenville, is shown as the carrier of the dead Stamp Act in its coffin on the way to burial. In the background, trade between the colonies and Britain is beginning again.

James Otis, depicted in this engraving, was an early advocate of resistance to British policies on taxation and regulation of trade, which many Americans believed to be unjust. Otis was called The Patriot because of his unwavering support for the rights of Americans against the British government.

justified their opposition with legal and philosophical arguments about their rights. For example, James Otis, a young lawyer in Boston, expressed particularly American ideas about individual rights. He recognized that the colonists' rights were rooted in English legal traditions, but he—and others—believed Americans also possessed rights because they were human beings.

In a widely read pamphlet, *The Rights of the British Colonies Asserted and Proved*, published in July 1764, Otis expressed ideas on rights that pointed the way to the American Revolution and Declaration of Independence in 1776. He said, "Every British subject born on the continent of America or in any other of the British dominions, is by the law of God and nature, by the common law, and by act of Parliament entitled to all the natural, essential, inherent, and inseparable rights of our fellow subjects in Great Britain."

James Otis and other American advocates of the natural rights of mankind agreed with such English social and political philosophers as John Locke and Algernon Sidney, who stressed constitutional limitations upon all branches of government in order to protect the natural rights of individuals. In Britain, however, Parliament, representing the people, had become supreme after 1689 in its contests for power with the king. Americans criticized the unlimited—or insufficiently limited—power that the Parliament exercised over them, which violated their belief in government by consent of the governed.

Conflict between Great Britain and its American colonies grew in scope and intensity. Colonial protests became more heated and obstinate. British responses became more unyielding and punitive. A peaceful settlement of differences seemed increasingly unlikely as the British cracked down against colonial resistance to their policies.

According to John Adams, the spark that fed the flame of revolution in 1775 was lit initially in 1761, at the Council Chamber of the Boston Town House. Adams, 26 years old at that time, observed judges of the Superior Court of Massachusetts assemble to hear and resolve a hot issue of the day. It involved the legality of a locally hated instrument of law enforcement, the general writ of assistance. In possession of a general writ of assistance, issued by a court of law, a British official could search anywhere at anytime for anything. Further, he could require a local constable or justice of the peace to assist him in the search. By contrast with the general writ of assistance, a typical search warrant was issued only after a sworn statement of probable cause or reasonable suspicion of wrongdoing. And such a warrant permitted officials to search only a specific place for specific goods.

Colonial merchants bristled as tax collectors, armed with general writs of assistance, conducted searches at will. In 1761, a group of merchants in Boston and Salem challenged the authority of the courts to issue general writs of assistance.

Other British laws that aroused resistance were those regulating and taxing personal and commercial activities in order to raise money to pay for the defense of the British empire. The American colonists resented enforcement of laws made by Parliament, a legislature in which they were not directly represented. Their popular slogan was, "No taxation without representation."

The Stamp Act, passed by Parliament in 1765, imposed a small tax on legal documents and several other items. Anyone obtaining a marriage license, birth certificate, or the deed to a piece of land was supposed to buy a revenue stamp to be placed on the document. Goods such as playing cards, newspapers, calendars, and almanacs were not to be sold without the revenue stamps.

While some colonists took direct action in the streets against the Stamp Act, others deliberated in government assemblies and drafted formal appeals to the British king and Parliament.

On May 30, 1765, the Virginia House of Burgesses was the first to vote its opposition to the Stamp Act. Patrick Henry presented the Virginia Resolves to the House of Burgesses on his 29th birthday. Henry, a tall, thin lawyer from the Virginia backcountry, gave a spellbinding speech with the kind of passion and fury exhibited four years earlier by James Otis in his protest against the general writs of assistance. Henry asserted that Virginians had no representatives in Parliament and no voice in making tax laws. Thus, the Stamp Act was illegal, and the colonists should not have to obey it. Even as Henry spoke, some observers shouted that he was a traitor, but his words stirred others, such as Thomas Jefferson, a 22-year-old law student, who heard Henry while standing at the doorway to the House of Burgesses.

Newspapers in the northern colonies printed the Virginia Resolves, and colonial leaders in Massachusetts made the next formal appeal against the Stamp Act. Led by James Otis, they called for delegates from all 13 colonies to meet at New York in a Stamp Act Congress. Delegates from nine colonies attended the meeting, where they called for repeal of the act.

Colonial resistance to the Stamp Act hurt businesses in Britain. Many Americans refused to buy British products and most at least cut back their purchases. Thus, exports to the American colonies declined by half. The British were losing profits. So a majority in Parliament voted in March 1766 to repeal the Stamp Act. While many colonists celebrated, others noted with alarm a new law, the Declaratory Act, which proclaimed Parliament's final authority over the colonies in all matters, even in disregard of hallowed traditions about the rights of individuals rooted in ancient laws. Furthermore, Parliament enacted new laws and commercial regulations. And law enforcers used the general writs of assistance to gather evidence against presumed lawbreakers, who were often tried without a jury in admiralty courts.

From 1766 to 1774 conflict escalated, and differences between the American colonists and the British seemed irreconcilable. Hot protests in Massachusetts led to a hard-hitting British response. To punish that colony, in 1774 Parliament enacted repressive regulations, which Americans called the Intolerable Acts. These punitive laws closed Boston Harbor, quartered British troops in private homes, and imposed British military rule on Massachusetts in place of the colonial legislative assembly elected by the voters.

Colonial leaders of Virginia, such as Patrick Henry and Thomas Jefferson, supported the protestors in Massachusetts. Members of the Virginia House of Burgesses—meeting in the Raleigh Tavern in Williamsburg after their British-appointed governor had disbanded them—voted to call a "congress" of all the colonies on the "continent."

In September 1774, the First Continental Congress met in Philadelphia to decide what the colonies should do to oppose the British. Representatives came from every colony except Georgia. This body passed the Declaration and Resolves of the Continental Congress to express American opposition to violations of individual rights in the colonies.

Members of the Continental Congress also agreed to boycott all trade with Britain. And they agreed to meet again, if necessary, to sustain their cause. Further, the Continental Congress began to act like a government and decided to form the Continental Association to enforce the boycott and other decisions made by the Congress.

Committees of Public Safety and Inspection sprang up in every colony to carry out the duties of the Continental Association. These committees organized units of armed militia—called Minutemen because they could be ready immediately to oppose the enemy. They drilled regularly to become ready to fight for their rights.

In 1774, the British punished the Massachusetts colonists by closing Boston harbor to all shipping of goods. This cartoon suggests that the British naval blockade denied the people of Boston their liberty, deprived them of food and other necessities, and made them dependent on the British for their survival.

Continuing clashes finally led to war on the morning of April 19, 1775, when more than 700 well-armed British soldiers confronted a short, thin line of colonial militiamen on a field at the center of Lexington, Massachusetts. These British troops had come from Boston to seize or destroy guns and ammunition that the colonial militia kept in Concord, six miles beyond Lexington. The red-coated soldiers stopped and, for a fateful moment, faced the militiamen. Suddenly, a shot was fired—"the shot heard 'round the world," wrote Ralph Waldo Emerson many years later—and a battle was underway. Who fired first? No one knows for sure, but each side blamed the other, and a revolutionary war began.

On May 10, 1775, less than a month after the battles at Lexington and Concord, the Second Continental Congress met in Philadelphia. The main topic of discussion was independence. For several months, representatives of the colonies debated whether to become 13 independent American states. At first, they sought reconciliation with the British government. But after failing to overcome deep differences, delegates to the Continental Congress decided to unite their colonies as the United States of America.

On July 4, 1776, the Continental Congress discussed Thomas Jefferson's draft of the Declaration of Independence and approved it with a few changes. The most significant change was the deletion of Jefferson's strong denunciation of the slave trade as an evil imposed upon the Americans by the king's government.

Americans in 1776 were the first people ever to found a nation upon principles of individual rights of the kind expressed in the Declaration of Independence. To be an American was to believe in equal rights under law as an inviolable possession of each person. And, in fact, the American states in 1776 were havens for enjoyment of individual rights, especially in comparison to other regions of the world. There were, however, striking contradictions that troubled many, embarrassed some, and outraged others.

Slavery existed in each of the 13 American states, despite the revolutionary American creed on rights. In 1776, about 20 percent of the American population (roughly 700,000 people out of nearly 4 million) was of African descent. Most were enslaved. Free African Americans made up only about 1 percent of the new nation's population.

Even without a denunciation of slavery, however, the Declaration of Independence was greeted with excitement by all when it was printed in newspapers and broadsides and distributed throughout the 13 colonies. But Americans were sharply divided about their political allegiances. According to John Adams, more than one-third of the people opposed independence. Many of them remained loyal to the king throughout the long war, which did not end until 1783, when Great Britain signed the Treaty of Paris to recognize the independence of the United States.

The War of Independence was also a political revolution, fundamentally changing how the country would be ruled. As King George III said, shortly before the clash at Lexington, "The die is now cast. The colonists must either triumph or submit." Levi Preston, a veteran of the Lexington battle, used different words, but he saw the conflict as the king did. "What we meant in going for those redcoats was this: we always had governed ourselves, and we always meant to. They didn't mean we should."

A short-run result of the war was the birth of a new, independent nation dedicated to principles about the rights of individuals set forth in founding-era documents such as the 1776 Declaration of Independence and the 1791 Bill of Rights. A long-term and ongoing consequence has been the emergence of struggles in the

United States and abroad to expand the range and reach of rights so that more people will be protected effectively by law against those who would oppress them.

American Protests

In a proceeding known as Lechmere's case, a brilliant young lawyer named James Otis represented a group of colonial merchants who opposed the general writs of assistance being used by British officials to conduct searches at will. The specific question of this case was about a technical point of the law—whether or not a general writ of assistance could be issued by the chief justice of the Massachusetts colony without prior authorization from the king in London. King George II, who recently had died, was the authority for the general writs of assistance in use. His successor, King George III, had not yet acted to renew this authority. Otis, however, used this opportunity to make a case against unlimited and unconstitutional use of power.

Otis's argument attacked a fundamental facet of British government after the Glorious Revolution of 1688—the

In this engraving, an angry mob of colonists tar and feather a British custom's officer, who was responsible for enforcing the Stamp Act. Americans took to the streets to protest the British Stamp Act, which they declared was "taxation without representation."

James Otis on Rights

In July 1764 James Otis expressed ideas on rights in a widely read pamphlet that pointed the way to the American Revolution and Declaration of Independence in 1775 and 1776:

The *end* of government being the *good* of mankind, points out its great duties: It is above all things to provide for the security, the quiet and happy enjoyment of life, liberty and property. . . .

In order to form an idea of the natural rights of the Colonists, I presume it will be granted that they are men, the common children of the same Creator with their brethren of Great Britain. . . .

Every British subject born on the continent of America or in any other of the British dominions, is by the law of God and nature, by the common law, and by act of parliament (exclusive of all charters from the Crown) entitled to all the natural, essential, inherent, and inseparable rights of our fellow subjects in Great Britain.

—James Otis, *The Rights of the British Colonies Asserted and Proved*, 1764

supremacy of Parliament. The English Bill of Rights of 1689 was directed only against the power of the Crown by Parliament on behalf of the people. But what if the people's representatives in Parliament, by majority decision of its members, acted against individual rights? According to Otis, such acts would be void, or unconstitutional, whenever they violated provisions of the English legal tradition rooted in the Magna Carta, the Petition of Right, the Bill of Rights, and common law. Although Otis lost his case, the principle for which he argued survived. Otis's claim that a person has the right to be secure in his home and possessions against arbitrary invasions by government officers was included in the 4th Amendment of the Constitution. John Adams, who was in the courtroom for Otis's speech on February 24, 1761, produced this record of the event.

This Writ is against the fundamental Principles of Law. The Priviledge of House. A Man, who is quiet, is as secure in his House, as a Prince in his Castle, not with standing all his Debts, and civil Prossesses of any kind. . . .

As to Acts of Parliament. An Act against the Constitution is void. . . . [A]nd if an Act of Parliament should be made, in the very Words of this Petition [to authorize the general writ of assistance], it would be void. The executive Courts must pass such Acts into disuse [declare them to be unconstitutional]. . . .

I will admit, that writs of one kind, may be legal, that is, special writs, directed to special officers, and to search certain houses, especially set forth in the writ, may be granted by the Court of Exchequer at home, upon oath made before the Lord Treasurer by the person, who asks, that he suspects such goods to be concealed in those very places he desired to search. . . . [Y]ou will find it adjudged that special warrants only are legal. . . . [T]he writ prayed for in this petition, being general, is illegal. . . .

[E]very one with this [general] writ may be a tyrant; . . . [and] a tyrant may in a legal manner also, controul, imprison or murder any one within the realm. In the next place, it is perpetual; there is no return, a man is accountable to no person for his doings, every man may reign secure in his petty tyranny, and spread terror and desolation around him. . . . Now one of the most essential branches of English liberty, is the freedom of one's house. A man's house is his castle; and while he is quiet, he is as well guarded as a prince in his castle. This writ, if it should be declared legal, would totally annihilate this privilege. . . .

No Acts of Parliament can establish such a writ . . . An act against the constitution is void.

Representatives from 9 of the 13 American colonies met in the City Hall of New York to convene the Stamp Act Congress. On October 19, 1765, they issued a set of resolves drafted by John Dickinson of Pennsylvania, which strongly opposed the Stamp Act because it was a tax imposed by a parliament in which Americans were not represented. They argued the tax was therefore unconstitutional and unjust and called for repeal of the hated act.

THE members of this Congress, sincerely devoted with the warmest sentiments of affection and duty to His Majesty's person and Government . . . esteem it our indispensable duty to make the following declarations of our humble opinion respecting the most essential rights and liberties of the colonists, and of the grievances

The Minutemen

The "Minutemen" were armed regiments of colonial volunteers. They stood ready to defend their communities against enemies "at a minute's notice." Units of these Minutemen were formed first in Massachusetts in response to repressive British actions during 1774. This term is especially associated with those men who defended Lexington and Concord against British soldiers on April 19, 1775.

More than 400 Minutemen stood against the British at the Old North Bridge in Concord, Massachusetts. And 100 years later, a marvelous bronze statue was placed at the Concord Bridge to honor the Minutemen. The sculptor was Daniel Chester French. Critics called the Concord Minuteman Memorial a masterpiece of the sculptor's art. Daniel Chester French's statue has remained a main attraction of the Minuteman National Historical Park.

An African American joins protesters on the streets of Boston in October 1765 to demonstrate against the hated Stamp Act.

Mercy Otis Warren and the American Revolution

In 1805, a *History of the Rise, Progress, and Termination of the American Revolution* was published in Boston. This three-volume work attracted many readers, who praised it as a valuable study of the American War for Independence and the events that came right after it. The author was a 77-year-old woman, Mercy Otis Warren.

In the 1800s, American women had few of the rights and opportunities they enjoy today. No matter, Mercy Otis Warren lived boldly, as if she had them. When their father hired a teacher for her brother, James, Mercy insisted on learning his lessons too. Mercy married James Warren, who was becoming a leader of the Sons of Liberty—an organization opposed to unpopular British laws in the 13 colonies—with his brother, Joseph. She was in the midst of protest activity against the British. Through her brother and husband, she became friends with John Hancock and the Adamses—John, his wife Abigail, and his cousin, Sam.

Personal tragedy struck in 1767, when James Otis was assaulted by a British customs agent and injured severely, with a deep gash in his head. James recovered, but the beating destroyed his mind. He died in 1783. Mercy took up her brother's cause and began to write essays, poems, and satirical plays in support of American rights.

In 1775, after the Revolutionary War began, Mercy decided to gather information so that she could write a history of the birth of the American nation. In her history, she said that freedom cannot be won once and for all. Thus, a major responsibility of American citizenship in every generation is to protect and extend the rights of individuals for which the American nation was created.

under which they labour, by reason of several late Acts of Parliament.

I. That His Majesty's subjects in these colonies owe the same allegiance to the Crown of Great Britain that is owing from his subjects born within the realm, and all due subordination to that august body the Parliament of Great Britain.

II. That His Majesty's liege subjects in these colonies are intitled to all the inherent rights and liberties of his natural born subjects within the kingdom of Great Britain.

III. That it is inseparably essential to the freedom of a people, and the undoubted right of Englishmen, that no taxes be imposed on them but with their own consent, given personally or by their representatives.

IV. That the people of these colonies are not, and from their local circumstances cannot be, represented in the House of Commons in Great Britain.

V. That the only representatives of the people of these colonies are persons chosen therein by themselves, and that no taxes ever have been, or can be constitutionally imposed on them, but by their respective legislatures.

VII. That trial by jury is the inherent and invaluable right of every British subject in these colonies.

VIII. That the late Act of Parliament, entitled *An Act for granting and applying certain stamp duties, and other duties, in the British colonies and plantations in America, etc.*, by imposing taxes on the inhabitants of these colonies; and the said Act, and several other Acts, by extending the jurisdiction of the courts of Admiralty beyond its ancient limits, have a manifest tendency to subvert the rights and liberties of the colonists. . . .

XIII. That it is the right of the British subjects in these colonies to petition the King or either House of Parliament.

Lastly, That it is the indispensable duty of these colonies . . . to procure the repeal of the Act for granting and applying certain stamp duties.

Prominent American leaders wrote letters of protest against British laws, and these were often printed and circulated throughout the colonies. John Dickinson of Pennsylvania, for example, wrote in 1767 the renowned "Letters from a Farmer in Pennsylvania to the Inhabitants of the British Colonies." These letters, published in newspapers and widely read, expressed resentment of British regulations that Dickinson, like others, viewed as unconstitutional and

destructive to the liberty of the colonies. In the 12th letter of his "Pennsylvania Farmer" series, Dickinson boldly rejected British tax laws as destructive of individual rights to property and liberty and called upon the inhabitants of Britain's American colonies to stand united against oppressive acts of Parliament.

Let these truths be indelibly impressed on our minds—that we cannot be happy without being free—that we cannot be free without being secure in our property—that we cannot be secure in our property if without our consent others may as by right take it away—that taxes imposed on us by Parliament do thus take it away—that duties laid for the sole purpose of raising money are taxes—that attempts to lay such duties should be instantly and firmly opposed—that this opposition can never be effectual unless it is the united effort of these Provinces—that therefore benevolence of temper towards each other and unanimity of councils are essential to the welfare of the whole—and lastly, that for this reason, every man amongst us who in any manner would encourage either dissension, diffidence, or indifference between these colonies is an enemy to himself and to his country.

Resolutions in Defense of Rights

In September 1774, the First Continental Congress met in Philadelphia and passed the Declaration and Resolves of the Continental Congress to express the American reaction to violations of individual rights in the colonies. The declaration conveyed the prevailing American belief in the fundamental rights of the people, as indicated by the title page of a New York printing that called this document the "Bill of Rights."

That the inhabitants of the English Colonies in North America, by the immutable laws of nature, the principles of the English Constitution, and the several charters or compacts, have the following rights:

1. That they are entitled to life, liberty, and property, and they have never ceded to any sovereign power whatever, a right to dispose of either without their consent.

2. That our ancestors, who first settled these colonies, were at the time of their emigration from the mother country, entitled to all the rights, liberties, and immunities of free and natural-born subjects within the realm of England.

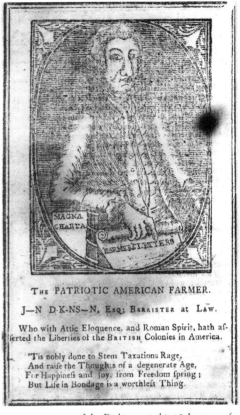

THE PATRIOTIC AMERICAN FARMER.

J—N D·K·NS—N, Esq; Barrister at Law.

Who with Attic Eloquence, and Roman Spirit, hath asserted the Liberties of the BRITISH Colonies in America.

'Tis nobly done to Stem Taxations Rage,
And raise the Thoughts of a degenerate Age,
For Happiness and Joy, from Freedom spring;
But Life in Bondage is a worthless Thing.

John Dickinson, in his 12 Letters of a Pennsylvania Farmer, denied the authority of the British Parliament to impose taxes on the American colonies. In this picture, published in a Boston almanac in 1772, Dickinson rests his elbow on the Magna Carta, as he displays his "Farmer's Letters."

3. That by such emigration they by no means forfeited, surrendered, or lost any of those rights, but that they were, and their descendants now are entitled to the exercise and enjoyment of all such of them, as their local and other circumstances enable them to exercise and enjoy.

4. That the foundation of English liberty, and of all free government, is a right in the people to participate in their legislative council: and as the English colonists are not represented, and from their local and other circumstances, cannot properly be represented in the British Parliament, they are entitled to a free and exclusive power of legislation in their several provincial legislatures, where their right of representation can alone be preserved, in all cases of taxation and internal polity. . . .

5. That the respective colonies are entitled to the common law of England, and more especially to the great and inestimable privilege of being tried by their peers of the vicinage, according to the course of that law.

6. That they are entitled to the benefit of such of the English statutes, as existed at the time of their colonization; and which they have, by experience, respectively found to be applicable to their several local and other circumstances.

7. That these, His Majesty's Colonies, are likewise entitled to all the immunities and privileges granted and confirmed to

The First Continental Congress met in Philadelphia from September 5 to October 26, 1774, to consider how the American colonies should jointly respond to repressive British actions. In this 1782 French illustration, Peyton Randolph of Virginia, the first president of the Congress, sits on an elevated chair to preside over a meeting of representatives from 12 of the 13 American colonies; Georgia did not participate.

them by royal charters, or secured by their several codes of provincial laws.

8. That they have a right peaceably to assemble, consider of their grievances, and petition the king; and that all prosecutions, prohibitory proclamations, and commitments for the same, are illegal.

9. That the keeping a standing army in these colonies, in times of peace, without the consent of the legislature of that colony in which such army is kept is against law.

10. It is indispensably necessary to good government, and rendered essential by the English Constitution, that the constituent branches of the legislature be independent of each other; that, therefore, the exercise of legislative power in several colonies, by a council appointed during pleasure, by the Crown, is unconstitutional, dangerous, and destructive to the freedom of American legislation.

All and each of which the aforesaid deputies, in behalf of themselves and their constituents, do claim, demand, and insist on, as their indubitable rights and liberties; which cannot be legally taken from them, altered or abridged by any power whatever, without their own consent, by their representatives in their several provincial legislatures.

On June 7, 1776, Richard Henry Lee of Virginia presented a decisive proposal to the Second Continental Congress, a "Resolution for Independence." Congress voted to approve it on July 2, 1776, which pointed the way to independence and union of the 13 American states.

Resolved
That these United Colonies are, and of right ought to be, free and independent States, that they are absolved from all allegiance to the British Crown, and that all political connection between them and the State of Great Britain is, and ought to be, totally dissolved.

That it is expedient forthwith to take the most effectual measures for forming foreign Alliances.

That a plan of confederation be prepared and transmitted to the respective Colonies for their consideration and approbation.

The Declaration of Independence

On June 11, 1776, the Continental Congress selected a committee of five to draft a document that would justify the independence of the united American states. The members

Thomas Paine and *Common Sense*

A mong the greatest patriots of the American Revolution was an immigrant from England, Thomas Paine. He came to Pennsylvania in November 1774, only about five months before the Revolutionary War began. Yet, no one more fervently boosted the American cause than Thomas Paine.

In January 1776, Paine published his widely praised pamphlet *Common Sense*, which brilliantly argued the case for American independence and pushed public opinion throughout the 13 states toward a formal and final separation from the mother country. Thomas Paine wrote:

"O ye that love mankind! Ye that dare oppose, not only the tyranny, but the tyrant, stand forth! Every spot of the old world is over-run with oppression. Freedom hath been hunted round the globe. Asia, and Africa, have long expelled her.—Europe regards her like a stranger, and England hath given her warning to depart. O! receive the fugitive, and prepare in time an asylum for mankind."

were John Adams, Benjamin Franklin, Thomas Jefferson, Robert Livingston, and Roger Sherman. Jefferson wrote the draft submitted to the Continental Congress, which approved it on July 4, 1776.

The idea of natural rights permeates the Declaration of Independence. In the second paragraph of the document, for example, Jefferson puts forth a theory of government that comes from *The Second Treatise of Government* by John Locke. According to this theory, all individuals are equal in their possession of certain natural rights, which the government is supposed to protect. These rights do not come from the government. Rather, they are part of human nature and, therefore, all human beings possess them. The primary purpose of government is to guarantee these rights.

A good government, according to this declaration, is one that effectively secures or protects these natural rights. Further, a good government is always based on the consent of the governed—the people who create the government, live under its authority, and possess the right to change it if the government does not serve the purpose for which it was created.

In the Declaration of Independence, there is a shift in American thinking away from the legal traditions of England to a conception of natural rights of mankind. The American documents of the 1760s, such as the resolutions of the Stamp Act Congress, refer to the English common law and charters as the foundations of rights. By contrast, the Declaration of Independence refers to the natural rights of all people—the "unalienable rights to life, liberty, and the pursuit of happiness."

WHEN in the course of human events, it becomes necessary for one people to dissolve the Political Bands which have connected them with another, and to assume among the Powers of the Earth the separate and equal Station to which the Laws of Nature and of Nature's God entitle them, a decent Respect to the Opinions of Mankind requires that they should declare the causes which impel them to the Separation.

We hold these Truths to be self-evident, that all Men are created equal, that they are endowed by their Creator with certain unalienable Rights, that among these are Life, Liberty, and the Pursuit of Happiness—That to secure these Rights, Governments are instituted among Men, deriving their just Powers from the

In this June 21, 1776, letter, Thomas Jefferson asked Benjamin Franklin to read his draft of the Declaration of Independence. He invited Franklin to "suggest such alterations as his more enlarged view of the subject will dictate."

Consent of the Governed. That whenever any Form of Government becomes destructive to these Ends, it is the Right of the People to alter or to abolish it, and to institute new Government, laying its Foundations on such Principles and organizing its Powers in such Form, as to them shall seem most likely to effect their Safety and Happiness. Prudence, indeed, will dictate that Governments long established should not be changed for light and transient causes; and accordingly all Experience hath shown, that Mankind are more disposed to suffer, while Evils are sufferable, than to right themselves by abolishing the Forms to which they are accustomed. But when a long Train of Abuses and Usurpations, pursuing invariably the same Object evinces a Design to reduce them under absolute Despotism, it is their Right, it is their Duty, to throw off such Government, and to provide new Guards for their future Security. Such has been the patient Sufferance of these Colonies; and such is now the Necessity which constrains them to alter their former Systems of Government. The History of the present King of Great Britain is a history of repeated Injuries and Usurpations, all having in direct Object the Establishment of an absolute Tyranny over these States. . . .

We, therefore, the Representatives of the united States of America, in General Congress, Assembled, appealing to the Supreme Judge of the world for the rectitude of our Intentions, do, in the Name, and by authority of the good People of these Colonies, solemnly publish and declare, That these United Colonies are, and of Right ought to be, Free and Independent States; that they are absolved from all allegiance to the British Crown, and that all political connection between them and the

[I]n the new Code of Laws which I suppose it will be necessary for you to make I desire you would Remember the Ladies, and be more generous and favorable to them than your ancestors. Do not put such unlimited power into the hands of the Husbands. Remember all Men would be tyrants if they could. If particular care and attention is not paid to the Ladies we are determined to foment a Rebellion, and will not hold ourselves bound by any Laws in which we have no voice, or Representation.

—Abigail Adams, letter to John Adams, March 31, 1776

The Liberty Bell

The bell known as the Liberty Bell was made in 1753 and was engraved with these words: "Proclaim liberty throughout all the land unto all the inhabitants thereof."

When the Declaration of Independence was read publicly in Philadelphia on July 8, 1776, it seemed right to ring the bell in celebration of the new nation. When British troops captured Philadelphia, the bell was taken away and hidden in Allentown, Pennsylvania. It was taken back to Independence Hall in 1778.

The bell cracked when it was rung in 1835. In 1976 it was taken down and moved to a special public place for display, near Independence Hall, where great Americans made their Declaration of Independence and Constitution.

State of Great Britain, is and ought to be totally dissolved; and that as Free and Independent States, they have full Power to levy War, conclude Peace, contract Alliances, establish Commerce, and to do all other Acts and Things which Independent States may of right do. And for the support of this Declaration, with a firm reliance on the Protection of Divine Providence, we mutually pledge to each other our Lives, our Fortunes, and our sacred Honor.

On January 13, 1777, seven African Americans petitioned the legislature of Massachusetts to secure their natural rights and those of slaves on equal terms with other inhabitants of the state. This petition was in agreement with the prevailing American belief that natural rights are the common possession of all human beings. The government cannot, therefore, justly deny these rights to anyone. The petitioners implied that officials of the Massachusetts government were hypocrites, given their professed beliefs in natural rights, unless they renounced slavery.

The General Court, or legislature, of Massachusetts accepted this petition and discussed it approvingly. Further, members of the General Court drafted a bill "for preventing the practice of holding persons in Slavery." But nothing came of it, and slavery continued in Massachusetts and other American states. Although this petition failed, it helped set the terms of a continuing American debate on the range and reach of principles about individual rights. The subsequent American movement to abolish slavery and secure the rights of former slaves developed in response to revolutionary statements about the natural rights of mankind. In 1783, the Superior Court of Massachusetts decided that slavery was illegal because it violated the state's Declaration of Rights.

The petition of a great number of blacks detained in a state of slavery in the bowels of a free and Christian country humbly shows that your petitioners apprehend that they have in common with all other men a natural and unalienable right to that freedom which the Great Parent of the universe has bestowed equally on all mankind and which they have never forfeited by any compact or agreement whatever. But they were unjustly dragged by the hand of cruel power from their dearest friends and some of them even torn from the embraces of their tender parents, from a populous, pleasant, and plentiful country and in violation of laws of

On July 9, 1776, after listening to a public reading of the Declaration of Independence, Americans in New York City pulled down and removed a statue of King George III. In this French engraving recording the event, African Americans are shown pulling at the ropes. Many African Americans hoped that the rights asserted during the American Revolution would extend to slaves.

nature and of nations and in defiance of all the tender feelings of humanity, brought here either to be sold like beasts of burden and, like them, condemned to slavery for life—among a people professing the mild religion of Jesus; a people not insensible of the secrets of rational being, nor without spirit to resent the unjust endeavors of others to reduce them to a state of bondage and subjection. Your Honor need not be informed that a life of slavery like that of your petitioners, deprived of every social privilege of everything requisite to render life tolerable, is far worse than nonexistence. . . .

[E]very principle from which America has acted in the course of their unhappy difficulties with Great Britain pleads stronger than a thousand arguments in favor of your petitioners.

They therefore humbly beseech Your Honors to give this petition its due weight and consideration, and cause an act of legislation to be passed whereby they may be restored to the enjoyments of that which is the natural right of all men, and that their children, who were born in this land of liberty, may not be held as slaves after they arrive at the age of twenty-one years. So may the inhabitants of this state, no longer chargeable with the inconsistency of acting themselves the part which they condemn and oppose in others, be prospered in their present glorious struggle for liberty and have those blessings for themselves.

Chapter Three

The Birth of the Bill of Rights

This engraving commends George Washington, first President of the United States, as a "supporter of the rights of Mankind." He is surrounded by the seals of the 13 states, with the seal of the United States at the top.

Americans have always seen their revolutionary war as a fight for rights that the British had denied them. But rights defended in war will be lost in peace if people fail to establish a good government in place of the one they overturned. Americans in 1776 were committed to the central principle of good government stated in their Declaration of Independence: "That to secure these rights [to life, liberty, and the pursuit of happiness] governments are instituted among men, deriving their just powers from the consent of the governed." As the war raged, they undertook the challenge of creating new governments for their newly independent states, in order to secure their rights.

No one had thought longer or deeper than John Adams about new constitutions and governments for the new American states. In his autobiography, he recalled that "almost every day, I had something to say about advising the States to institute Governments." And Adams was so respected that leaders from several states asked for his thoughts, which he readily offered. For example, Richard Henry Lee wanted Adams's advice on writing a constitution for Virginia. In a long letter to Lee, Adams emphasized the idea of separation and balance of powers among three branches of government as the way to protect the people's rights against the ever-present threat of tyranny. Adams wrote, "A Legislative, an Executive and a judicial power comprehend the whole of what is meant and understood by Government. It is by balancing each of these Powers against the other two, that the Effort in human Nature toward Tyranny can alone be checked and restrained and any degree of Freedom preserved in the constitution."

A short time later, in April 1776, Adams used the ideas in this letter as the basis for a widely circulated pamphlet, *Thoughts on Government*, which greatly influenced constitution-making in the new American

John Adams was a deep thinker about the theory and practice of constitutional government. His ideas on limited government, the rule of law, and separation of powers influenced several of the original state constitutions and the 1787 U.S. Constitution.

states. The Second Continental Congress, meeting in Philadelphia in May, responded to Adams's pleas that new governments should be established in the 13 British colonies soon to become the 13 United States of America. The Congress on May 10 passed Adams's resolution on the formation of state governments, thereby prompting an extraordinary burst of constitution making among the states, which preceded and followed the Declaration of Independence in July 1776.

Virginia readily responded to the congressional resolution, and its Declaration of Rights became a model for others. Some of the states added rights not included in the Virginia document and unlike Virginia were not constrained by the need to protect the institution of slavery from the appeal of declarations about natural rights. The Pennsylvania Declaration of Rights, for instance, unequivocally states that the primary purpose of government is "to enable the individuals who compose it to enjoy their natural rights." It was also the first one to guarantee freedom of speech. And it notably guaranteed the right to legal protection against invasion of privacy and seizure of property by government officials, a forerunner of the 4th Amendment to the U.S. Constitution. In addition, the Pennsylvania Declaration stated that "the people have a right to bear arms for the defense of themselves and the states." This is an antecedent of the 2nd Amendment to the U.S. Constitution. Further, this declaration guaranteed the right to legal counsel for persons accused of a crime, which was later included in the Constitution's 6th Amendment.

From 1776 until 1780, the 13 new American states wrote constitutions. Most of them included declarations of rights at the start of the document. These constitutions were designed primarily to protect the rights of the people who created them, but they also influenced the contents of the U.S. Constitution of 1787 and the Bill of Rights of 1791, the fulfillment of an American revolution for rights. The various state declarations included nearly all the rights found later in the Bill of Rights.

As the states made their constitutions, delegates to the Continental Congress drafted a plan of government for the entire United States, the Articles of Confederation. Under the Articles, each state kept its sovereignty—the supreme power to make and enforce rules. The Congress had few powers, with little capacity to carry them out. The United States was really a loose alliance of 13 practically sovereign states. Weaknesses in the national government under the Articles of Confederation led to serious problems. There was no power in the Confederation to maintain law and order throughout the country or to provide for the common defense against foreign enemies.

Because Americans had recently fought a war against an overbearing British government, they were reluctant to grant very much power to their own new government. They were determined to protect their rights mainly by limiting the government's power. They understood that the rights of individuals are at risk if the government is too strong and if there are insufficient limitations upon it. They seemed unaware that the rights of individuals also are at risk if the government is too weak to protect them from enemies, foreign or domestic, who would threaten their personal safety, property, and liberty.

James Madison of Virginia and other American leaders, such as Alexander Hamilton of New York, urged Congress to call a convention of delegates from the 13 states to strengthen the government of the United States. Congress convened a meeting in Philadelphia in May 1787 to consider reforms. George Washington led Virginia's delegation, which also included Madison. Eventually, 55 delegates from 12 states took part. Only Rhode Island did not send representatives.

From May 25 until September 17, 1787, the delegates to the Constitutional Convention met at the State House in Philadelphia, where the Continental Congress had declared independence and drafted the Articles of Confederation. Now they made the Constitution of the United States of America to provide an effective federal government for the country. The delegates

This illustration of the Pennsylvania State House in Philadelphia appeared in the July 1787 issue of the Columbian *magazine. On the centennial of the* Declaration of Independence *in 1876, it became a national museum and is known today as Independence Hall.*

agreed on their main objective—to make a constitution for the United States that truly would secure their rights and thereby fulfill the purpose of the American Revolution.

The Constitution produced by the convention empowered the federal government to maintain law and order for the safety and security of the people. However, principles of separated powers, checks and balances, and federalism were included in the Constitution to limit the powers of that government. The government was also limited to the powers granted to it by the Constitution; powers not granted to the national government by the people were reserved to the state governments or to the people. The ultimate purpose of all these limitations was to protect the rights of individuals against misuse of power. The Constitution makers understood that a government with too little power could not protect the people's rights, but a government with too much power could abuse the people. They therefore tried to make a constitutional government that was neither too strong nor too weak so that the rights of individuals would be secured.

On September 17, the last day of the Constitutional Convention, 39 men representing 12 states signed the Constitution. George Mason, the primary author of the 1776 Virginia Declaration of Rights, was one of three who refused to sign it. He had drawn up a list of objections, one of which was that the Constitution did not include a federal bill of rights. Mason's objections began to circulate, first as a handwritten document and then as a newspaper editorial and printed pamphlet. On September 28, the Continental Congress voted unanimously to send the proposed Constitution to the legislature of each of the 13 states "in Order to be submitted to a convention of Delegates chosen in each state by the people thereof." In this way, Congress asked each state to convene a special ratifying convention to approve or reject the Constitution. If nine state ratifying conventions approved it, this Constitution would become the supreme law of the United States of America.

The idea of rights was, from the start, at the center of the national debate on the Constitution. Mason and other opponents of the Constitution, the Anti-Federalists, feared that ratification of the Constitution would put their rights at risk. Defenders of the Constitution, the Federalists, such as Alexander Hamilton of New York and James Madison of Virginia, supported ratification. In response to Mason's objections, they pointed to protections provided for in the Constitution, such as the right to a trial by jury.

In the *Federalist Papers*, Hamilton and Madison argued that basic principles of the Constitution—such as separation of powers, checks and balances, popular election of legislators, and limited grants of power to the federal government—would be sufficient to protect the people's rights and liberties. Further, they recognized that the federal government under the Constitution could not negate liberties and rights in the state constitutions because it had not been granted the power to do so; the federal government, for example, had not been granted the power to make laws denying freedom of the press. So the Federalists believed there was no need to add a bill of rights to the Constitution.

Objection to the lack of a bill of rights, however, haunted the Federalists until they gave in and promised that, if the Constitution were ratified, they would make sure to add a bill of rights to it. This trade-off was a key to Federalist victories in the ratifying conventions of several states, such as Massachusetts, South Carolina, New Hampshire, Virginia, New York, and North Carolina. As the ratification struggle continued, James Madison began to change his mind about adding a bill of rights to the Constitution and realized that this would be the price of ratification. During and after the Virginia ratifying convention, Madison publicly committed himself to the cause of a bill of rights, but only if its provisions would not change the basic structure of the federal government. Above all, he wanted to prevent any reduction in the power of the federal government in its relationship with the several state governments.

The Constitution was approved in 1788 by state ratifying conventions. In 1789, a new federal government was instituted under the Constitution of the United States of America. James Madison, representing his district of Virginia in the U.S. House of Representatives, proposed a bill of rights during the First Federal Congress, as promised. On September 25, 1789, after weeks of deliberations and debate, more than two-thirds of both houses of Congress agreed to 12 constitutional amendments derived from Madison's list. On October 2, President George Washington sent the 12 proposed amendments to the states for their approval. Article 5 of the Constitution says that constitutional amendments may be proposed by two-thirds of both houses of Congress. They cannot be ratified unless three-fourths of the states approve them. By December 15, 1791, 10 of the 12 amendments were ratified by the states and became the part of the Constitution known as the Bill of Rights.

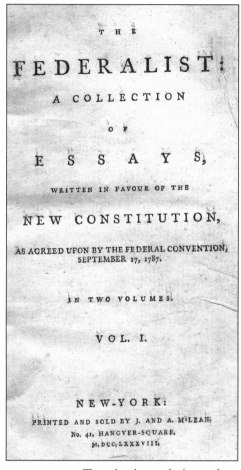

This is the title page of volume 1 of The Federalist, a collection of 85 papers in favor of ratifying the 1787 U.S. Constitution. Alexander Hamilton edited this 2-volume set and was the author of 51 of the papers.

The birth of an American Bill of Rights was the consequence of a long series of events that began in England in 1215 and ended in America in 1791. The Bill of Rights was, however, primarily a product of the process by which Americans made their original state and federal constitutions.

Rights in the New American States

A Virginia convention was organized in mid-May of 1776 with the mission of drafting a Declaration of Rights and constitution for the state government. George Mason, a wealthy landowner in Fairfax County, became the primary writer of the Virginia declaration and the state constitution that followed it.

In six days, Mason completed his draft of a declaration and submitted it to the convention for discussion and approval. Two significant criticisms came forward. First, most representatives objected to Mason's sweeping statement of natural rights in Section 1 of his work: "That all men are *born* equally free and independent, and have certain inherent rights." They substituted the words "by nature" for "born" and added, after "inherent rights," the phrase "when they enter into a state of society." This was done to satisfy the concerns of Virginia slave owners. It would be impossible by the laws of that time for a slave to enter into the society of Virginia. Thus, they could legally (according to this revised Declaration of Rights) be denied the rights guaranteed for others by the constitutional government of the state.

A second criticism was raised against Section 16, which pertained to free expression of religious beliefs. The critic, in this instance, was young James Madison, 25 years old in 1776, who wrote in his *Autobiography* that he was "initiated into the political career" through participation in the committee that drafted the Virginia Declaration of Rights. "Being young," wrote Madison, he did not have a leading part in the debate, but he added an important clause to the final article of the document, which asserted the fundamental importance of the right to "free exercise of religion." The Virginia Declaration of Rights reflected an American consensus on the rights of individuals that developed from the centuries-old English legal tradition and the more than 160 years of the American colonial experience.

That all men have a natural and unalienable right to worship Almighty God, according to the dictates of their own consciences and understanding; and that no man ought or of right can be compelled to attend any religious worship, or erect or support any place of worship, or maintain any ministry contrary to, or against, his own free will and consent; nor can any man, who acknowledges the being of a God, be justly deprived or abridged of any civil right as a citizen, on account of his religious sentiments or peculiar mode of religious worship; and that no authority can, or ought to be vested in, or assumed by any power whatever, that shall in any case interfere with, or in any manner controul the right of conscience in the free exercise of religious worship.

—Article 2 of the Pennsylvania Declaration of Rights, 1776

A third element of this document was the idea of natural rights, found in the philosophy of John Locke, and stated in Sections 1 through 3 of the Virginia Declaration of Rights, which was drafted and approved more than three weeks before July 4, 1776. The language in this section is very similar to the second paragraph of the Declaration of Independence. Both documents proclaim that the primary purpose of government, based on consent of the governed, is to secure the natural rights of individuals.

A Declaration of Rights made by the Representatives of the good people of Virginia, assembled in full and free Convention; which rights do pertain to them and their posterity, as the basis and foundation of government.

1. That all men are by nature equally free and independent, and have certain inherent rights, of which, when they enter into a state of society, they cannot, by any compact, deprive or divest their posterity; namely, the enjoyment of life and liberty, with the means of acquiring and possessing property, and pursuing and obtaining happiness and safety.

2. That all power is vested in, and consequently derived from, the People; that magistrates are their trustees and servants, and at all times amenable to them.

3. That Government is, or ought to be, instituted for the common benefit, protection, and security of the people, nation, or community; of all the various modes and forms of Government, that is best which is capable of producing the greatest degree of happiness and safety, and is most effectually secured against the danger of mal-administration; and that, when any Government shall be found inadequate or contrary to these purposes, a majority of the community hath an indubitable, unalienable, and indefeasible right to reform, alter, or abolish it, in such manner as shall be judged most conducive to the publick weal.

4. That no man, or set of men, are entitled to exclusive or separate emoluments or privileges from the community, but in consideration of publick services; which,

This 1778 British cartoon ridiculed American proclamations about the rights of individuals and the evils of British tyranny, such as those expressed in the Declaration of Independence. A prostrate African American represents the denial of liberty to enslaved people, and the American soldiers at the right are depicted as miserable and degraded.

A VIEW IN AMERICA IN 1778

not being descendible, neither ought the offices of Magistrate, Legislator, or Judge, to be hereditary.

5. That the Legislative and Executive powers of the State should be separate and distinct from the Judicative; and that the members of the two first may be restrained from oppression, by feeling and participating the burdens of the people, they should, at fixed periods, be reduced to a private station, return into that body from which they were originally taken, and the vacancies be supplied by frequent, certain, and regular elections, in which all, or any part of the former members, to be again eligible, or ineligible, as the law shall direct.

6. That elections of members to serve as Representative of the people, in Assembly, ought to be free; and that all men, having sufficient evidence of permanent common interest with, and attachment to, the community, have the right of suffrage, and cannot be taxed or deprived of their property for publick uses without their own consent or that of their Representative so elected, nor bound by any law to which they have not, in like manner, assented, for the publick good.

7. That all power of suspending laws, or the execution of laws, by any authority, without consent of the Representatives of the people, is injurious to their rights, and ought not to be exercised.

8. That in all capital or criminal prosecutions a man hath a right to demand the cause and nature of his accusation, to be confronted with the accusers and witnesses, to call for evidence in his favour, and to a speedy trial by an impartial jury of his vicinage, without whose unanimous consent he cannot be found guilty, nor can he be compelled to give evidence against himself; that no man be deprived of his liberty except by the law of the land, or the judgment of his peers.

9. That excessive bail ought not to be required, nor excessive fines imposed, nor cruel and unusual punishments inflicted.

10. That general warrants, whereby an officer or messenger may be commended to search suspected places without evidence of a fact committed, or to seize any person or persons not named, or whose offence is not particularly described and supported by evidence, are grievous and oppressive, and ought not to be granted.

11. That in controversies respecting property, and in suits between man and man, the ancient trial by Jury is preferable to any other, and ought to be held sacred.

12. That the freedom of the Press is one of the great bulwarks of liberty, and can never be restrained but by despotick Governments.

13. That a well-regulated Militia, composed of the body of the people, trained to arms, is the proper, natural, and safe defence of a free State; that Standing Armies, in time of peace, should be avoided, as dangerous to liberty; and that in all cases, the military should be under strict subordination to, and governed by, the civil power.

14. That the people have a right to uniform Government; and, therefore, that no Government separate from, or independent of, the Government of Virginia, ought to be erected or established within the limits thereof.

15. That no free Government, or the blessings of liberty, can be preserved to any people but by a firm adherence to justice, moderation, temperance, frugality, and virtue, and by frequent recurrence to fundamental principles.

16. That Religion, or the duty which we owe to our Creator, and the manner of discharging it, can be directed only by reason and conviction, not by force or violence; and, therefore, all men are equally entitled to the free exercise of religion, according to the dictates of conscience; and that it is the mutual duty of all to practise Christian forbearance, love, and charity, towards each other.

John Adams believed that individual rights cannot be protected by an eloquently worded declaration alone. Rather, the machinery of government, set forth in a constitution, must work effectively to protect those rights. The 1780 Massachusetts Constitution, written mostly by Adams, was designed to limit and empower the government for the ultimate purpose of protecting rights set forth in a Declaration of Rights, which Adams also drafted. It is the only one of the original American state constitutions still in use today.

The Massachusetts Constitution had a strong influence on the U.S. Constitution and the Bill of Rights. The preamble to the Massachusetts document declares two standards for good government that were established during the era of the American Revolution: government by consent of the governed, and government for the purpose of protecting the natural rights and promoting the common good of the governed.

PREAMBLE

The end of the institution, maintenance and administration of government, is to secure the existence of the body-politic; to protect it; and to furnish the individuals who compose it, with the power of enjoying, in safety and tranquility, their natural rights,

ALL men are born free and equal, and have certain natural, essential, and unalienable rights; among which may be reckoned the right of enjoying and defending their lives and liberties; that of acquiring, possessing, and protecting property; in fine, that of seeking and obtaining their safety and happiness.

—Article 1 of the Massachusetts Declaration of Rights, 1780

A Constitution or Frame of Government for the Commonwealth of MASSACHUSETTS.

PREAMBLE.

THE end of the institution, maintenance and administration of government, is to secure the existence of the body-politic; to protect it; and to furnish the individuals who compose it, with the power of enjoying, in safety and tranquility, their natural rights, and the blessings of life: And whenever these great objects are not obtained, the people have a right to alter the government, and to take measures necessary for their safety, prosperity and happiness.

The body-politic is formed by a voluntary association of individuals: It is a social compact, by which the whole people covenants with each citizen, and each citizen with the whole people, that all shall be governed by certain laws for the common good. It is the duty of the people, therefore, in framing a Constitution of Government, to provide for an equitable mode of making laws, as well as for an impartial interpretation, and a faithful execution of them; that every man may, at all times, find his security in them.

WE, therefore, the people of Massachusetts, acknowledging with grateful hearts, the goodness of the Great Legislature of the Universe, in affording us, in the course of His Providence, an opportunity, deliberately and peaceably, without fraud, violence or surprize, of entering into an original, explicit, and solemn compact with each other; and of forming a new Constitution of Civil Government, for ourselves and posterity; and devoutly imploring His direction in so interesting a design, DO agree upon, ordain and establish, the following *Declaration of Rights, and Frame of Government*, as the CONSTITUTION of the COMMONWEALTH of MASSACHUSETTS.

PART THE FIRST.

A DECLARATION of the RIGHTS of the Inhabitants of the Commonwealth of MASSACHUSETTS.

Art. I. ALL men are born free and equal, and have certain natural, essential and unalienable rights; among which may be reckoned the right of enjoying and defending their lives and liberties; that of acquiring, possessing, and protecting property; in fine, that of seeking and obtaining their safety and happiness.

II. It is the right as well as the duty of all men in society, publicly, and at stated seasons, to worship the SUPREME BEING, the great creator and preserver of the universe. And no subject shall be hurt, molested, or restrained, in his person, liberty, or estate, for worshipping GOD in the manner and season most

In 1779, the eligible voters of Massachusetts elected representatives to a constitutional convention, which appointed a three person committee—John Adams, Samuel Adams, and James Bowdoin—to draft a constitution for the state's government. The Massachusetts Constitution of 1780, written mainly by John Adams, is the only original American state constitution still in use.

and the blessings of life: And whenever these great objects are not obtained, the people have a right to alter the government, and to take measures necessary for their safety, prosperity and happiness.

The body-politic is formed by a voluntary association of individuals: It is a social compact, by which the whole people covenants with each citizen, and each citizen with the whole people, that all shall be governed by certain laws for the common good. It is the duty of the people, therefore, in framing a Constitution of Government, to provide for an equitable mode of making laws, as well as for an impartial interpretation, and a faithful execution of them; that every man may, at all times, find his security in them.

We, therefore, the people of Massachusetts, acknowledging, with grateful hearts, the goodness of the Great Legislator of the Universe, in affording us, in the course of His providence, an opportunity, deliberately and peaceably, without fraud, violence or surprise, of entering into an original, explicit, and solemn compact with each other; and of forming a new Constitution of Civil Government, for ourselves and posterity; and devoutly imploring His direction in so interesting a design, DO agree upon, ordain and establish, the following *Declaration of Rights, and Frame of Government*, as the CONSTITUTION of the COMMONWEALTH of MASSACHUSETTS.

In 1786, George Washington noted with dismay the weakness of the national government in the United States. Members of Congress were more loyal to their states than to their country. Most citizens seemed to consider their own state first and to think of other states almost as foreign lands. The central government did not have enough authority to build national unity, to defend the country against enemies, and to enforce law and order adequately throughout the land.

Washington feared anarchy, and he warned that loss of individual rights and freedom would follow a breakdown of law and order. On August 1, 1786, Washington expressed his worries about a crisis in government in a letter to John Jay of New York.

Your sentiments, that our affairs are drawing rapidly to a crisis, accord with my own. What the event will be, is also beyond the reach of my foresight. We have errors to correct. We have probably had too good an opinion of human nature in forming our Confederation. Experience has taught us, that men will not adopt and carry into execution measures the best calculated for their own good, without the intervention of a coercive power. I do not conceive we can exist long as a nation without having lodged somewhere a power, which will pervade the whole Union in as energetic a manner as the authority of the State governments extends over the several States. . .

To be fearful of investing Congress, constituted as that body is, with ample authorities for national purposes, appears to me to be the very climax of popular absurdity and madness.

Rights in the U.S. Constitution

Gouverneur Morris, a delegate from Pennsylvania to the Constitutional Convention in 1787, wrote a preamble that stated the purposes of government addressed by the new Constitution. It declares that "domestic tranquility" and "common defence" are important ends of government, as are rights to "the blessings of liberty." These words reflected the general agreement among Americans that constitutional government should provide order and liberty under law for people of their time and future generations.

We, the people of the United States, in order to form a more perfect Union, establish justice, insure domestic tranquility, provide for the common defence, promote the general welfare, and secure the blessings of liberty to ourselves and our posterity, do ordain and establish this Constitution for the United States of America.

On September 12, 1787, near the end of the Constitutional Convention, George Mason of Virginia proposed that a committee should be named to prepare a bill of rights. He was supported by Elbridge Gerry, a statesman from Massachusetts, but Roger Sherman, a representative from Connecticut,

The Northwest Ordinance of 1787

During the summer of 1787, the Constitutional Convention in Philadelphia was writing the U.S. Constitution. At the same time, the soon-to-be defunct Congress of the Articles of Confederation was meeting in New York City to enact the Northwest Ordinance. This Ordinance of 1787 was a plan for establishing government and making new states in the territory north and west of the Ohio River. Five states eventually were created from this Northwest Territory: Ohio (1803), Indiana (1816), Illinois (1818), Michigan (1837), and Wisconsin (1848).

In six Articles of Compact, the Ordinance of 1787 also guaranteed rights not included in the U.S. Constitution until ratification in 1791 of the Bill of Rights and amendments 13 and 14 in 1865 and 1868. For example, freedom of religion, due process in legal proceedings, trial by jury, protection of private property, sanctity of contracts, free public education, and protection against cruel and unusual punishments were proclaimed as inviolable rights of inhabitants of the Northwest Territory. Further, slavery was prohibited. On July 13, 1787, the Confederation Congress passed the Northwest Ordinance. In 1789, the First Federal Congress under the U.S. Constitution reaffirmed the Ordinance of 1787.

argued, "The State Declarations of Rights are not repealed by this Constitution; and being in force are sufficient." Mason pointed to Article 6 of the Constitution and replied, "The laws of the United States are to be paramount to State Bills of Rights." He was worried that the U.S. government under this new Constitution would have the power to override state guarantees of rights. According to Mason, a federal bill of rights was needed to limit the federal government's power. Every state delegation at the Constitutional Convention voted against George Mason's proposal.

Mason was furious. The next day, Mason scowled as he studied the printed draft of the Constitution prepared by the Committee of Style. He turned over the draft and started to write on the back his "Objections to this Constitution of Government." His main objection was, of course, "There is no Declaration of Rights."

There is no Declaration of Rights; and the Laws of the general Government being paramount to the Laws and Constitutions of the several States, the Declaration of Rights in the separate States are no Security. . . .

In the House of Representatives there is not the Substance, but the Shadow only of Representation; which can never produce proper Information in the Legislature, or inspire Confidence in the People: the Laws will therefore be generally made by Men little concern'd in, and unacquainted with their Effects and Consequences. . . .

[The Senate] with their . . . great Powers . . . will destroy any Balance in the Government, and will enable them to accomplish what Usurpations they please upon the Rights and Libertys of the People.

The Judiciary of the United States is so constructed and extended, as to absorb and destroy the Judiciarys of the several States . . . thereby rendering Law . . . and Justice as unattainable, by a great part of the Community. . . .

Under their own Construction of the general Clause at the End of the enumerated powers [Article 1, Section 8, Clause 18: the "Necessary and Proper" clause], the Congress may grant monopolies in Trade and Commerce, constitute new Crimes, inflict unusual and severe punishments, and extend their Power as far as they shall think proper; so that the State Legislatures have no security for the powers now presumed to remain to them; or the People for their Rights.

There is no Declaration of any kind for preserving the Liberty of the Press, the Trial by Jury in civil Causes; nor against the Danger of standing Armys in time of Peace. . . .

This Government will commence in a moderate Aristocracy; it is at present impossible to foresee whether it will, in its Operation, produce a Monarchy, or a corrupt, oppressive Aristocracy; it will most probably vibrate some years between the two, and then terminate in the one or the other.

The Federalists, who supported ratification of the Constitution, pointed to several sections as evidence that the document sufficiently protected individual rights.

Article 1, Section 9, protects the privilege of the writ of habeas corpus. Such a writ requires officials to bring a person whom they have arrested before a judge in a court of law. The officials must convince the judge that there are lawful reasons for holding the person. If the judge finds their reasons unlawful, then the court frees the suspect. The writ of habeas corpus protects individuals against government officials who might want to jail them because they belong to unpopular groups or criticize the government.

Article 1, Section 9, also prohibits enactment of bills of attainder and ex post facto laws. A bill of attainder is a law that punishes individuals without a trial or fair hearing in a court of law. An ex post facto law makes an act a crime even if it was committed before the law was enacted. The Federalists argued that other articles of the Constitution, also listed below, outlined further protections.

George Mason objected to the 1787 U.S. Constitution because "there is no declaration of rights." He refused to sign the document on September 17, 1787, the last day of the Constitutional Convention. Mason said that it is necessary to "attend to the rights of every class of the people."

Article 1, Section 9

. . . The Privilege of the Writ of Habeas Corpus shall not be suspended, unless when in Cases of Rebellion or Invasion the public Safety may require it.

No Bill of Attainder or ex post facto Law shall be passed. . . .

Article 1, Section 10

. . . No State shall . . . pass any Bill of Attainder, ex post facto Law, or Law impairing the Obligation of Contracts, or grant any Title of Nobility. . . .

Article 3, Section 2

. . . The Trial of all Crimes, except in Cases of Impeachment, shall be by Jury; and such Trial shall be held in the State where the said Crimes shall have been committed; but when not committed

This page of George Washington's copy of the draft Constitution of the United States has his handwritten notes in the margin. The delegates unanimously selected Washington to preside at the Constitutional Convention. Subsequently he urged ratification of the 1787 Constitution but he admitted, "the warmest friends and the best supporters the Constitution has do not contend that it is free from imperfections."

WE the People of the States of New-Hampſhire, Maſſachuſetts, Rhode-Iſland and Providence Plantations, Connecticut, New-York, New-Jerſey, Pennſylvania, Delaware, Maryland, Virginia, North-Carolina, South-Carolina, and Georgia, do ordain, declare and eſtabliſh the following Conſtitution for the Government of Ourſelves and our Poſterity.

ARTICLE I.

The ſtile of this Government ſhall be, " The United States of America."

II.

The Government ſhall conſiſt of ſupreme legiſlative, executive and judicial powers.

III.

The legiſlative power ſhall be veſted in a Congreſs, to conſiſt of two ſeparate and diſtinct bodies of men, a Houſe of Repreſentatives, and a Senate; each of which ſhall, in all caſes, have a negative on the other. The Legiſlature ſhall meet on the firſt Monday in December in every year.

IV.

Sect. 1. The Members of the Houſe of Repreſentatives ſhall be choſen every ſecond year, by the people of the ſeveral States comprehended within this Union. The qualifications of the electors ſhall be the ſame, from time to time, as thoſe of the electors in the ſeveral States, of the moſt numerous branch of their own legiſlatures.

Sect. 2. Every Member of the Houſe of Repreſentatives ſhall be of the age of twenty-five years at leaſt; ſhall have been a citizen in the United States for at leaſt ▓▓▓ years before his election; and ſhall be, at the time of his election, ▓▓▓▓▓▓ of the State in which he ſhall be choſen.

Sect. 3. The Houſe of Repreſentatives ſhall, at its firſt formation, and until the number of citizens and inhabitants ſhall be taken in the manner herein after deſcribed, conſiſt of ſixty-five Members, of whom three ſhall be choſen in New-Hampſhire, eight in Maſſachuſetts, one in Rhode-Iſland and Providence Plantations, five in Connecticut, ſix in New-York, four in New-Jerſey, eight in Pennſylvania, one in Delaware, ſix in Maryland, ten in Virginia, five in North-Carolina, five in South-Carolina, and three in Georgia.

within any State, the Trial shall be at such Place or Places as the Congress may by Law have directed. . . .

Article 3, Section 3

Treason against the United States, shall consist only in levying War against them, or in adhering to their Enemies, giving them Aid and Comfort. No Person shall be convicted of Treason unless on the Testimony of two Witnesses to the same overt Act, or on Confession in open Court.

The Congress shall have Power to declare the Punishment of Treason, but no Attainder of Treason shall work Corruption of Blood, or Forfeiture except during the Life of the Person attainted. . . .

Article 6

. . . [N]o religious Test shall ever be required as a Qualification to any Office or public Trust under the United States.

The vigor of government is essential to the security of liberty.
—Alexander Hamilton,
The Federalist,
Number 1, 1787

Constitutional Amendments

On October 17, 1788, before his election to the House of Representatives, James Madison wrote to Thomas Jefferson to explain his conversion to the cause of including a bill of rights in the Constitution. Madison, however, continued to believe that a bill of rights would not be an effective safeguard for the people's liberties unless it were embedded in a well-constructed constitutional government that could enforce it. Otherwise, a bill of rights would be a mere "parchment barrier" to tyranny, not an enforceable instrument for individual rights and liberties. So he continued to emphasize the fundamental importance of such constitutional principles as separation of powers and checks and balances among the branches of the federal government and the division of powers between the federal and state governments. These means to limited government and the rule of law were of paramount importance in Madison's scheme to secure the rights of individuals to life, liberty, property, and the pursuit of happiness.

**   In this letter to Jefferson, Madison emphasized the potential tyranny of the majority as the main threat to individual rights in a government based on popular sovereignty, the consent of the governed. A primary purpose of the Constitution was to limit power from any source, including the will of the majority, in order to protect the rights of individuals against tyranny. Madison wanted government to involve majority rule of duly elected representatives of the people, but the majority's power must be limited. If not, the rights of those the majority disliked would be compromised or lost. Madison equally opposed the despotism of a monarch (the tyranny of one), a hereditary aristocracy (the tyranny of the few), and a majority of the people (the tyranny of the majority).**

The States which have adopted the new Constitution are all proceeding to the arrangements for putting it into action. . . .

    The little pamphlet herewith inclosed will give you a collective view of the alterations which have been proposed for the new Constitution. . . . It is true . . . that among the advocates for the Constitution there are some who wish for further guards to public liberty and individual rights. As far as these may consist of

W hen a majority is included in a faction, the form of popular government . . . enables it to sacrifice to its ruling passion or interest both the public good and the rights of other citizens. To secure the public good and private rights against the danger of such a [majority] faction, and at the same time to preserve the spirit and the form of popular government, is then the great object to which our inquiries are directed.. . .

—James Madison, *The Federalist*, Number 10, 1787

James Madison, called the Father of the Bill of Rights, recommended constitutional amendments on individual rights to the U.S. Congress on June 8, 1789. He said, "Government is instituted and ought to be exercised for the benefit of the people, which consists in the enjoyment of life and liberty, with the right of acquiring and using property, and generally of pursuing and obtaining happiness and safety."

A bill of rights is what the people are entitled to against every government on earth, general or particular, and what no just government should refuse or rest on inference.

—Thomas Jefferson, letter to James Madison, December 20, 1787

a constitutional declaration of the most essential rights, it is probable they will be added; though there are many who think such addition unnecessary, and not a few who think it misplaced in such a Constitution. . . .

My own opinion has always been in favor of a bill of rights; provided it be so framed as not to imply powers not meant to be included in the enumeration. At the same time I have never thought the omission a material defect, nor been anxious to supply it even by subsequent amendment, for any other reason than that it is anxiously desired by others. I have favored it because I supposed it might be of use, and if properly executed could not be of disservice. . . .

[E]xperience proves the inefficacy of a bill of rights on those occasions when its controul is most needed. Repeated violations of these parchment barriers have been committed by overbearing majorities in every State. In Virginia I have seen the bill of rights violated in every instance where it has been opposed to a popular current [the will of the majority of the people]. . . .

Wherever the real power in a Government lies, there is the danger of oppression. In our Governments the real power lies in the majority of the Community, and the invasion of private rights is *chiefly* to be apprehended, not from acts of Government contrary to the sense of its constituents, but from acts in which the Government is the mere instrument of the major number of the constituents. This is a truth of great importance, but not yet sufficiently attended to. . . . Wherever there is an interest and power to do wrong, wrong will generally be done, and not less readily by a powerful and interested party [constituting a majority of the people] than by a powerful and interested prince. . . .

Where the power is in the few it is natural for them to sacrifice the many to their own partialities and corruptions. Where the power, as with us, is in the many not in the few, the danger can not be very great that the few will be thus favored. It is much more to be dreaded that the few will be unnecessarily sacrificed to the many.

On June 8, 1789, James Madison spoke to the House of Representatives and proposed several amendments to the Constitution. His proposals were influenced by the 1776 Virginia Declaration of Rights. Madison recommended that his proposals be inserted into sections of the Constitution rather than appended to it. Roger Sherman of Connecticut,

that the will of the Majority should always prevail. if they approve the proposed Convention in all it's parts, I shall concur in it cheerfully, in hopes that they will amend it whenever they shall find it work wrong. I think our governments will remain virtuous for many centuries; as long as they are chiefly agricultural; and this will be as long as there shall be vacant lands in any part of America. When they get piled upon one another in large cities, as in Europe, they will become corrupt. above all things I hope the education of the common people will be attended to; convinced that on their good sense we may rely with the most security for the preservation of a due degree of liberty. I have tired you by this time with my disquisitions & will therefore only add assurances of the sincerity of those sentiments of esteem & attachment with which I am. Dear Sir your affectionate friend & servant

Th: Jefferson

P.S. the instability of our laws is really an immense evil. I think it would be well to provide in our constitutions that there shall always be a twelvemonth between the ingrossing a bill & passing it: that it should then be offered to it's passage without changing a word: and that if circumstances should be thought to require a speedier passage, it should take two thirds of both houses instead of a bare majority.

During the Constitutional Convention and the subsequent contest of the ratification of the 1787 Constitution, Thomas Jefferson was in Paris, where he served as a representative of the United States to the government of France. James Madison sent Jefferson a copy of the 1787 Constitution and asked his opinion of it. In a December 20, 1787, letter to Madison, Jefferson replied that he generally approved the proposed Constitution, but he wished that a bill of rights would be added to it.

however, rallied opposition to this recommendation, and the House of Representatives decided that the proposals should be appended to the Constitution as a separate Bill of Rights. The states ratified 10 of the 12 amendments as of December 15, 1791. They became part of the Constitution and are known as the Bill of Rights.

Amendment 1

Congress shall make no law respecting an establishment of religion, or prohibiting the free exercise thereof; or abridging the freedom of speech, or of the press, or the right of the people peaceably to assemble, and to petition the Government for a redress of grievances.

If they [the amendments in the Bill of Rights] are incorporated into the Constitution, independent tribunals of justice will consider themselves in a peculiar manner the guardians of those rights.

—James Madison,
Annals of Congress, 1789

From August 25 to September 9, 1789, the United States Senate deliberated about 17 constitutional amendments on rights that were proposed by the House of Representatives. Using this working draft of the House amendments, the Senate reduced their number to 12 and modified them in style and wording.

CONGRESS OF THE UNITED STATES.

In the HOUSE *of* REPRESENTATIVES,

Monday, 24th August, 1789,

RESOLVED, BY THE SENATE AND HOUSE OF REPRESENTA-
TIVES OF THE UNITED STATES OF AMERICA IN CONGRESS
ASSEMBLED, two thirds of both Houfes ~~deeming it neceffary~~. That
the following Articles be propofed to the Legiflature of the feveral
States, as Amendments to the Conftitution of the United States, all
or any of which Articles, when ratified by three fourths of the faid
Legiflatures, to be valid to all intents and purpofes as part of the
faid Conftitution—Viz.

ARTICLES in addition to, and amendment of, the Conftitution of
the United States of America, propofed by Congrefs, and ratified
by the Legiflatures of the feveral States, purfuant to the fifth Article of the original Conftitution.

ARTICLE THE FIRST.

After the firft enumeration, required by the firft Article of the
Conftitution, there fhall be one Reprefentative for every thirty thoufand, until the number fhall amount to one hundred, ~~after which~~
the proportion fhall be fo regulated by Congrefs, that there fhall
be not lefs than one hundred Reprefentatives, nor lefs than one Reprefentative for every forty thoufand perfons, until the number of
Reprefentatives fhall amount to two hundred, after which the proportion fhall be fo regulated by Congrefs, that there fhall not be lefs
than two hundred Reprefentatives, nor lefs than one Reprefentative
for every fifty thoufand perfons.

ARTICLE THE SECOND.

No law varying the compenfation ~~to the members of Congrefs,~~
fhall take effect, until an election of Reprefentatives fhall have intervened.

ARTICLE THE THIRD.

Congrefs fhall make no law eftablifhing ~~religion or prohibiting~~
~~the free exercife thereof, nor fhall~~

ARTICLE THE FOURTH.

The Freedom of Speech, and of the Prefs, and the right of the
People peaceably to affemble, and to apply to the Government for a redrefs of grievances, ~~fhall~~
~~not be infringed.~~

Amendment 2

A well regulated Militia, being necessary to the security of a free State, the right of the people to keep and bear Arms, shall not be infringed.

Amendment 3

No Soldier shall, in time of peace be quartered in any house, without the consent of the Owner, nor in time of war, but in a manner to be prescribed by law.

Amendment 4

The right of the people to be secure in their persons, houses, papers, and effects, against unreasonable searches and seizures, shall not be violated, and no Warrants shall issue, but upon probable cause, supported by Oath or affirmation, and particularly describing the place to be searched, and the persons or things to be seized.

Amendment 5

No person shall be held to answer for a capital, or otherwise infamous crime, unless on a presentment or indictment of a Grand Jury, except in cases arising in the land or naval forces, or in the Militia, when in actual service in time of War or public danger; nor shall any person be subject for the same offence to be twice put in jeopardy of life or limb, nor shall be compelled in any criminal case to be a witness against himself, nor be deprived of life, liberty, or property, without due process of law; nor shall private property be taken for public use, without just compensation.

Amendment 6

In all criminal prosecutions, the accused shall enjoy the right to a speedy and public trial, by an impartial jury of the State and district wherein the crime shall have been committed; which district shall have been previously ascertained by law, and to be informed of the nature and cause of the accusation; to be confronted with the witnesses against him; to have compulsory process for obtaining witnesses in his favor, and to have the Assistance of Counsel for his defence.

Amendment 7

In Suits at common law, where the value in controversy shall exceed twenty dollars, the right of trial by jury shall be preserved, and no fact tried by a jury, shall be otherwise re-examined in any Court of the United States, than according to the rules of the common law.

Amendment 8

Excessive bail shall not be required, nor excessive fines imposed, nor cruel and unusual punishments inflicted.

Amendment 9

The enumeration in the Constitution of certain rights shall not be construed to deny or disparage others retained by the people.

Amendment 10

The powers not delegated to the United States by the Constitution, nor prohibited by it to the States, are reserved to the States respectively, or to the people.

The Bill of Rights at the National Archives

The Bill of Rights, written in 1789 and ratified in 1791, is kept at the National Archives in Washington, D.C. There were 15 original copies of the Bill of Rights, but the only copy on permanent public display is in the Exhibition Hall of the National Archives. It is exhibited with original copies of the two other most important founding documents of the United States of America: the 1776 Declaration of Independence and the 1787 Constitution. The old and faded documents are kept in bronze and glass cases, where they are sealed in helium to protect them from damaging elements of the environment. Thousands of visitors come each year to the Exhibition Hall to see these charters of American freedom. Each night at closing time, a guard pushes a button to trigger an electric mechanism that lowers the cases into a fireproof and bombproof vault 20 feet below. A huge lid bangs shut, and these precious pieces of our history are safely put away for the night.

LOOK ON THIS PICTURE,   AND ON THIS.

See what a grace was seated on this brow.
An eye like Mars to threaten and command,
A combination, and a form, indeed,
Where every God did seem to set his seal,
To give the world assurance of a man.

THIS WAS____

ORDER
LAW
RELIGION

HERE IS____

____ *like a mildew'd ear,*
Blasting his wholesome brother____

Vide Hamlt.

New-York, June, 1807.

Chapter Four

The Bill of Rights Marginalized

T he U.S. Congress, from 1789 to 1792, successfully launched the federal government under provisions of the Constitution. During this time, Congressman James Madison was often in Philadelphia, the temporary national capital, where he discussed political and constitutional issues with his closest friend and political ally, Thomas Jefferson, who served the federal government as the secretary of state under President George Washington. Madison and Jefferson asked Philip Freneau, a writer and editor, to join them in Philadelphia, where Madison influenced him to begin publication of a newspaper on current political and constitutional issues. Thus, the *National Gazette* was born and became an outlet for essays by Madison and others with like-minded political ideas.

Madison, whom some called "Father of the Bill of Rights," used the pages of the *National Gazette* to inform and instruct citizens about public issues and principles of constitutional government. In an essay published on December 20, 1792—"Who Are the Best Keepers of the People's Liberties?"—Madison stressed that "mankind are capable of governing themselves" by responsibly electing their representatives in government and holding them accountable to the purposes of their constitutional government. First among these purposes was protection of the natural rights of the people who had established the government. And first among the responsibilities of citizens, said Madison, was continued vigilance and action in support of their rights.

Madison had always believed that individual rights listed in charters like the Bill of Rights were only "parchment barriers"—mere pieces of paper against the formidable forces of oppression. The only effective barrier against abusive power, he argued, was the machinery

In this 1807 political cartoon George Washington's virtues are compared with those of Republican Party leader Thomas Jefferson. Washington's portrait rests on books entitled Order, Law, *and* Religion. *Jefferson rests on the works of Voltaire, Thomas Paine, and other advocates of social change that many Federalists considered a threat to hallowed tradition.*

of a well-constructed constitution, which worked only when the people properly used and maintained it. According to Madison, the people are the "best keepers of the people's liberties." In order to enjoy their rights, they must be ready to defend them. From the ratification of the Bill of Rights in 1791 until today, many Americans, in line with Madison's advice, have protested the unjust denial of rights to unpopular or unprotected individuals and groups.

Essays in the *National Gazette* roused citizens to form a new political party, the Republicans—sometimes called Democratic-Republicans—led by Madison and Jefferson. (This party was a forerunner of the modern-day Democrats.) They wished to promote the principles of free government that Madison and Jefferson held dear. On the other side was the Federalist Party led by Alexander Hamilton, secretary of the treasury, and favored by President George Washington. Federalist ideas were promoted through the *Gazette of the United States*, published by John Fenno, a friend of Hamilton.

In the summer of 1792, sharp differences erupted between these two original political parties of the United States. Freneau's *National Gazette* slammed Hamilton and his Federalist followers. In return, Fenno's *Gazette of the United States* harshly criticized the ideas and actions of Madison, Jefferson, and their growing Republican Party. Freedom of speech and press, declared inviolable in the first article of the Bill of Rights, seemed to be flourishing. However, the intensely expressed differences of the rival political parties alarmed some leaders, including Washington and his successor, John Adams, who feared that such animosity would disrupt political stability and order.

In 1798, the Federalist Party controlled all branches of the federal government, but the Republicans were gaining popular support. President Adams and the Federalist majority in Congress were concerned about how to maintain their power against the unrelenting criticism of the Republicans. A confrontation on the floor of the House of Representatives revealed how extreme the political party strife had become. Matthew Lyon, a Republican representative from Vermont, and Roger Griswold, a Federalist representative from Connecticut, battled verbally and physically in front of the assembled House. Griswold attacked Lyon with his cane, and Lyon fought back with fire tongs.

Political party differences within the United States were made more severe by military conflicts abroad between Britain and France. The Federalists tended to favor Britain, while the Republicans preferred France. For a short period in 1798, it seemed that the United States would declare war against France. The threat of war, and political party conflicts about it, prompted Congress to pass four laws to suppress disorderly dissent: the Alien and Sedition Acts.

Two of the Alien Acts gave the President power to deport noncitizens whom he believed dangerous to the country's welfare. Another Alien Act made it very difficult for a foreigner to become a citizen. It created a Naturalization Law that required an alien to live in the United States for 14 years, rather than 5, to become eligible for citizenship. The Sedition Act made it unlawful to express some kinds of criticisms of federal government officials. It was now a crime to express in public "any false, scandalous, and malicious writing or writings against the Governments of the United States, with intent to defame . . . or to bring them . . . into contempt or disrepute."

The Sedition Act was quickly used to squelch dissident speech. (The Alien Acts were never enforced.) Matthew Lyon was among the first to suffer. He made severe denunciations of Adams and his Federalist opponents in Vermont, and the result was four months in jail and a $1,000 fine. The voters, however, reelected him to Congress while he was serving his sentence. Republicans were alarmed as they watched the federal courts equate the right of free speech with unlawful resistance to the government. Several Republican newspaper editors were punished for writing articles against Federalist officials.

Republican Party leaders appealed to the people and their state governments, instead of the Supreme Court, with claims that the Sedition Act was unconstitutional and thereby null and void. In 1798 the Supreme Court's power of judicial review of an act of Congress had not yet been established. (This would happen in 1803.) And conviction under the Sedition Act brought no cases on appeal to the Supreme Court. Further, the lower federal courts were not inclined to raise the question of constitutionality with regard to the Sedition Act. Republican leaders therefore hoped to rouse the public to protest against laws that were unconstitutional violations of the Bill of Rights and to influence the government to revoke them.

James Madison and Thomas Jefferson penned arguments against the Sedition Act known as the Kentucky and Virginia Resolutions, because the legislatures of these two states adopted

The Jeffersonian Republicans celebrated their sweeping victory in the election of 1800, which led to their party's control of Congress and the Presidency. In this Republican victory banner, the American eagle announces that Jefferson is the President and John Adams "No More." The Federalist Party never recovered from this electoral defeat.

and proclaimed them. The resolutions declared the Sedition Act to be "void and of no force" because it violated the Constitution. The resolutions held that whenever the federal government exceeded its constitutional powers, each state had the right to decide whether or not to obey. The Kentucky Resolution, for example, declared that if the federal courts would not judge the Sedition Act unconstitutional, then the state government of Kentucky would do so. In practice, this meant that the state would refuse to enforce such a law within its borders. Most states ignored or opposed the Kentucky and Virginia Resolutions, so these documents had no immediate force in resolving the question of whether or not the Sedition Act was constitutional.

The American people decided the fate of the Sedition Act during the Presidential and congressional elections of 1800. The voters repudiated the Federalist Party by electing a large majority of Republicans to represent them in Congress, and Thomas Jefferson became President in place of the defeated Federalist Party leader, John Adams. The citizens as voters had rejected the Federalist Party and its Sedition Act.

An article in a Federalist newspaper, the *Columbian Centinel*, had warned that to elect Jefferson would be "equivalent to a Revolution." Jefferson rather liked the idea that he stood for revolutionary ideas. So he adopted the would-be insult and claimed, upon winning the Presidency, that he had wrought "the revolution of 1800." But that election was a peaceful and orderly transfer of power from one party to another according to the supreme law of the land, the Constitution. This was an extraordinary event in the world of 1800, where questions about who should rule typically were settled by brute force, not by peaceful, lawful, and orderly procedures based on the will of the people.

Majority rule with protection of minority rights was a fundamental founding principle of American constitutional government. In line with this principle, the new Republican majority in Congress rejected the Sedition Act by failing to renew it upon its expiration in March 1801. And Jefferson pardoned all those who had been convicted under the act.

In his final major move as President, John Adams had appointed John Marshall to be chief justice of the United States. From 1801 until his death in 1835, Marshall dominated the Supreme Court so thoroughly that it was often informally called the Marshall Court. The first key decision of the Marshall Court occurred in the case of *Marbury* v. *Madison* (1803). Marshall's assertion in this case of the power of judicial review eventually made the Court a primary guardian of the people's rights.

Judicial review is the power of the Supreme Court to overturn acts of the government that violate the Constitution. For example,

The text of the Sedition Act, passed by Congress on July 14, 1798, restricted political speech against the President and the federal government. James Madison responded in the Virginia Resolutions that the act "ought to produce universal alarm, because it is leveled against the right of freely examining public characters and measures, and of free communication among the people thereon, which has been justly deemed the only effectual guardian of every other right."

if Congress enacts a statute that contradicts any part of the Constitution, such as the right to free speech found in the Bill of Rights, and if a case involving that law comes before the Court, it can use its power of judicial review to declare that law void. For more than 100 years after Marshall established the power of judicial review against coordinate branches of the Federal government, the Supreme Court rarely used it.

In 1833, in the case of *Barron* v. *Baltimore*, the Supreme Court under Marshall effectively limited the range and reach of the Bill of Rights in American life. The case was brought by John Barron of Baltimore, who invoked his 5th Amendment rights to private property. Barron owned docks and warehouses on the harbor, but a city construction project was ruining his business by causing debris to pile up under his wharf. Barron sued the city government of Baltimore to compensate him for financial losses.

Barron based his claim on a clause in the 5th Amendment that says that "private property" shall not "be taken for public use without just compensation." His claim against the city government, part of the state of Maryland, raised important constitutional questions: Can the 5th Amendment, or any part of the Bill of Rights, be used to limit the power of city or state governments? Or does the Bill of Rights restrain only the government of the United States?

Barron's suit was initially brought to his county court, which awarded him $4,500 in damages. The city of Baltimore appealed this decision to the Maryland Court of Appeals, which reversed the lower court's decision. Barron then appealed to the U.S. Supreme Court, which rendered a unanimous opinion written by Chief Justice Marshall. The court rejected Barron's claim to "just compensation." Marshall said that the Bill of Rights applied only to the federal government. The 5th Amendment could not be used to require the city of Baltimore to pay Barron. According to Marshall, the Supreme Court had no jurisdiction in this case. So the Court let stand the decision of the Maryland Court of Appeals, which had ruled against Barron.

After the *Barron* ruling, people denied their constitutional rights by a state government could not appeal for help to the federal government, as they can today. The state constitutions included bills of rights similar to amendments 1 through 10 of the U.S. Constitution, but these rights were occasionally violated. And when large, vocal majorities appeared to deny free speech rights, for example, to unpopular individuals, the constitutional violations were sometimes permitted and not punished. In some states, individual rights, even for unpopular people, were faithfully protected. But in others, strong majorities were allowed to exercise tyranny over unpopular minorities.

Newspapers and magazines that printed highly unpopular opinions or facts were sometimes censored by local and state governments, and their editors and reporters were shunned and insulted. Publications and writers that opposed slavery and criticized slave owners were special targets of censorship. On the night of November 7, 1837, in Alton, Illinois, for example, the tyranny of the majority became deadly.

Slavery was illegal in Illinois, but pro-slavery opinions were common, and in southern Illinois, the majority clearly favored slavery. The proximity of Alton to two slave states across the Illinois border, Kentucky and Missouri, contributed to the strong pro-slavery views of most people in this Mississippi River town. For more than a year, the citizens of Alton had complained about Elijah Lovejoy and the newspaper he published, the *Alton Observer*. Lovejoy so strongly believed in freedom that he could not abide slavery, and he vehemently expressed antislavery opinions in his newspaper. During a protest against Lovejoy's right to free speech and press, a mob assaulted and killed the abolitionist editor.

The divisive questions of slavery and the rights of black people came to a head in the 1857 Supreme Court case of *Scott* v. *Sandford*, known as the Dred Scott case. In 1854 Dred Scott, a slave, had traveled with his owner from Missouri, a slave state, to Illinois, a free state. Later, Scott went with his master to the Wisconsin Territory (now part of Minnesota), where the Missouri Compromise of 1820, a federal law, had forbidden slavery. Scott was then taken back to Missouri, where he brought suit against his owner, claiming he was a free person because of his residence in areas where slavery was illegal.

In his notorious opinion for the Court, Chief Justice Roger B. Taney ruled against Scott on all counts and claimed that neither Scott nor any other black person could have the rights and privileges of a citizen of the United States. For the first time since *Marbury* v. *Madison*, the Court had used its power of judicial review to declare unconstitutional an act of Congress (the Missouri Compromise). Further, the Court denied to a black man his rights to liberty and due process of law in the Bill of Rights.

From the time the Bill of Rights was adopted until the Civil War, however, there were few federal court cases dealing with the rights of individuals set forth in those amendments. And the U.S. Supreme Court was not involved at all in cases pertaining to 1st Amendment

What, to the American slave, is your Fourth of July? I answer: a day that reveals to him, more than all other days of the year, the gross injustice and cruelty to which he is the constant victim.

—Frederick Douglass,
Independence Day speech,
Rochester, New York,
July 5, 1852

freedoms or rights of the criminally accused, with which it has been extensively engaged during the 20th century.

The Sedition Act Controversy

Enforcement of the Sedition Act of 1798 appeared to be a direct violation of the 1st Amendment to the Constitution, which said, "Congress shall make no law . . . abridging the freedom of speech, or of the press." However, this law was upheld by three justices of the U.S. Supreme Court, who did double duty by also serving as federal circuit court judges for cases involving people accused of violating federal laws. Thomas Paterson, for example, was a Supreme Court justice who, in October 1798, presided at the federal circuit court trial of Congressman Matthew Lyon, whose severe criticisms of the Federalists had led to a charge of violating the Sedition Act. In his instructions to the jury, Justice Paterson said that this court was not the place to decide whether or not the Sedition Act was constitutional. Rather, he charged the jury with deciding only if Matthew Lyon had broken the law.

[PATERSON, Circuit Justice charging jury]. You have nothing whatever to do with the constitutionality or unconstitutionality of the sedition law. Congress has said that the author and publisher of seditious libels is to be punished; and until this law is declared null and void by a tribunal competent for the purpose, its validity cannot be disputed. . . . The only question you are to determine is, that which the record submits to you. Did Mr. Lyon publish the

This political cartoon caricatures the fight that broke out on the floor of the House of Representatives in February 1798 between Matthew Lyon, a Republican from Vermont and Roger Griswold, a Federalist from Connecticut. Griswold attacks Lyons with his cane, and Lyons, fights back with fire tongs. Later, Lyons was one of 25 people convicted under the terms of the Sedition Act of 1798.

writing given in the indictment? Did he do so seditiously? On the first point, the evidence is undisputed, and in fact, he himself concedes the fact of publication as to a large portion of libellous matter. As to the second point, you will have to consider whether language such as that here complained of could have been uttered with any other intent than that of making odious or contemptible the president and government, and bringing them both into disrepute. If you find such is the case, the offence is made out, and you must render a verdict of guilty. . . . As to yourselves, one point, in addition, in exercising the functions allotted to you, you must keep in mind; and that is, that in order to render a verdict of guilty, you must be satisfied beyond all reasonable substantial doubt that the hypothesis of innocence is unsustainable. Keeping these instructions in your mind, you will proceed to deliberate on your verdict.

In the original Kentucky and Virginia Resolutions, written to oppose the Alien and Sedition Acts, James Madison and Thomas Jefferson argued that a state could disobey a federal law if that law violated the Constitution. In a second Kentucky Resolution, issued in 1799, Jefferson was careful to emphasize the duty of citizens and their states to remain loyal supporters of their Constitution and federal union. But he continued to claim that the Alien and Sedition laws were unconstitutional violations of the Bill of Rights. And he continued to urge citizens to take responsibility for their rights by staging public protests and signing petitions against violations of the Bill of Rights.

[Resolved] . . . That this commonwealth [Kentucky] does, under the most deliberate reconsideration, declare, that the said Alien and Sedition Laws are, in their opinion, palpable violations of the said Constitution; and, however cheerfully it may be disposed to surrender its opinion to a majority of its sister states, in matters of ordinary or doubtful policy, yet, in momentous regulations like the present, which so vitally wound the best rights of the citizen, it would consider a silent acquiescence as highly criminal: That although this commonwealth, as a party to the federal compact, will bow to the laws of the Union, yet it does, at the same time declare, that it will not now, or ever hereafter, cease to oppose in a constitutional manner, every attempt at what quarter soever offered, to violate that compact. And, finally, in order that no pretext or arguments may be drawn from a supposed acquiescence, on the part of this commonwealth in the constitutionality of those laws, and be thereby used as precedents for similar future violations of the federal compact—this commonwealth does now enter against them its solemn protest.

In his Inaugural Address on March 4, 1801, President Thomas Jefferson reminded Americans of their constitutional commitment to individual rights, especially the right to free speech and press that recently had been threatened by the Sedition Act. He also reaffirmed the people's right to self-government based on majority rule.

During the contest of opinion through which we have passed the animation of discussions and of exertions has sometimes worn an aspect which might impose on strangers unused to think freely and to speak and to write what they think; but this being now decided by the voice of the nation, announced according to the rules of the Constitution, all will, of course, arrange themselves under the will of the law, and unite in common efforts for the common good. All, too, will bear in mind this sacred principle, that though the will of the majority is in all cases to prevail, that will to be rightful must be reasonable; that the minority possess their equal rights, which equal law must protect, and to violate would be oppression.

Landmark Opinions of Chief Justice Marshall

In the case of *Marbury* v. *Madison* (1803), Chief Justice John Marshall declared that a part of the Judiciary Act, passed by Congress in 1789, violated the Constitution. It was therefore unconstitutional, or void. Even though the Constitution does not specifically say that the federal courts have the power of judicial review, Marshall, in his opinion for this case, established the Supreme Court's power to review the federal government's actions. (The Court's power of judicial review of state government actions had been established by the Judiciary Act of 1789.) Long after Marshall's time, the Court relied on judicial review many times to protect the constitutional rights of Americans.

The question, whether an act, repugnant to the constitution, can become the law of the land, is a question deeply interesting to the United States. . . .

James Madison on Property

In the March 27, 1792 issue of the National Gazette, James Madison published a striking statement, a testimonial on rights titled "Property." This essay keenly explained philosophical foundations of the American Bill of Rights, which Madison derived from the 17th-century works of an English writer, John Locke. Like Locke in his Two Treatises of Government, Madison said that the main purpose of government is "to protect property of every sort." Like Locke, Madison broadly defined property to include not only the objects one owned—such as land, buildings, money, or machines—but "everything to which a man may attach a value and have a right"—such as his rights to life, liberty, and "the free use of his faculties [abilities] and free choice of the objects on which to employ them."

In a word, as a man is said to have a right to his property, he may be equally said to have a property in his rights. Where an excess of power prevails, property of no sort is duly respected. No man is safe in his opinions, his person, his faculties, or his possessions. Where there is an excess of liberty, the effect is the same, though from an opposite cause. Government is instituted to protect property of every sort, as well that which lies in the various rights of individuals. . . . This being the end of government, that alone is a just government which *impartially* secures to every man whatever is his *own*.

Certainly all those who have framed written constitutions contemplate them as forming the fundamental and paramount law of the nation, and, consequently, the theory of every such government must be, that an act of the legislature, repugnant to the constitution, is void. . . .

It is emphatically the province and duty of the judicial department to say what the law is. Those who apply the rule to particular cases, must of necessity expound and interpret that rule. If two laws conflict with each other, the courts must decide on the operation of each.

So if a law be in opposition to the constitution, if both the law and the constitution apply to a particular case, so that the court must either decide that case conformably to the law, disregarding the constitution, or conformably to the constitution, disregarding the law; the court must determine which of these conflicting rules governs the case. This is of the very essence of judicial duty.

If, then, the courts are to regard the constitution, and the constitution is superior to any ordinary act of the legislature, the constitution, and not such ordinary act, must govern the case to which they both apply. . . .

Thus, the particular phraseology of the constitution of the United States confirms and strengthens the principle, supposed to be essential to all written constitutions, that a law repugnant to the constitution is void and that courts, as well as other departments, are bound by that instrument.

James Madison had proposed to Congress in 1789 that certain parts of the Bill of Rights should be applied to the state governments. A majority of the House of Representatives voted in favor of this proposal, but the Senate rejected it. Chief Justice John Marshall's opinion in the case of *Barron* v. *Baltimore* (1883) established the widely held view that the federal Bill of Rights was intended by its framers in 1789 to bind the U.S. government but not the state governments. The Supreme Court denied John Barron's claim, based on the 5th Amendment, that the city of Baltimore owed him "just compensation" for causing damage to his property.

The question thus presented is, we think, of great importance, but not of much difficulty.

The constitution was ordained and established by the people of the United States for themselves, for their own government, and not for the governments of the individual states. Each state

THE PROVIDENTIAL DETECTION

In this anti-Republican caricature, the American eagle, a symbol of the United States, stops Thomas Jefferson from burning the Constitution on the "Altar of Gallic Despotism"—a reference to the French Revolution. Federalist Party leaders charged Jefferson and his followers with partiality to France during its war with Britain, whom the Federalists favored in the conflict.

John Marshall became chief justice of the United States in 1801 and served in this position until his death in 1835, the longest tenure of any chief justice. Marshall's strong leadership and masterful legal opinions established the authority of the Supreme Court in relation to the other branches of the federal government. John Adams, the President who appointed Marshall, said near the end of his life in 1826, "My gift of John Marshall to the people of the United States was the greatest act of my life."

established a constitution for itself, and, in the constitution, provided such limitations and restrictions on the powers of its particular government as its judgment dictated. The people of the United States framed such a government for the United States as they supposed best adapted to their situation, and best calculated to promote their interests. The powers they conferred on this government were to be exercised by itself; and the limitations on power, if expressed in general terms, are naturally, and, we think, necessarily applicable to the government created by the instrument. They are limitations of power granted in the instrument itself; not of distinct governments, framed by different persons and for different purposes.

If these propositions be correct, the fifth amendment must be understood as restraining the power of the general government, not as applicable to the states. In their several constitutions they have imposed such restrictions on their respective governments as their own wisdom suggested; such as they deemed most proper for themselves. It is a subject on which they judge exclusively, and with which others interfere no farther than they are supposed to have a common interest. . . .

These amendments [the Bill of Rights] contain no expression indicating an intention to apply them to the state governments. This court cannot so apply them.

We are of the opinion that the provision in the fifth amendment to the constitution, declaring that private property shall not be taken for public use without just compensation, is intended solely as a limitation on the exercise of power by the government of the United States, and is not applicable to the legislation of the states.

Contradiction of Ideals

In July 1837, citizens of Alton, Illinois, held a town meeting to decide what to do about Elijah Lovejoy's unpopular antislavery newspaper, the *Alton Observer*. The majority appointed a committee to meet with Lovejoy and ask him to stop publishing articles against slavery. Lovejoy refused to give up his rights to freedom of speech and press, which were guaranteed by the state constitution. Lovejoy's opponents responded by invading his office and smashing his printing press. With the financial support of friends, Lovejoy bought a new press and resumed publication of his antislavery newspaper. Once again, opponents ransacked his offices and

destroyed his equipment. And once again, Lovejoy ordered a new printing press.

The majority in Alton, however, was determined to deny Lovejoy's rights to liberty, and he had nowhere to turn for help. Neither his city nor state government would protect his rights against the tyrannical majority. And the U.S. Bill of Rights, according to the Supreme Court, could not be used to settle conflicts about rights in the states. On November 3, 1837, a few town leaders met with Lovejoy and admitted that the local government would not protect his rights to property and liberty. They advised him to leave town. He refused, and a riotous mob assaulted him and his property. This time, Lovejoy forcibly resisted, and they killed him. So Elijah Lovejoy was a martyr to the cause of liberty, a victim of the majority's unrestrained passion.

Newspaper editors from New York to Chicago lamented the barbarous denial of Elijah Lovejoy's rights to free speech and press—and to liberty and life. The most poignant memorial came in 1838 from Lovejoy's friend, the Reverend Edward Beecher. Like James Madison at an earlier time, Beecher placed the primary responsibility for protecting individual rights on the citizens of the land. Rights always would be secure if most citizens would act boldly to defend them. In his memorial to Lovejoy, Reverend Beecher discussed the paradoxical principle of majority rule and protection of minority rights, which Thomas Jefferson had once proclaimed as the foundation of government in America. And he praised the courage and devotion to human rights of a white abolitionist who gave his life in the cause of freedom for enslaved black people.

[T]hat all printing presses are under the protection of law has been heretofore considered the settled order of things in this state. . . .

But it is said the majority of the citizens of Alton did not wish the press located there. What then? Have a majority a right to drive out a minority if they happen in the exercise of inalienable rights to do what they do not like; and if they will not go, murder them? And is it every editor's duty to give up all his civil rights at the voice of the majority, and flee?

But this is not all. It is not a mere question of an editor's rights. All parties in the state have a right to the advantages of prominent commercial points. If any place is in a center of communication,

[A] Bill of Rights is an important protection against unjust and oppressive conduct on the part of the people themselves. The prescriptions in favor of liberty ought to be leveled against that quarter, where the greatest danger lies, namely, that which possesses the highest prerogative of power. But this is not found in the executive or legislative departments of government; but in the body of the people, operating by the majority against the minority.

—Joseph Story, justice of the U.S. Supreme Court, *A Familiar Exposition of the Constitution of the United States,* 1840

This woodcut, made in 1838, shows the pro-slavery riot of November 7, 1837 in Alton, Illinois, which resulted in the death of abolitionist journalist and publisher Elijah Lovejoy. He had declared in his newspaper the Alton Observer, "We distinctly avow it to be our settled purpose, never, while life lasts, to yield to this new system of attempting to destroy, by means of mob violence, the right of conscience, the freedom of opinion, and of the press."

like Alton, it is the best location for a paper; and any set of men in the state have a right, if they wish, to establish a paper there. Had it been a political paper in which citizens all over the state were interested, what would have been said of an effort to drive it away because the majority of Alton were opposed to its views?

But it is said "that it was injurious to the interests of the place to have it there." This allegation is both false and absurd. If its views were false, it was easy to answer them; but if true, can it be injurious to know the truth?. . . Is it then injurious to any place to be known as the decided friend of free inquiry and the fearless protector of the rights of speech?. . .

On whom, then, does the guilt of these transactions fall? First, on the guilty agents; and next, on all who excited, instigated, or countenanced them in their deeds. All who have aided to stigmatize with unjust reproach an innocent, meritorious, and suffering portion of their fellow citizens. Profligate editors, at the East and at the West, have a large account to render to God for these bloody deeds. All professedly religious men who have by rendering their fellow citizens odious in the eyes of an infuriated mob stimulated their hatred and urged them on. All who have refused to fear God more than man, and who, through fear of popular odium, have failed to oppose and rebuke the workers of iniquity. All who have allowed their prejudices against unpopular sentiments to render them traitorous to the great principles of human society and to the holy cause of God.

The antislavery crusade continued alongside another struggle to ensure the rights of all Americans—the women's rights movement. There were, in fact, close connections between these two movements, which overlapped in membership and leadership. Prominent women's rights advocates, such as Elizabeth Cady Stanton and Lucretia Mott, participated in the World Anti-Slavery Convention in London in 1840. There, they were outraged when male leaders at the convention prevented women from participating equally. The women, for example, were required to sit behind a barrier, out of the way of men.

Their humiliating experience in London prompted Stanton and Mott to act decisively for women's rights in the United States. They convened the first public meeting to demand equal rights under the law for women. In this groundbreaking convention at Seneca Falls, New York, in 1848, they issued a Declaration of Sentiments and Resolutions calling for equal rights in voting, employment, property rights, and family relationships. This declaration was anchored in the words and principles of the Declaration of Independence.

1. DECLARATION OF SENTIMENTS

When, in the course of human events, it becomes necessary for one portion of the family of man to assume among the people of the earth a position different from that which they have hitherto occupied, but one to which the laws of nature and of nature's God entitle them, a decent respect to the opinions of mankind requires that they should declare the causes that impel them to such a course.

We hold these truths to be self-evident: that all men and women are created equal; that they are endowed by their Creator with certain inalienable rights; that among these are life, liberty, and the pursuit of happiness; that to secure these rights governments are instituted, deriving their just powers from the consent of the governed. . . .

The history of mankind is a history of repeated injuries and usurpations on the part of man toward woman, having in direct object the establishment of an absolute tyranny over her. To prove this, let facts be submitted to a candid world.

He had never permitted her to exercise her inalienable right to the elective franchise.

He has compelled her to submit to laws, in the formation of which she had no voice.

Mere circumstances of sex does not give to man higher rights . . . than to women.
—Angelina Grimké, letter to Catherine E. Beecher, October 2, 1837

this resolution is particularly interesting to me & am glad that it has been read here — ... suppose no one will pretend to deny but that they are true — and that there are men in our midst county and city who have become so imbued with the idea of man's superiority, that he does assume the prerogative of judging for his wife in everything almost even if she need some addition to her wardrobe — he must be the judge before he will allow her to have the means to make the purchase — when in reality it rightfully belongs to her as to him — she either received it from ... inheritance or contributed her full share of labour to produce it — in some instances the husband has taken the hard earnings of his wife to get the poisonous draught of intoxication, and in turn receive his kick and unkind words — and if there is any means of redress, it is fraught with many difficulties and unpleasant things that I think it much better to avoid the first evil than to seek its remedy. I have been surprised some times to see how supercilious some men do grow after marriage — entirely unlike what they were or appeared to be) before marriage — this is all calculated to bring about a very unharmonious state of society —

A Bush
E McC secretary

During the month following the July 1848 Seneca Falls convention another convention on women's rights was held in Rochester, New York. Frederick Douglass, the African American abolitionist leader, attended both conventions. These notes, taken at the Rochester Women's Rights Convention, were written on the backside of a printed prospectus for Douglass's anti-slavery newspaper, the North Star.

He has withheld from her rights which are given to the most ignorant and degraded men—both natives and foreigners.

Having deprived her of this first right of a citizen, the elective franchise, thereby leaving her without representation in the halls of legislation, he has oppressed her on all sides.

He had made her, if married, in the eye of the law, civilly dead.

He had taken from her all right in property, even to the wages she earns.

He had made her, morally, an irresponsible being, as she can commit many crimes with impunity, provided they be done in the presence of her husband. In the covenant of marriage, she is compelled to promise obedience to her husband, he becoming, to all intents and purposes, her master—the law giving him power to deprive her of her liberty, and to administer chastisement.

He has so framed the laws of divorce, as to what shall be the proper causes, and in case of separation, to whom the guardianship of the children shall be given, as to be wholly regardless of the happiness of women—the law, in all cases, going upon a false supposition of the supremacy of man, and giving all power into his hands.

After depriving her of all rights as a married woman, if single, and the owner of property, he has taxed her to support a government which recognizes her only when her property can be made profitable to it.

He has monopolized nearly all the profitable employments, and from those she is permitted to follow, she receives but a scanty remuneration. He closes against her all the avenues to wealth and distinction which he considers most honorable to himself. As a teacher of theology, medicine, or law, she is not known.

He has denied her the facilities for obtaining a thorough education, all colleges being closed against her.

He allows her in Church, as well as State, but a subordinate position, claiming Apostolic authority for her exclusion from the ministry, and, with some exceptions, from any public participation in the affairs of the Church.

He has created a false public sentiment by giving to the world a different code of morals for men and women, by which moral delinquencies which exclude women from society, are not only tolerated, but deemed of little account in man.

He has usurped the prerogative of Jehovah himself, claiming it as his right to assign for her a sphere of action, when that belongs to her conscience and to her God.

He has endeavored, in every way that he could, to destroy her confidence in her own powers, to lessen her self-respect and to make her willing to lead a dependent and abject life.

Now, in view of this entire disfranchisement of one-half the people of this country, their social and religious degradation—in view of the unjust laws above mentioned, and because women do feel themselves aggrieved, oppressed, and fraudulently deprived of their most sacred rights, we insist that they have immediate admission to all the rights and privileges which belong to them as citizens of the United States.

In entering upon the great work before us, we anticipate no small amount of misconception, misrepresentation, and ridicule; but we shall use every instrumentality within our power to effect our object. We shall employ agents, circulate tracts, petition the State and National legislatures, and endeavor to enlist the pulpit and the press in our behalf. We hope this Convention will be followed by a series of Conventions embracing every part of the country.

2. RESOLUTIONS

. . . *Resolved,* That all laws which prevent woman from occupying such a station in society as her conscience shall dictate, or which place her in a position inferior to that of man, are contrary to the great precept of nature, and therefore of no force or authority.

We are assembled to protest against a form of government, existing without the consent of the governed to declare our right to be free as man is free.
—Elizabeth Cady Stanton, speech at Seneca Falls, New York, July 19, 1848

This 1838 coin advocates freedom for African American women using an adaptation of the popular abolitionist motif of a kneeling, chained slave who implores "Am I not a man and a brother?" Nineteenth-century women struggling for their rights found common cause with the slaves' struggle for freedom and many were also abolitionists as well as advocates for women's rights.

Resolved, That woman is man's equal—was intended to be so by the Creator, and the highest good of the race demands that she should be recognized as such.

Resolved, That the women of this country ought to be enlightened in regard to the laws under which they live, that they may no longer publish their degradation by declaring themselves satisfied with their present position, nor their ignorance, by asserting that they have all the rights they want.

Resolved, That inasmuch as man, while claiming for himself intellectual superiority, does accord to woman moral superiority, it is pre-eminently his duty to encourage her to speak and teach, as she has an opportunity, in all religious assemblies.

Resolved, That the same amount of virtue, delicacy, and refinement of behavior that is required of woman in the social state, should also be required of man, and the same transgressions should be visited with equal severity on both man and woman.

Resolved, That the objection of indelicacy and impropriety, which is so often brought against woman when she addresses a public audience, comes with a very ill-grace from those who encourage, by their attendance, her appearance on the stage, in the concert, or in feats of the circus.

Resolved, That woman has too long rested satisfied in the circumscribed limits which corrupt customs and a perverted application of the Scriptures have marked out for her, and that it is time she should move in the enlarged sphere which her great Creator has assigned her.

Resolved, That it is the duty of the women of this country to secure to themselves their sacred right to the elective franchise.

Resolved, That the equality of human rights results necessarily from the fact of the identity of the race in capabilities and responsibilities.

Resolved, That the speedy success of our cause depends upon the zealous and untiring efforts of both men and women, for the overthrow of the monopoly of the pulpit, and for the securing to women an equal participation with men in the various trades, professions, and commerce.

Resolved, therefore, That, being invested by the creator with the same capabilities, and the same consciousness of responsibility for their exercise, it is demonstrably the right and duty of woman, equally with man, to promote every righteous cause by every righteous means; and especially in regard to the great subjects of morals and religion, it is self-evidently her right to participate with her brother in teaching them, both in private and in public, by

writing and by speaking, by any instrumentalities proper to be used, and in any assemblies proper to be held; and this being a self-evident truth growing out of the divinely implanted principles of human nature, any custom or authority adverse to it, whether modern or wearing the hoary sanction of antiquity, is to be regarded as a self-evident falsehood, and at war with mankind.

The Dred Scott Case

The Dred Scott case (1857) involved a Missouri slave's claim that he was a free man because his owner had taken him to part of the country where slavery had been outlawed by the Missouri Compromise. The case raised three issues: (1) Was Scott a citizen of Missouri and therefore able to bring suit in a federal court of law? (2) Was Scott legally free because of his period of residence in a free state and territory? (3) Was the Missouri Compromise, a federal law prohibiting slavery in northern regions of the United States, constitutional and thereby a valid basis for Scott's claim to freedom? The Court decided against Scott on all three questions.

In his opinion for the Court, Chief Justice Roger Taney held that blacks did not have the privileges of U.S. citizens, but this ruling was contested by two dissenters on the Court: Benjamin Curtis and John McLean. A nationwide conflict concerning the Dred Scott case was an ominous prelude to the Civil War, which came four years later in 1861. A brief

Frederick Douglass, Champion of Equal Rights

Frederick Douglass rose from slavery to become a great champion of equal rights to liberty under the law. He escaped from slavery in 1838 and joined the abolitionist movement. Douglass quickly became a noted public speaker in the cause of human freedom.

During the Civil War, Douglass was an adviser to President Lincoln and influenced the President to issue the Emancipation Proclamation. Then he helped Lincoln to decide to permit blacks to fight in the armed forces of the Union. Douglass urged black Americans to join the Federal armies. His two sons were among the first to respond.

During the years of Reconstruction, Douglass worked to protect the rights of former slaves. He also was concerned about equal rights of women, black and white. He was a member of the National Woman Suffrage Association, and Elizabeth Cady Stanton and Susan B. Anthony often turned to Douglass for advice and support.

excerpt from Chief Justice Taney's lengthy opinion for the Court is presented below, followed by an excerpt from the dissent by Curtis.

Mr. Chief Justice Taney delivered the opinion of the court.

. . . The question is simply this: Can a negro, whose ancestors were imported into this country, and sold as slaves, become a member of the political community formed and brought into existence by the Constitution of the United States, and as such become entitled to all the rights, and privileges, and immunities, by that instrument to the citizen guaranteed? One of which rights is the privilege of suing in a court of the United States in the cases specified in the Constitution. . . .

In discussing this question, we must not confound the rights of citizenship which a state may confer within its own limits, and the rights of citizenship as a member of the Union. It does not by any means follow, because he has all the rights and privileges of a citizen of a State, that he must be a citizen of the United States. He may have all of the rights and privileges of the citizen of a State, and yet not be entitled to the rights and privileges of a citizen in any other State. For, previous to the adoption of the Constitution of the United States, every State had the undoubted right to confer on whomsoever it pleased the character of citizen, and endow him with all its rights. . . .

In the opinion of the court, the legislation and histories of the times, and the language used in the Declaration of Independence, show, that neither the class of persons who had been imported as slaves, nor their descendants, whether they had become free or not, were then acknowledged as a part of the people, nor intended to be included in the general words used in that memorable instrument. . . .

They had for more than a century before been regarded as beings of an inferior order, and altogether unfit to associate with the white race, either in social or political relations; and so far inferior that they had no rights which the white man was bound to respect. . . .

[T]he court is of opinion that . . . Dred Scott was not a citizen of Missouri within the meaning of the Constitution of the United States, and not entitled as such to sue in its courts; and, consequently, that the Circuit Court had no jurisdiction of the case. . . .

Upon these considerations, it is the opinion of the court that the Act of Congress which prohibited a citizen from holding and owning property of this kind in the territory of the United States

> Dred Scott — Pleff in Er
> vs
> John F. A. Sandford
>   In error to the Circuit Court of the
> United States for the District of
> Missouri. —
>   This cause came on to be
> heard on the transcript of the record
> from the Circuit Court of the United
> States for the District of Missouri and
> was argued by counsel — On Consider
> ation whereof, it is now here ordered
> and adjudged by this Court that the
> judgment of the said Circuit Court
> in this cause be and the same is
> hereby reversed for the want of juris-
> diction in that Court, and that this
> cause be and the same is hereby
> remanded to the said Circuit Court
> with directions to dismiss the case
> for the want of jurisdiction in that
> Court. —
>   Pr. Mr Ch. Jus. Taney
>   6th March 1857.

On March 6, 1857, Chief Justice Roger B. Taney publicly stated the Supreme Court's judgment in Scott v. Sandford. This judgment denied Dred Scott's plea for freedom and asserted that black people could not be citizens of the United States. This decision, considered by legal experts to be the worst ever made by the Court, was overturned by the 13th and 14th Amendments.

north of the line therein mentioned, is not warranted by the Constitution, and is therefore void; and that neither Dred Scott himself, nor any of his family, were made free by being carried into this territory; even if they had been carried there by the owner, with the intention of becoming a permanent resident. . . .

Justice Benjamin Curtis's dissent was a brilliant refutation of every major point of Taney's opinion for the Court. Antislavery Americans pointed to this dissent as they condemned the Court's decision in the _Dred Scott_ case. Proslavery Americans condemned Justice Curtis as they praised the Court's decision.

A house divided against itself cannot stand. I believe this Government cannot endure, permanently, half slave and half free.

—Abraham Lincoln, speech, Springfield, Illinois, June 16, 1858

This family of slaves lived on the plantation of J. J. Smith in Beaufort, South Carolina, before and during the Civil War.

I dissent from the opinion pronounced by the Chief Justice, and from the judgment which the majority of the court think it proper to render in this case. . . .

To determine whether any free persons, descended from Africans held in slavery, were citizens of the United States under the Confederation, and consequently at the time of the adoption of the Constitution of the United States, it is only necessary to know whether any such persons were citizens of either of the States under the Confederation, at the time of the adoption of the Constitution.

Of this there can be no doubt. At the time of the ratification of the Articles of Confederation, all free native-born inhabitants of the States of New Hampshire, Massachusetts, New York, New Jersey, and North Carolina, though descended from African slaves, were not only citizens of those States, but such of them as had the other necessary qualifications possessed the franchise of electors, on equal terms with other citizens. . . .

Did the Constitution of the United States deprive them or their descendants of citizenship?

That Constitution was ordained and established by the people of the United States through the action, in each State, of those persons who were qualified by its laws to act thereon, in behalf of themselves and all other citizens of that State. In some of the States, as we have seen, colored persons were among those qualified by law to act on this subject. These colored persons were not only included in the body of "the people of the United States by whom the Constitution was ordained and established," but in at least five of the States they had the power to act, and doubtless did act, by their suffrages, upon the question of its adoption. It would be strange, if we were to find in that instrument anything which deprived of their citizenship any part of the people of the United States who were among those by whom it was established.

I can find nothing in the Constitution which deprives of their citizenship any class of persons who were citizens of the United States at the time of its adoption; or who should be native-born citizens of any State after its adoption; nor any power enabling Congress to disfranchise persons born on the soil of any State, and entitled to citizenship to such State by its constitution and laws. And my opinion is, that, under the Constitution of the United States, every free person born on the soil of the State, who is a citizen of that State by force of its Constitution or laws, is also a citizen of the United States. . . .

It has been often asserted that the Constitution was made exclusively by and for the white race. It has already been shown that in five of the thirteen original States, colored persons then possessed the elective franchise, and were among those by whom the Constitution was ordained and established. If so, it is not true, in point of fact, that the Constitution was made exclusively by the white race. And that it was made exclusively for the white race is, in my opinion, not only an assumption not warranted by anything in the Constitution, but contradicted by its opening declaration, that it was ordained and established by the people of the United States, for themselves and their posterity. And as free colored persons were then citizens of at least five States, and so in every sense part of the people of the United States, they were among those for whom and whose posterity of the Constitution was ordained and established.

I dissent, therefore, from that part of the opinion of the majority of the court, in which it is held that a person of African descent cannot be a citizen of the United States; and I regret I must go further, and dissent both from what I deem their assumption of authority to examine the constitutionality of the act of Congress commonly called the Missouri Compromise act, and the grounds and conclusions announced in their opinion. . . .

I am of opinion that so much of the several acts of Congress as prohibited slavery and involuntary servitude within that part of the Territory of Wisconsin lying north of 36 degrees 30 feet north latitude, and west of the river Mississippi, were constitutional and valid laws.

I think the authors of that notable instrument [the Declaration of Independence] intended to include all men, but they did not mean to declare all men equal in all respects. . . . They defined with tolerable distinctness in what they did consider all men created equal— equal in certain inalienable rights, among which are life, liberty, and the pursuit of happiness. . . . They meant to set up a standard maxim for free society which should be familiar to all: constantly looked to, constantly labored for, and even, though never perfectly attained, constantly approximated, and thereby constantly spreading and deepening its influence and augmenting the happiness and value of life to all people, of all colors, everywhere.

—Abraham Lincoln, speech, Alton, Illinois, October 15, 1858

"To Thine Own Self Be True."

[61]

April 24, 1875

Chapter Five

Rights Renewed and Denied

Conflict over slavery and rights caused the Civil War, as the Southern states seceded from the United States and fought to preserve their slave-based way of life. The Northern states rallied around the federal Union and fought to prevent its breakup.

As the war continued, a new spirit infused the Union side. It was expressed by troops marching to the tune of "The Battle Hymn of the Republic" and singing: "Let us die to make men free." Freedom for enslaved people was the message of the Emancipation Proclamation issued by President Abraham Lincoln at the beginning of 1863. The right to freedom and the end of slavery became primary war aims of the Union forces during the Civil War.

Lincoln viewed the war as a supreme test of the ideals of the nation's founding documents, especially the Declaration of Independence and the Bill of Rights. He hoped that after the war there would be a renewal of the principle that all people have an equal right to life, liberty, and the pursuit of happiness.

Soon after the Confederate States were defeated, Congress began a program of reform to bring equal rights to former slaves. Three basic changes in the Constitution were made with the addition of the 13th, 14th, and 15th amendments. Lincoln, who was killed by an assassin, was not present to witness these changes.

The 13th Amendment abolished slavery throughout the United States. Lincoln's earlier Emancipation Proclamation was a limited wartime act that had abolished slavery only within any state or territory in rebellion against the United States of America. In 1865, Congress enacted on February 1—and the states ratified on December 18—the

This engraving shows Columbia, representing the United States, handing the 1875 Civil Rights Act to black Americans. This federal law protected blacks from unjust discrimination by state and local government and by private businesses, such as hotels, theaters, and restaurants. However, the U.S. Supreme Court declared this law unconstitutional in the Civil Rights Cases in 1883.

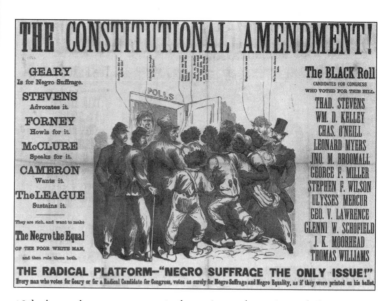

13th Amendment to pervasively and conclusively end slavery in a nation that had always claimed to be "the land of the free."

The 14th Amendment, passed by Congress on June 16, 1866, and ratified by the states on July 28, 1868, protected the citizenship and rights of African Americans on equal terms with other Americans, and it guaranteed that no state "shall make or enforce any law which shall abridge the privileges or immunities" of U.S. citizens. The 15th Amendment guaranteed the right to vote to former slaves and blacks by stating that this right cannot be denied "on account of race, color, or previous condition of servitude."

In 1866, during the congressional debates on the proposed 14th Amendment, its main author, Congressman John Bingham of Ohio, said that he wanted to apply the Bill of Rights to the state governments. The objective, he said, was to guarantee by the Constitution the privileges and immunities, the fundamental rights, of all citizens whenever they are denied by the unconstitutional acts of any state government. Only a few years later, however, a majority of the Supreme Court ignored the clearly expressed intentions of the 14th Amendment's framers. In the first decision on that amendment to come before the Court, the Slaughterhouse Cases (1873), five of the nine justices rejected Bingham's expectation that the new amendment "incorporated" the Bill of Rights and thereby extended its provisions to the state governments.

If the Court in this case had broadly interpreted the "privileges and immunities" clause, as its authors in Congress had intended, then this provision of the 14th Amendment would have been a powerful instrument for securing the rights of all people in the

United States. The Court's rejection of this idea, however, made that clause practically useless as a guarantee that the U.S. government could be called upon to protect those rights listed in the Bill of Rights against abuses by the state governments.

The Court's decision in the Slaughterhouse Cases was only one in a series of setbacks for those Americans in need of the Civil War amendments to protect their rights against hostile state governments. Both women and blacks were denied their rights to liberty and equality, in contradiction of the hopes Lincoln had expressed for "a new birth of freedom" after the war.

Leaders of the movement for women's rights were bitterly disappointed that the Constitution's 15th Amendment did not guarantee their right to vote. Some, like Susan B. Anthony of New York, decided to protest. So, in defiance of her state's election laws, she went to a polling place and boldly attempted to cast a vote in the national election of 1872. As she expected, Anthony was arrested, brought to trial in Rochester, New York, and fined $100.

Like Anthony, Virginia Minor, a resident of Missouri, decided to act on her beliefs by testing the constitutionality of her state's election laws, which also prohibited women from voting. When she attempted to vote in a national election, Minor was arrested, convicted, and punished. She contested the state court's decision and argued that as a citizen of the United States, the state of Missouri could not, according to the 14th Amendment, deprive her of the right to vote because this right was guaranteed under the "privileges and immunities" clause. The case went on appeal to the Supreme Court in 1875, but the Court refused to recognize that women possessed constitutional rights on equal terms with men.

Section 5 of the 14th Amendment gives Congress the authority to make laws necessary to carry out provisions of that amendment, such as the clause in Section 1 that guarantees to all people that no state government shall deprive them of "the equal protection of the laws." On March 1, 1875, Congress enacted the Civil Rights Act to prohibit racial discrimination in the use of facilities open to the general public, such as railroad transportation, hotels, restaurants, and theaters. This was an attempt by Congress to counteract widespread discrimination against black Americans, who were being denied their constitutional rights.

The Civil Rights Act of 1875 led to the *Civil Rights Cases* of 1883—five related cases about the constitutionality of that federal law. In all five situations, the U.S. government had enforced the Civil Rights Act against owners of private facilities—a railroad company, theater owners, and innkeepers. In each instance, a black American had been denied the same accommodations or services as those enjoyed by white Americans, which was clearly a violation of the federal law. The defendants, however, argued that the Civil Rights Act was an unconstitutional regulation of their private property. In response, the plaintiffs held that the act was valid under the terms of the recently enacted 14th Amendment.

The Court, by an 8-to-1 vote, agreed with the defendants and frustrated once more the faith that black Americans had placed in the Civil War amendments. According to Justice Joseph Bradley, writing for the Court, the Civil Rights Act of 1875 was unconstitutional because it attempted to regulate the private behavior of persons, an action beyond the scope of the 14th Amendment.

Justice John Marshall Harlan strongly objected to the Court's opinion, and in his sharply worded dissent, he argued for a broad interpretation of the 13th and 14th amendments. He claimed that the federal government has the authority and responsibility to protect individuals against racial discrimination in their access to privately owned facilities serving the public. Harlan's lone dissent in the *Civil Rights Cases* spoke to the future and was vindicated by his 20th-century successors on the Supreme Court.

Public opinion in the 1880s, however, sided with Bradley's majority decision. In several significant rulings before the end of the 19th century, the Supreme Court practically disabled the 14th and 15th amendments as effective guarantees for Americans in need of protection of their rights. Blacks, in particular, were often denied by dubious legal means their right to vote and their right to fair treatment under the law.

A significant legal setback to the cause of equal rights came in the case of *Plessy* v. *Ferguson* (1896), which upheld state laws, mostly in the South, that segregated blacks from whites in their use of public facilities, such as schools, trains, theaters, parks, and hospitals. This case arose because a group of black leaders in Louisiana founded a Citizens' Committee deliberately to test the constitutionality of their state's Separate Car Law, which racially segregated passengers in railroad cars. Acting for the Citizens' Committee, Homer Plessy, a racially mixed Louisiana resident, bought a first-class ticket for a train and took a seat in the railroad car reserved for whites. When Plessy refused to move to the "colored only" coach, he was arrested for violating a state law.

The Citizens' Committee and Plessy claimed the Louisiana segregation law denied him the "equal protection of the laws" guaranteed by the 14th Amendment. Plessy's lawyers also claimed that the state law violated the 13th Amendment by destroying the legal equality of the races and, in effect, reintroducing slavery. The Court ruled, 7 to 1, against Plessy and held that the "equal protection of the laws" clause allowed a state to provide "separate but equal" facilities for blacks. This doctrine legally justified racial segregation in many states for the next half-century and resulted in massive denial of constitutional rights to black Americans. Once again, Justice John Marshall Harlan dissented.

African Americans were bitterly disappointed by the Supreme Court's decision in this case and earlier ones. One of the strongest protestors was Frederick Douglass. Born into slavery, Douglass had escaped to freedom and achieved prominence as a leader of the abolitionist movement. During the Civil War, he was an adviser to President Lincoln. After the war, and until his death in 1895, he was a powerful advocate for the constitutional rights of black Americans, and he called for blacks to organize and demand those rights.

The distinct but complementary remedies for injustices offered by Harlan and Douglass were later used by 20th-century advocates of the Bill of Rights. As Douglass had urged, black Americans and their white allies would actively organize, protest, and demand redress of their grievances about rights. And as Harlan had called for in his forward-looking dissents, the Supreme Court would overturn the flawed legal judgments of the past. So Douglass, a former slave from Maryland, and Harlan, a former slave owner from Kentucky, were together harbingers of a future when the Bill of Rights would dramatically move from the margins to the center of American political and civic life.

Rights Proclaimed and Restricted

A pivotal battle of the Civil War occurred at Gettysburg, Pennsylvania, during three days, from July 1 to 3, 1863. It was hard fought and one of the bloodiest battles of the war. The Union army drove the Confederate forces from the field in a victory that signaled the eventual final defeat and surrender of the Confederate States of America in 1865.

On November 19, 1863, at a ceremony to dedicate a cemetery for those killed in the battle, President Lincoln spoke to the crowd. In 10 sentences, he reminded his fellow Americans of their nation's exceptional founding principles—its creed—which had distinguished their country's

"Lessons of the Hour," delivered on several occasions during 1892 and 1893, was Frederick Douglass's last major speech in defense of the rights of black Americans before he died in 1895. His speech about the "so-called but mis-called Negro problem" focused on the state of affairs in the South, where mob violence, disenfranchisement, and tenant farming denied African Americans their basic rights.

birth and growth from that of any other nation on earth. At the core of this creed was the idea of "unalienable rights" to liberty possessed equally by each person. This is the meaning of "equality" in the Declaration of Independence to which Lincoln referred in his Gettysburg Address.

At the end of his brief but brilliant speech, Lincoln called for a renewal of dedication among Americans to their founding principles of liberty and equality. And he asked for something more—"a new birth of freedom." The Gettysburg Address was a call to those who would make a second founding of the United States of America. And this time, Americans might more genuinely and inclusively fulfill the original principles of their Constitution and Bill of Rights.

Four score and seven years ago our fathers brought forth on this continent, a new nation, conceived in Liberty, and dedicated to the proposition that all men are created equal.

Now we are engaged in a great civil war, testing whether that nation, or any nation so conceived and so dedicated, can long endure. We are met on a great battle-field of that war. We have

All persons held as slaves within any State . . . in rebellion . . . shall be . . .free.

—President Abraham Lincoln, Emancipation Proclamation, January 1, 1863 come to dedicate a portion of that field, as a final resting place for those who here gave their lives that that nation might live. It is altogether fitting and proper that we should do this.

But, in a larger sense, we can not dedicate—we can not consecrate—we can not hallow—this ground. The brave men, living and dead, who struggled here, have consecrated it, far above our poor power to add or detract. The world will little note, nor long remember what we say here, but it can never forget what they did here. It is for us the living, rather, to be dedicated here to the unfinished work which they who fought here have thus far so nobly advanced. It is rather for us to be here dedicated to the great task remaining before us—that from these honored dead we take increased devotion to that cause for which they gave the last full measure of devotion—that we here highly resolve that these dead shall not have died in vain—that this nation, under God, shall have a new birth of freedom—and that government of the people, by the people, for the people, shall not perish from the earth.

Known as the Civil War Amendments, the 13th, 14th, and 15th Amendments to the U.S. Constitution abolished slavery and secured the rights of black Americans as U.S. citizens. The 14th Amendment was written to protect the rights of freed slaves against state governments that might abuse them in response to the will of the majority. The creator of Section 1 of the 14th Amendment was Congressman John Bingham of Ohio, a Republican Party leader in the House of Representatives.

Bingham noted that the Supreme Court in 1833, in the case of *Barron* v. *Baltimore*, had decided that the Bill of Rights applied only to the national government and not to the states. A constitutional amendment was required, said Bingham, to make the Bill of Rights binding on the states. He recalled that in 1789 another member of the House of Representatives—James Madison of Virginia—had urged that a provision be added to the Bill of Rights to ban infringement by state governments of certain basic rights, such as freedom of religion, speech, and press, and the right to a trial by jury.

Congress in 1789 had rejected Madison's proposal. Congress in 1866, according to Bingham, had another chance to do what Madison had wanted and more in the cause of individual rights. Bingham's peers agreed with him and clearly intended for the 14th Amendment to become an instrument for expanding the range and reach of the Bill of Rights to all

The [Emancipation] Proclamation is an incalculable element of strength to the Union cause. . . . It perfects the purposes of the Declaration of Independence.
—Newspaper publisher Rufus Blanchard, from an 1863 broadside

I urge the [14th] Amendment for the enforcement of these essential provisions of your Constitution, divine in their justice, sublime in their humanity, which declare that all men are equal in the rights of life and liberty before the majesty of American law.

—John Bingham, Ohio Representative, 14th Amendment sponsor, 1866

people in all parts of the United States and in regard to all levels of government.

The 15th Amendment guaranteed the right to vote to former slaves and black Americans. The words of this amendment reflected a continuing commitment to the idea of natural rights expressed in the Declaration of Independence. Section 1 of the 15th Amendment does not say that the government grants this right to vote to certain people. Rather, the writers of the amendment assumed, as did John Locke and Thomas Jefferson, that certain natural rights are possessed equally by all persons just because they are human beings.

Thus, the 15th Amendment does say that the right to vote "shall not be denied or abridged"—by any government, national or state, within the United States—because of a person's "race, color, or previous condition of servitude." Rather than granting the right to vote, the 15th Amendment says that the government cannot justly take that right away from a certain group of people.

AMENDMENT XIII [Ratified in 1865]
Section 1. Neither slavery nor involuntary servitude, except as a punishment for crime whereof the party shall have been duly convicted, shall exist within the United States, or any place subject to their jurisdiction.

Section 2. Congress shall have power to enforce this article by appropriate legislation.

AMENDMENT XIV [Ratified in 1868]
Section 1. All persons born or naturalized in the United States, and subject to the jurisdiction thereof, are citizens of the United States and of the State wherein they reside. No State shall make or enforce any law which shall abridge the privileges or immunities of citizens of the United States; nor shall any State deprive any person of life, liberty, or property, without due process of law; nor deny to any person within its jurisdiction the equal protection of the laws.

Section 5. The Congress shall have power to enforce, by appropriate legislation, the provisions of this article.

AMENDMENT XV [Ratified in 1870]
Section 1. The right of citizens of the United States to vote shall not be denied or abridged by the United States or by any State on account of race, color, or previous condition of servitude.

Section 2. The Congress shall have power to enforce this article by appropriate legislation.

The details and overt issues of the Slaughterhouse Cases (1873) were about the rights of local stockyard workers in New Orleans. The Supreme Court was asked to decide whether or not the "privileges and immunities" clause of the 14th Amendment "incorporated," or included, the Bill of Rights and thereby applied it to state governments. If so, the U.S. Bill of Rights could be used to protect the rights of workers in New Orleans against the power of the Louisiana state government. In a close vote of 5 to 4, the Court upheld the Louisiana law at issue and decided against the claim of the stockyard workers.

Writing for the Court, Justice Samuel Miller narrowly interpreted the 14th Amendment provision that reads, "No State shall make or enforce any law which shall abridge the privileges or immunities of citizens of the United States." A slim Supreme Court majority decided that provisions of the Bill of Rights were not among these "privileges and immunities."

MR. JUSTICE MILLER delivered the opinion of the Court. . . .

. . . Was it the purpose of the Fourteenth Amendment, by the simple declaration that no State could make or enforce any law which shall abridge the privileges and immunities of *citizens of the United States,* to transfer the security and protection of all the civil rights which we have mentioned, from the States to the Federal government? And where it is declared that Congress shall have the power to enforce that article, was it intended to bring within the power of Congress the entire domain of civil rights heretofore belonging exclusively to the States? . . .

[S]uch a construction followed by the reversal of the judgments of the Supreme Court of Louisiana in these cases, would constitute this court a perpetual censor upon all legislation of the States, on the civil rights of their own citizens, with authority to nullify such as it did not approve as consistent with those rights, as they existed at the time of the adoption of this amendment. The argument we admit is not always the most conclusive which is drawn from the consequences urged against the adoption of a particular construction of an instrument. But when, as in the case before us, these consequences are so serious, so far-reaching and pervading, so great a departure from the structure and spirit of our

Let us now refer to the provisions of the proposed [14th] Amendment. The first section prohibits the States from abridging the privileges and immunities of citizens of the United States, or unlawfully depriving them of life, liberty, or property, or of denying to any person within their jurisdiction as the equal protection of the laws.

I can hardly believe that any person can be found who will not admit that every one of these provisions is just. They are all asserted, in some form or another, in our DECLARATION or organic law. But the Constitution limits only the action of Congress, and is not a limitation on the States. This amendment supplies that defect, and allows Congress to correct the unjust legislation of the States, so far that the law which operates upon one man shall operate equally upon all.

—Thaddeus Stevens, Pennsylvania Representative, 1866

This drawing shows the stockyard of the Crescent City Livestock Landing and Slaughterhouse Company of New Orleans, which was the place of origin of the landmark Slaughterhouse *cases decided by the Supreme Court in 1873. The cases were brought to the Court by butchers who claimed that a Louisiana law had deprived them of their right "to exercise their trade." The butchers challenged the law under the 13th and 14th Amendments, but the Court ruled against them.*

institutions; when the effect is to fetter and degrade the State governments by subjecting them to the control of Congress, in the exercise of powers heretofore universally conceded to them of the most ordinary and fundamental character; when in fact it radically changes the whole theory of the relations of the State and Federal governments to each other and of both these governments to the people; the argument has a force that is irresistible, in the absence of language which expresses such a purpose too clearly to admit or doubt.

We are convinced that no such results were intended by the Congress which proposed these amendments, nor by the legislatures of the States which ratified them.

Rights Denied to Women

Myra Bradwell, a resident of Illinois, was denied a license to practice law solely because of her status as a married woman. She brought suit against the state and claimed that her rights guaranteed by the newly ratified 14th Amendment had been denied. As a citizen of the United States, who was qualified to practice law, Bradwell argued that the state of Illinois was abridging her constitutional rights under the "privileges and immunities" clause of the 14th Amendment. The justices of the Illinois Supreme Court, however, decided against her application for certification as a lawyer. She appealed to the Supreme Court of the United States. In *Bradwell* v. *Illinois* (1873), the Court relied upon its ruling in the *Slaughterhouse Cases* to deny Myra Bradwell protection under the Constitution's 14th Amendment.

MR. JUSTICE MILLER delivered the opinion of the Court.

. . .[T]he plaintiff asserted her right to a license on the grounds, among others, that she was a citizen of the United States, and that having been a citizen of Vermont at one time, she was, in the State of Illinois, entitled to any right granted to citizens of the latter State. . . .

The fourteenth amendment declares that citizens of the United States are citizens of the State within which they reside; therefore the plaintiff was, at the time of making her application, a citizen of the United States and a citizen of the State of Illinois.

We do not here mean to say that there may not be a temporary residence in one State, with intent to return to another, which will not create citizenship in the former. But the plaintiff states nothing to take her case out of the definition of citizenship of a State as defined by the first section of the fourteenth amendment.

In regard to that amendment counsel for the plaintiff in this court truly says that there are certain privileges and immunities which belong to a citizen of the United States as such; otherwise it would be nonsense for the fourteenth amendment to prohibit a State from abridging them, and he proceeds to argue that admission to the bar of a State of a person who possesses the requisite learning and character is one of those which a State may not deny.

In this latter proposition we are not able to concur with counsel. We agree with him that there are privileges and immunities belonging to citizens of the United States, in that relation and character, and that it is these and these alone which a State is forbidden to abridge. But the right to admission to practice in the courts of a State is not one of them. This right in no sense depends on citizenship of the United States. It has not, as far as we know, ever been made in any State, or in any case, to depend on citizenship at all. Certainly many prominent and distinguished lawyers have been admitted to practice, both in the State and Federal courts, who were not citizens of the United States or of any State. But, on whatever basis this right may be placed, so far as it can have any relation to citizenship at all, it would seem that, as to the courts of a State, it would relate to citizenship of the State, and as to Federal courts, it would relate to citizenship of the United States.

The opinion just delivered in the *Slaughter-House Cases* renders elaborate argument in the present case unnecessary; for, unless we are wholly and radically mistaken in the principles on which these cases are decided, the right to control and regulate the granting of license to practice law in the courts of a State is one

Although the Supreme Court ruled against Myra Bradwell's appeal for a license to practice law in Bradwell v. Illinois (1873), *she remained active in the legal profession. She was an honorary member of the Illinois State Bar Association since 1872 and served as its vice president for four terms. In 1890, the Illinois Supreme Court acting on its own volition approved Bradwell's original application for a license to practice law and in 1892 she was granted the right to appear as a lawyer before the U.S. Supreme Court.*

Susan B. Anthony and the Woman Suffrage Movement

Susan B. Anthony believed that the right to vote was the key to other civil rights for women. If women could vote, they might influence government officials to make laws that opened opportunities for women. So she worked for more than 50 years in the cause of woman suffrage. Every year she asked members of Congress to pass a "Women's Right to Vote" amendment to the Constitution, which came to be known as the Susan B. Anthony Amendment.

From 1892 to 1900, Anthony was president of the National American Woman Suffrage Association. When she stepped down from active leadership of the women's rights movement, she was 80 years old. In 1920, 14 years after Anthony's death, her great goal was achieved. The 19th Amendment to the Constitution was ratified to protect the right of women to vote throughout the United States.

[W]omen have learned the value of organization and united, systematic work in securing the best and speediest results. . . . Until woman has obtained that right protective of all other rights—the ballot—this agitation must still go on, absorbing the time and the energy of our best and strongest women.

—Susan B. Anthony, *Arena,* 1897

of these powers which are not transferred for its protection to the Federal government, and its exercise is in no manner governed or controlled by citizenship of the United States in the party seeking such license.

It is unnecessary to repeat the argument on which the judgment in those cases is founded. It is sufficient to say they are conclusive of the present case.

Judgment affirmed.

In a widely reported speech, Susan B. Anthony attracted nationwide attention to her prosecution for merely attempting to vote in the national election of 1872 in New York State. Although she was arrested and fined, she was able to use the occasion to publicly protest the injustice of denying women their natural rights, including the right to vote. Anthony's cause was ultimately vindicated in 1920 with the ratification of the Constitution's 19th Amendment, which guarantees to women their right to vote.

Friends and Fellow Citizens:—I stand before you to-night under indictment for the alleged crime of having voted at the last presidential election, without having a lawful right to vote. It shall be my work this evening to prove to you that in thus voting, I not only committed no crime, but, instead, simply exercised my *citizen's rights,* guaranteed to me and all United States citizens by the National Constitution, beyond the power of any State to deny.

The preamble of the Federal Constitution says:

"We, the people of the United States, in order to form a more perfect union, establish justice, insure *domestic* tranquility, provide for the common defense, promote the general welfare, and secure the blessings of liberty to ourselves and our posterity, do ordain and establish this Constitution for the United States of America."

It was we, the people; not we, the white male citizens; nor yet we, the male citizens; but we, the whole people, who formed the Union. And we formed it, not to give the blessings of liberty, but to secure them; not to the half of ourselves and the half of our posterity, but to the whole people—women as well as men. And it is a downright mockery to talk to women of their enjoyment of the blessings of liberty while they are denied the use of the only means of securing them provided by this democratic-republican government—the ballot.

For any State to make sex a qualification that must ever result in the disfranchisement of one entire half of the people is to pass a bill of attainder, or an *ex post facto* law, and is therefore a violation of the supreme law of the land. By it the blessings of liberty are for ever withheld from women and their female posterity. To them this government has no just powers derived from the consent of the governed. To them this government is not a democracy. It is not a republic. It is an odious aristocracy; a hateful oligarchy of sex; the most hateful aristocracy ever established on the face of the globe; an oligarchy of wealth, where the rich govern the poor. An oligarchy of learning, where the educated govern the ignorant . . . might be endured; but this oligarchy of sex, which makes father, brothers, husband, sons, the oligarchs over the mother and sisters, the wife and daughters of every household—which ordains all men sovereigns, all women subjects, carries dissension, discord and rebellion into every home of the nation.

Webster, Worcester and Bouvier all define a citizen to be a person in the United States, entitled to vote and hold office.

The only question left to be settled now is: Are women persons? And I hardly believe any of our opponents will have the hardihood to say they are not. Being persons, then, women are citizens; and no State has a right to make any law, or to enforce any old law, that shall abridge their privileges or immunities. Hence, every discrimination against women in the constitutions and laws of the several States is to-day null and void.

In *Minor* v. *Happersett* (1875), the Supreme Court once again refused to recognize that women possessed constitutional rights on equal terms with men. It ruled against Virginia Minor in her appeal for the right to vote. She had argued that the state of Missouri could not prohibit her from voting because, as a citizen of the United States, she was protected by the "privileges and immunities" clause of the 14th Amendment. Yet again, an appeal to the Constitution's 14th Amendment failed to yield a decision favorable to the principle that all persons equally possess certain rights under the

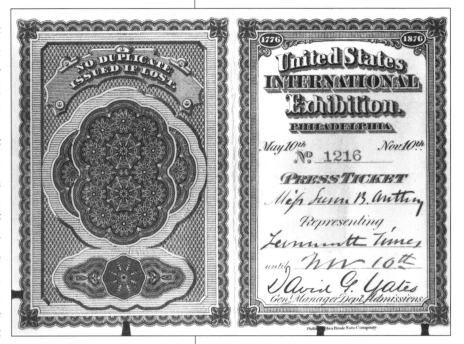

On July 4, 1886, Susan B. Anthony used this press pass to gain entry to the Centennial Celebration of the Declaration of Independence in Philadelphia. Denied the opportunity to officially participate, she interrupted the celebration to present a "Declaration of Women's Rights" to the presiding officer. Anthony and her supporters then left the hall and gathered in front of the Liberty Bell where she read her Declaration to a cheering crowd.

Constitution. Chief Justice Morrisson R. Waite delivered the opinion of the Court.

The question is presented in this case, whether, since the adoption of the Fourteenth Amendment, a woman, who is a citizen of the United States and of the State of Missouri, is a voter in that State, notwithstanding the provision of the constitution and laws of the State, which confine the right of suffrage to men alone. . . .

The Amendment did not add to the privileges and immunities of a citizen. It simply furnished an additional guaranty for the protection of such as he already had. No new voters were necessarily made by it. Indirectly it may have had that effect, because it may have increased the number of citizens entitled to suffrage under the constitution and laws of the States, but it operates for this purpose, if at all, through the States and the state laws, and not directly upon the citizen.

It is clear therefore, we think, that the Constitution has not added the rights of suffrage to the privileges and immunities of citizenship as they existed at the time it was adopted. This makes it proper to inquire whether suffrage was co-extensive with the citizenship of the States at the time of its adoption. If it was, then it may with force be argued that suffrage was one of the rights which belonged to citizenship, and in the enjoyment of which every citizen must be protected. But if it was not, the contrary may with propriety be assumed. . . .

[I]n respect to suffrage in the several States it cannot for a moment be doubted that if it had been intended to make all citizens of the United States voters, the framers of the Constitution would not have left it to implication.

Rights Denied to African Americans

Writing for the Court in the *Civil Rights Cases* (1883), Justice Joseph Bradley claimed the Civil Rights Act of 1875—which prohibited racial discrimination in public facilities—was unconstitutional because it attempted to regulate the private behavior of persons, an action beyond the scope of the 14th Amendment.

It is obvious that the primary and important question in all the cases is the constitutionality of the law, for if the law is unconstitutional, none of the prosecutions can stand. . . .

[I]t is the purpose of the law to declare that, in the enjoyment of the accommodations and privileges of inns, public conveyances, theatres, and other places of public amusement, no distinction shall be made between citizens of different race or color or between those who have, and those who have not, been slaves. . . .

Has Congress constitutional power to make such a law?. . .

When a man has emerged from slavery, and, by the aid of beneficent legislation, has shaken off the inseparable concomitants of that state, there must be some stage in the progress of his elevation when he takes the rank of a mere citizen and ceases to be the special favorite of the laws, and when his rights as a citizen or a man are to be protected in the ordinary modes by which other men's rights are protected. . . .

On the whole, we are of opinion that no countenance of authority for the passage of the law in question can be found in either the Thirteenth or Fourteenth Amendment of the Constitution, and no other ground of authority for its passage being suggested, it must necessarily be declared void, at least so far as its operation in the several States is concerned.

In this political cartoon, Thomas Nast, the leading cartoonist of his time, expressed his disgust with the unfair and illegal treatment of black Americans after the Civil War. Nast's cartoon shows that the constitutionally guaranteed rights of blacks were routinely violated by organizations of white racists, such as the White League and the Ku Klux Klan.

As the only dissenter, Justice John Marshall Harlan strongly objected to the Court's opinion. He argued for a broad interpretation of the 13th and 14th amendments and claimed that the federal government should protect individuals against racial discrimination in facilities serving the public. He pointed out, for example, "that roads and railroads were established by the authority of these states" and theaters operated under state government licenses. Therefore, Harlan argued, the state's association with these facilities justified federal action to guarantee equal opportunity for all to use the facilities. Further, Harlan objected to Bradley's statement that former slaves had become the "special favorite of the laws." During the remaining years of the 19th century, Justice Harlan was the Court's lonely dissenting voice in favor of broad applications of the Civil War amendments.

MR. JUSTICE HARLAN dissenting.

The opinion in these cases proceeds, it seems to me, upon grounds entirely too narrow and artificial. I cannot resist the conclusion that the substance and spirit of the recent amendments of the Constitution have been sacrificed by a subtle and ingenious verbal criticism. . . .

I am of the opinion that such discrimination practised by corporations and individuals in the exercise of their public or *quasi*-public functions is a badge of servitude the imposition of which Congress may prevent under its power, by appropriate legislation, to enforce the Thirteenth Amendment; and, consequently, without reference to its enlarged power under the Fourteenth Amendment, the act of March 1, 1875, is not, in my judgment, repugnant to the Constitution. . . .

It is, I submit, scarcely just to say that the colored race has been the special favorite of the laws. The statute of 1875, now adjudged to be unconstitutional, is for the benefit of citizens of every race and color. What the nation, through Congress, has sought to accomplish in reference to that race is what had already been done in every State of the Union for the white race—to secure and protect rights belonging to them as freemen and citizens; nothing more. . . .

If the constitutional amendments [13th and 14th amendments] be enforced according to the intent with which, as I conceive, they were adopted, there cannot be, in this republic, any class of human beings in practical subjection to another class with power in the latter to dole out to the former just such privileges as they may choose to grant. The supreme law of the land has decreed that no authority shall be exercised in this country upon the basis of discrimination, in respect of civil rights, against freeman and citizens because of their race, color, or previous condition of servitude. . . .

For the reasons stated, I feel constrained to withhold my assent.

Frederick Douglass noted with dismay the plight of black Americans after the Civil War. They had believed in the principles of America's founding documents about immutable and universal rights, and they had expected to enjoy and take responsibility for their constitutional rights on equal terms with other Americans. It did not happen, and they were bitter but not defeated. Douglass described the lamentable treatment of African Americans in a speech on September 24, 1883, when he urged them to act boldly to defend and use their rights against those who would deny them.

It is our lot to live among a people whose laws, traditions, and prejudices have been against us for centuries, and from these they are not yet free. . . . Though we have had war, reconstruction, and abolition as a nation, we still linger in the shadow and blight of an extinct institution. Though the colored man is no longer subject to be bought and sold, he is still surrounded by an adverse sentiment which fetters all his movements. . . . The color line meets him everywhere, and in a measure shuts him out from all respectable and profitable trades and callings. . . .

If liberty, with us, is yet but a name, our citizenship is but a sham, and our suffrage thus far only a cruel mockery, we may yet congratulate ourselves upon the fact that the laws and institutions of the country are sound, just, and liberal. There is hope for a people when their laws are righteous, whether for the moment they conform to their requirements or not. But until this nation shall make its practice accord with its Constitution and its righteous laws, it will not do to reproach the colored people of this country. . . .

If the 6 million colored people of this country, armed with the Constitution of the United States, with a million votes of their own to lean upon and millions of white men at their back, whose hearts are responsive to the claims of humanity, have not sufficient spirit and wisdom to organize and combine to defend themselves from outrage, discrimination, and oppression, it will be idle for them to expect that the Republican Party or any other political party will organize and combine for them or care what becomes of them. Men may combine to prevent cruelty to animals, for they are dumb and cannot speak for themselves; but we are men and must speak for ourselves, or we shall not be spoken for at all.

In the case of *Plessy* v. *Ferguson* (1896), Justice Henry Brown presented the majority opinion of the Supreme Court, which ruled that the "equal protection of the laws" clause of the 14th Amendment allowed a state to provide "separate but equal" facilities for blacks, thereby legally justifying racial segregation. In this case, Homer Plessy lost his fight against segregated railroad cars in Louisiana.

The object of the [14th] amendment was undoubtedly to enforce the absolute equality of the two races before the law, but in the nature of things it could not have been intended to abolish distinctions based upon color, or to enforce social as distinguished from political equality, or a commingling of the two races upon

JIM CROW LAW.

UPHELD BY THE UNITED STATES SUPREME COURT.

Statute Within the Competency of the Louisiana Legislature and Railroads—Must Furnish Separate Cars for Whites and Blacks.

Washington, May 18.—The Supreme Court today in an opinion read by Justice Brown, sustained the constitutionality of the law in Louisiana requiring the railroads of that State to provide separate cars for white and colored passengers. There was no interstate, commerce feature in the case for the railroad upon which the incident occurred giving rise to case—Plessey vs. Ferguson—East Louisiana railroad, was and is operated wholly within the State, to the laws of Congress of many of the States. The opinion states that by the analogy of the laws of Congress, and of many of states requiring establishment of separate schools for children of two races and other similar laws, the statute in question was within competency of Louisiana Legislature, exercising the police power of the State. The judgment of the Supreme Court of State upholding law was therefore upheld.

Mr. Justice Harlan announced a very vigorous dissent saying that he saw nothing but mischief in all such laws. In his view of the case, no power in the land had right to regulate the enjoyment of civil rights upon the basis of race. It would be just as reasonable and proper, he said, for states to pass laws requiring separate cars to be furnished for Catholic and Protestants, or for descendants of those of Teutonic race and those of Latin race.

A newspaper article of May 18, 1896, announced the U.S. Supreme Court's decision in Plessy v. Ferguson, which upheld a Louisiana law for racial segregation. Such statutes were called "Jim Crow laws" to signify that they applied to black persons. Jim Crow, a generic name for a black American, was derived from a popular minstrel show produced initially in 1828.

terms unsatisfactory to either. Laws permitting, and even requiring, their separation in places where they are liable to be brought into contact do not necessarily imply the inferiority of either race to the other, and have been generally, if not universally, recognized as within the competency of the state legislatures in the exercise of their police power. The most common instance of this is connected with the establishment of separate schools for white and colored children, which has been held to be a valid exercise of the legislative power even by courts of states where the political rights of the colored race have been longest and most earnestly enforced. . . .

We consider the underlying fallacy of the plaintiff's argument to consist in the assumption that the enforced separation of the two races stamps the colored race with a badge of inferiority. If this be so, it is not by reason of anything found in the act, but solely because the colored race chooses to put that construction upon it. . . .

The argument also assumes that social prejudices may be overcome by legislation, and that equal rights cannot be secured to the Negro except by an enforced commingling of the two races. We cannot accept this proposition. If the two races are to meet upon terms of social equality, it must be the result of natural affinities, a mutual appreciation of each other's merits, and a voluntary consent of individuals. . . . Legislation is powerless to eradicate racial instincts or to abolish distinctions based upon physical differences, and the attempt to do so can only result in accentuating the difficulties of the present situation. If the civil and political rights of both races be equal, one cannot be inferior to the other civilly or politically. If one race be inferior to the other socially, the Constitution of the United States cannot put them upon the same plane. . . .

The judgment of the court below is, therefore, *affirmed.*

In *Plessy v. Ferguson*, once again Justice John Marshall Harlan dissented from an opinion that failed, in his view, to properly interpret provisions of the Civil War amendments to protect vulnerable minorities from the tyranny of a majority. He strongly criticized the Court for failing to protect fundamental rights of blacks or other Americans to liberty and equal treatment before the law. Though ignored, and at times reviled, for his opposition to the majority, Harlan's voice was prophetic. The majority today has accepted his

dissents, not the majority opinions of his contemporaries, as the correct view on how to interpret and apply the Civil War amendments.

It was said in argument that the statute of Louisiana does not discriminate against either race, but prescribes a rule applicable alike to white and colored citizens. But this argument does not meet the difficulty. Everyone knows that the statute in question had its origin in the purpose, not so much to exclude white persons from railroad cars occupied by blacks, as to exclude colored people from coaches occupied by or assigned to white persons. Railroad corporations of Louisiana did not make discrimination among whites in the matter of accommodation for travelers. The thing to accomplish was, under the guise of giving equal accommodation for whites and blacks, to compel the latter to keep to themselves while traveling in railroad passenger coaches. No one would be so wanting in candor as to assert the contrary. The fundamental objection, therefore, to the statute is that it interferes with the personal freedom of citizens. . . .

If a white man and a black man choose to occupy the same public conveyance on a public highway, it is their right to do so, and no government proceeding alone on grounds of race can prevent it without infringing the personal liberty of each. . . .

The white race deems itself to be the dominant race in this country. . . . But in view of the Constitution, in the eye of the law, there is in this country no superior, dominant, ruling class of citizens. There is no caste here. Our Constitution is color-blind and neither knows nor tolerates classes among citizens. In respect of civil rights, all citizens are equal before the law. The humblest is the peer of the most powerful. The law regards man as man and takes no account of his surroundings or of his color when his civil rights as guaranteed by the supreme law of the land are involved. It is therefore to be regretted that this high tribunal, the final expositor of the fundamental law of the land, has reached the conclusion that it is competent for a state to regulate the enjoyment by citizens of their civil rights solely upon the basis of race. . . .

The arbitrary separation of citizens, on the basis of race, while they are on a public highway, is a badge of servitude wholly inconsistent with the civil freedom and the equality before the law established by the Constitution. It cannot be justified upon any legal grounds.

John Marshall Harlan, A Dissenter in the Cause of Equal Justice Under Law

John Marshall Harlan served as an associate justice of the U.S. Supreme Court from 1877 to 1911. A former slaveholder from Kentucky, Harlan was a staunch defender of the constitutional rights of former slaves in cases before the Court. In two landmark decisions, the *Civil Rights Cases* (1883) and *Plessy* v. *Ferguson* (1896), Justice Harlan wrote memorable dissenting opinions in support of the rights of black Americans.

He strongly believed that the equal protection clause of the 14th Amendment meant full equality for black persons in their dealings with state governments. Thus, he opposed racial segregation sanctioned by state governments and supported federal government actions to stop it.

Justice Harlan emphasized that the 14th Amendment does not allow state governments to know the race of those entitled to the protection of their constitutional rights. He wrote: "Have we become so inoculated with prejudice of race that an American government . . . can make distinctions between citizens [with regard to their constitutional rights] simply because of their respective races?"

Harlan's grandson, John Marshall Harlan II, became a Supreme Court justice in 1955 and served until 1971.

Chapter Six

A Resurgence of Rights

In an acclaimed 19th-century book on government, world-renowned social scientist Henry Sumner Maine described the U.S. Bill of Rights as a "certain number of amendments on comparatively unimportant points." Today, no one would believe that statement. During the 20th century, both the federal judiciary and the general public have been quite concerned about how the Bill of Rights should be used to resolve continuing controversies involving freedom of expression, equitable relationships among diverse groups of Americans, and the rights of those accused of crimes. Further, the Bill of Rights has become both a symbol and a practical tool for people seeking liberty and justice under the U.S. Constitution.

In the 20th century, issues involving the Bill of Rights became prominent during U.S. involvement in World War I. Challenging issues were raised about limits on individual freedoms imposed by the federal government in its attempt to maintain national security. In response to potential threats of enemies during wartime, Congress passed the Espionage Act of 1917 and the Sedition Act of 1918. These laws made it a federal crime to distribute materials urging resistance to the government or to impugn the government and its leaders. Disruptive public protests were also banned. Critics of these laws argued that they were unconstitutional limits on the rights to liberty guaranteed in the Constitution's 1st Amendment. Tension arose between the government's responsibility to provide both national security and protection for constitutional rights.

This constitutional issue was reminiscent of controversies surrounding the Sedition Act of 1798. Unlike the earlier crisis, however, this issue went to the U.S. Supreme Court. The cases involved two antiwar activists, Charles Schenck and Jacob Abrams. Writing for the Court in *Schenck* v. *United States* (1919), Justice Oliver Wendell Holmes

This poster, designed by the Iowa Art Program WPA, announces a citywide forum or open meeting at Roosevelt High School in Des Moines, Iowa, on January 22, 1940. The speaker, Max Lerner, addressed the public issue of limitations on individual liberties during periods of national crisis or emergency.

Jr. said that when spoken or written words "create a clear and present danger" of bringing about evils that Congress had the authority to prevent, the government may limit freedom of speech.

This decision indicated that the 1st Amendment protection of free speech may under certain conditions be limited, such as when national security is threatened. But the difficulty in deciding exactly when and how to limit free speech in favor of national security was shown in another case, *Abrams* v. *United States* (1919). This time, Holmes wrote a dissenting opinion that modified his previously stated "clear and present danger" rule.

In the *Abrams* case, which involved a person's conviction under both the Espionage Act and the Sedition Act, Holmes argued that in order to limit speech, a "clear and present danger" must be directly connected to specific actions. If imminent danger cannot be demonstrated, then speech cannot be lawfully limited. Holmes's dissent in this case, which provided greater latitude for freedom of expression, was accepted by the Court in *Brandenburg* v. *Ohio* in 1969.

The next significant free speech case, *Gitlow* v. *New York* (1925), pertained to a state sedition law and not a federal statute. Once more, the Supreme Court permitted legal limitations on free speech. In deciding this case, however, the Court departed from the common understanding that the Bill of Rights restrained only the federal government and not the state governments. This time, the Court held that 1st Amendment guarantees of free speech and press could be used to prevent state governments from curtailing individual rights.

In New York, Benjamin Gitlow was arrested and convicted for violating the state's Criminal Anarchy Law, which made it a crime to advocate violent overthrow of the government. Gitlow appealed his conviction on the grounds that the state of New York had unlawfully denied his 1st Amendment right to free speech under the due process clause of the 14th Amendment.

A much earlier Supreme Court decision, *Barron* v. *Baltimore* (1833), had confirmed the common understanding that the federal Bill of Rights imposed limitations only upon the government of the United States and not the state governments. The 1st Amendment freedoms of religion, speech, press, assembly, and petition, for example, checked only the federal government; state governments retained the power to deal with these matters according to their own constitutions and statutes.

When the 14th Amendment was ratified in 1868, however, it established new limitations upon state governments. During the remainder of the 19th century and the first quarter of the 20th century, the Supreme Court tended to interpret this amendment narrowly and did not use it to enhance significantly the constitutional rights of individuals.

In the *Gitlow* case, the claim was put forward that the due process clause of the 14th Amendment could be used to limit state governments' power to abridge the rights to free speech and press. The Supreme Court upheld Gitlow's conviction and the constitutionality of the state of New York's Criminal Anarchy Law. However, the Court also held that the 1st Amendment rights of free speech and press could be applied to the states through the 14th Amendment, which says that "No state shall . . . deprive any person of life, liberty, or property, without due process of law."

According to the Court, the 1st Amendment freedoms "are among the fundamental personal rights and 'liberties' protected by the due process clause of the Fourteenth Amendment from impairment by the states." Thus, the Court said that the due process clause of the 14th Amendment could be used to "incorporate," or absorb, the free speech and press guarantees of the 1st Amendment and apply them against the power of a state government in order to protect an individual's rights.

This "incorporation doctrine" would allow the 14th Amendment to be used in future cases to apply provisions of the federal Bill of Rights to state governments. This was a turning point in the constitutional history of the United States; ever since that decision, the Bill of Rights has become more prominent in the lives of Americans.

In 1931, the Supreme Court did what it claimed it could do in the *Gitlow* case. In *Stromberg* v. *California,* the Court decided to use the incorporation doctrine. This case involved a 19-year-old camp counselor, Yetta Stromberg, who worked at a summer camp for children in San Bernardino County, California.

Stromberg required the children in her care to make a replica of the red flag of the Soviet Union, to raise the flag in a public ceremony, and to recite a pledge in honor of the values symbolized by the flag. By conducting this activity, Stromberg violated a California law that prohibited display of a red flag "as an emblem of opposition to organized government." After her conviction in a California state court, Stromberg appealed to the U.S. Supreme Court. The Supreme Court, relying on the incorporation doctrine, overturned California's conviction of Yetta Stromberg.

The second occasion for the Court's use of the incorporation doctrine in relationship to the 1st Amendment involved a 1925

Jacob Abrams (far right) and these other Russian immigrants distributed leaflets criticizing President Woodrow Wilson and the U.S. government and praising the new communist government in Russia. They were arrested and convicted f · violating two federal laws: the Espionage Act of 1917 and the Sedition Act of 1918. The Supreme Court upheld their conviction in Abrams v. United States *(1919).*

Minnesota statute, the Public Nuisance Abatement Law. It declared that anyone who published a "malicious, scandalous and defamatory newspaper, magazine, or other periodical" was guilty of a crime, which the state government could punish by fines or imprisonment. This law authorized a form of government censorship called prior restraint, which allows government officials to stop a newspaper or magazine in advance from publishing materials of which they disapprove.

Jay Near, publisher of the *Saturday Press*, was arrested and convicted for violating the Minnesota law because his newspaper regularly attacked government officials in Minneapolis. Near's attorney claimed that the law allowed prior restraint and thus violated the 14th Amendment. He argued that the Constitution's guarantee of freedom of the press was a fundamental right. No state could take the right away through prior restraint. In *Near* v. *Minnesota* (1931), the Supreme Court ruled that the Minnesota Public Nuisance Abatement Law was a prior restraint on the press and therefore an unconstitutional violation of the Constitution's 1st Amendment guarantee of the right to freedom of the press. And this 1st Amendment right was applicable to the state of Minnesota through its incorporation under the 14th Amendment.

In 1937, the Supreme Court made its next key decision to incorporate a provision of the Bill of Rights: the right to peaceable assembly. Dirk DeJonge, a member of the Communist Party of the United States, was arrested and convicted of breaking the state of Oregon's Criminal Syndicalism Act, which made it a crime to become a member of an organization that advocated violent or other unlawful methods of political revolution. According to this law, it was even a crime to assemble voluntarily with any group that teaches violent political revolution.

DeJonge's lawyers appealed his conviction on the grounds that the state Criminal Syndicalism Act violated the 1st Amendment's guarantee of the right to peaceable assembly to protest against the government. They also argued that the incorporation doctrine used by the Court in the *Stromberg* and *Near* cases should also be applied in DeJonge's case. The Supreme Court decided in favor of DeJonge.

One year after that case, the Court stated its preferred freedoms doctrine in a footnote to the opinion in *United States* v. *Carolene Products*. The "preferred freedoms" are those necessary to enable effective participation in a democracy, such as the rights to free speech, press, and assembly. The Court affirmed the incorporation doctrine and the fundamental importance of individual rights relative to laws that would limit those rights. The Preferred Freedoms Doctrine was a signal that laws restricting fundamental political rights guaranteed by the Bill of Rights would be viewed with great suspicion as possibly dangerous to the well being of a constitutional democracy. This doctrine has had a deep and abiding influence on the development of individual rights, especially rights of free expression in the 1st Amendment.

The 1st Amendment right to free exercise of religion was at issue in two cases involving laws that required a daily Pledge of Allegiance and salute to the flag of the United States in public schools. One case, *Minersville School District* v. *Gobitis* (1940) originated in Pennsylvania. The second case was *West Virginia State Board of Education* v. *Barnette* (1943). In both cases, students of the Jehovah's Witnesses faith refused to comply with the flag-salute ceremonies required by law in their public schools. Their religion held that saluting and pledging an oath to the flag was like worshiping a graven image or idol, an offense against God. In both cases, the students were punished for refusing to obey the flag-salute laws, and these cases eventually went to the Supreme Court.

The issue before the Court in both cases was whether or not public school officials could require Jehovah's Witnesses to participate in a ceremony that contradicted their religious beliefs. Did the flag-salute laws violate the 1st and 14th Amendment rights to free speech and to free exercise of religion? In both cases, the Court recognized the validity of the incorporation doctrine with regard to the 1st Amendment right to free exercise of religion, a principle that had been established earlier in *Cantwell* v. *Connecticut* (1940). So the issue now was whether a state or local government could limit this freedom by enacting flag-salute laws that Jehovah's Witnesses could not obey without violating their religious beliefs.

In the *Gobitis* case, the Court upheld the flag-salute law as a constitutional and therefore a legitimate limit on the right to free exercise of religion of Jehovah's Witnesses. Only three years later, however, the Court reversed this decision in the *Barnette* case. During the period from 1940 to 1943, the membership of the Supreme Court changed, which was a factor in overruling the *Gobitis* decision. But some members of the Court, after additional reflection and study, had decided that the rights to freedom of speech and free exercise of religion must be respected among those for whom compliance with the flag-salute would be a serious violation of religious belief.

The *Barnette* case set a precedent that the Supreme Court has followed to this day. And it was one more case—in a series that began in 1931 with decisions in the cases of *Stromberg* and *Near*—in which the Court acted to protect 1st Amendment freedoms against attempts by state governments to limit them. The central story about rights in the 20th century has been the Supreme Court's use of the 14th Amendment to apply the federal Bill of Rights to the state governments. The Court has used its incorporation doctrine to overturn more than 1,200 state laws as unconstitutional violations of individual rights. By contrast, the Supreme Court has voided only a few acts of the federal government as unconstitutional infringements of individual rights.

The main issues associated with actions of the federal government have been about national security and the tension between the need to protect the country and the need to secure individual rights. For example, after Japan's 1941 attack on Pearl Harbor, Hawaii, the federal government acted quickly to defend the nation, which became the top national priority. But this put the constitutional rights of some citizens in jeopardy when more than 100,000 Americans of Japanese ancestry were removed from their homes on the Pacific Coast of the United States and sent to internment camps in the interior of the country. Most of them spent the duration of the war confined in one of these camps, even though they were U.S. citizens who had done nothing to harm the country.

On November 5, 1935, Billy Gobitas wrote a letter to the school directors of Minersville, Pennsylvania, explaining that as member of the Jehovah's Witnesses he believes saluting the flag is forbidden by his religion. In Minersville School District v. Gobitis *(the family's name was misspelled in the Court records) the decision upheld compulsory flag salute ceremonies in public schools.*

unto the third and fourth generation of them that hate me. I am a true follower of Christ. I do not salute the flag because I do not love my country, but I love my country and I love God more and I must obey His commandments.

Your Pupil,
Billy Gobitas

The 5th Amendment claims, "No person shall be . . . deprived of life, liberty, or property without due process of law." Did the national emergency of World War II permit the federal government to suspend the constitutional rights of Japanese Americans? Two cases involving this question came to the Supreme Court: *Hirabayashi* v. *United States* (1943) and *Korematsu* v. *United States* (1944).

The Supreme Court upheld the exclusion of Japanese Americans from the Pacific coastal region. The needs of national security in a time of crisis, it said, justified the exclusion orders. The constitutional war powers of the president and Congress provided the legal basis for the majority decision. The cases of *Hirabayashi* and *Korematsu* are the only ones since 1938, when the Preferred Freedoms Doctrine was stated, in which a law specifically restricting the rights of a racial minority group was upheld.

Freedom and National Security during World War I

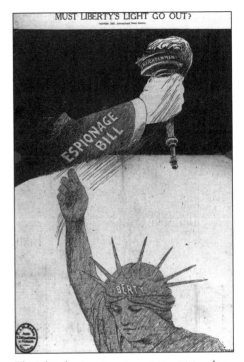

This political cartoon presents a negative opinion about the limits on free speech that were imposed during World War I. The torch of "enlightenment" is taken from the Statute of Liberty by the federal Espionage Act of 1917, which barred any act of interference with the federal government's capacity to carry out the war.

Charles Schenck, an outspoken critic of U.S. participation in the World War I, printed and mailed thousands of leaflets to men eligible for the military draft that denounced the draft law and urged resistance to the national war effort. Federal authorities arrested Schenck and convicted him of violating the Espionage Act. Schenck claimed that his 1st Amendment rights had been violated by enforcement of an unconstitutional federal law, and he appealed his conviction to the Supreme Court, which decided unanimously against him.

Writing for the Court in *Schenck* v. *United States* in 1919, Justice Oliver Wendell Holmes Jr. argued that during peacetime the 1st Amendment would have protected Charles Schenck's freedom to condemn the government's military policies by distributing antiwar pamphlets. But during a wartime emergency, urging men to resist the draft law presented a "clear and present danger" to the security of the nation, which Congress had the duty to oppose.

It well may be that the prohibition of laws abridging the freedom of speech is not confined to previous restraints, although to prevent them may have been the main purpose. . . . We admit that in many places and in ordinary times the defendants in saying all that was said in the circular would have been within their

Oliver Wendell Holmes Jr., Defender of Constitutional Rights to Liberty

President Theodore Roosevelt appointed Oliver Wendell Holmes Jr. to the Court in 1902, when he was 61 years old. He served until 1932. Justice Holmes was called "the great dissenter," because he dissented from the majority whenever he felt the Court was not defending the rights to freedom of individuals.

In *United States* v. *Schwimmer* (1929), Holmes defended the right to free speech of a person whose ideas he disliked. He explained: "If there is any principle of the Constitution that more imperatively calls for attachment than any other it is the principle of free thought— not free thought for those who agree with us but freedom for the thought that we hate." Holmes believed that free speech and a free press, protected by law, were cornerstones of liberty. As long as judges and the citizenry together guarded these civil liberties, Americans would be safe from tyranny.

constitutional rights. But the character of every act depends upon the circumstances in which it is done. . . . The most stringent protection of free speech would not protect a man in falsely shouting fire in a theatre and causing a panic. It does not even protect a man from an injunction against uttering words that may have all the effect of force. . . . The question in every case is whether the words used are used in such circumstances and are of such a nature as to create a clear and present danger that they will bring about the substantive evils that Congress has a right to prevent. It is a question of proximity and degree. When a nation is at war many things that might be said in time of peace are such a hindrance to its effort that their utterance will not be endured so long as men fight and that no Court could regard them as protected by any constitutional right.

Later that year, Holmes modified his position when he wrote the dissenting opinion in *Abrams* v. *United States*. In this case, he argued that in order to limit free speech, a "clear and present danger" must be imminent, and he concluded his dissent with a strong defense of free speech that stressed the "free trade in ideas" as the foundation of liberty and democracy.

I do not doubt for a moment that . . . the United States constitutionally may punish speech that produces or is intended to produce a clear and imminent danger that will bring about forthwith certain substantive evils that the United States constitutionally may seek to prevent. The power undoubtedly is greater in time of war than in time of peace because war opens dangers that do not exist at other times.

But as against dangers peculiar to war, as against others, the principle of the right to free speech is always the same. It is only the present danger of immediate evil or an intent to bring it about that warrants Congress in setting a limit to the expression of opinion where private rights are not concerned. Congress certainly cannot forbid all effort to change the mind of the country. Now nobody can suppose that the surreptitious publishing of a silly leaflet by an unknown man, without more, would present any immediate danger that its opinions would hinder the success of the government arms or have any appreciable tendency to do so. . . .

But when men have realized that time has upset many fighting faiths, they may come to believe even more than they believe the very foundations of their own conduct that the ultimate good desired is better reached by free trade in ideas—that the best test of truth is the power of the thought to get itself accepted in the competition of the market, and that truth is the only ground upon which their wishes safely can be carried out. That at any rate is the theory of our Constitution.

In the case of *Gitlow* v. *New York* (1925), the Supreme Court upheld Benjamin Gitlow's conviction, under the state of New York's Criminal Anarchy Law, for advocating violent over-throw of the government. At the same time, the Court also held that the 1st Amendment rights of free speech and press could be applied to the states through the 14th Amendment.

This case became the foundation for the Supreme Court's incorporation doctrine, by which the due process clause of the 14th Amendment could be used to stop state governments from abridging the 1st Amendment rights of individuals. The incorporation doctrine was used repeatedly in the following decades to expand the range and reach of the Bill of Rights to the states. Justice Sanford wrote the majority opionion.

The precise question presented, and the only question which we can consider under this writ of error, then, is whether the statute, as construed and applied in this case by the state courts, deprived the defendant of his liberty of expression in violation of the due process clause of the Fourteenth Amendment. . . .

The Manifesto [published by Gitlow and his codefendants], plainly, is neither the statement of abstract doctrine nor, as suggested by counsel, mere prediction that industrial disturbances and revolutionary mass strikes will result spontaneously in an inevitable process of evolution in the economic system. It advocates and urges in fervent language mass action which shall progressively foment industrial disturbances and through political mass strikes and revolutionary mass action overthrow and destroy organized parliamentary government. . . .

The means advocated for bringing about the destruction of organized parliamentary government, namely, mass industrial revolts usurping the functions of municipal government, political mass strikes directed against the parliamentary state, and revolutionary mass action for its final destruction, necessarily imply the use of force and violence, and in their essential nature are inherently unlawful in a constitutional government of law and order. That the jury were warranted in finding that the Manifesto

The constitutional guarantees of free speech and free press do not permit a State to forbid or proscribe advocacy of the use of force or of law violation except where such advocacy is directed to inciting or producing imminent lawless action and is likely to incite or produce such action.

—U.S. Supreme Court,
Brandenburg v. *Ohio* (1969)

advocated not merely the abstract doctrine of overthrowing organized government by force, violence and unlawful means, but action to that end, is clear.

For present purposes we may and do assume that freedom of speech and of the press—which are protected by the First Amendment from abridgment by Congress—are among the fundamental personal rights and "liberties" protected by the due process clause of the Fourteenth Amendment from impairment by the States. . . .

It is a fundamental principle, long established, that the freedom of speech and of the press which is secured by the Constitution, does not confer an absolute right to speak or publish, without responsibility, whatever one may choose, or an unrestricted and unbridled license that gives immunity for every possible use of language and prevents the punishment of those who abuse this freedom. . . .

We cannot hold that the present statute is an arbitrary or unreasonable exercise of the police power of the State unwarrantably infringing the freedom of speech or press; and we must and do sustain its constitutionality.

The Incorporation Doctrine

Chief Justice Charles Evans Hughes, writing for the Supreme Court in the case of _Stromberg_ v. _California_ (1931), overturned that state's conviction of camp counselor Yetta Stromberg for displaying a Soviet flag and having children salute it. Stromberg claimed that by enforcing its "red flag" law, the state of California had denied her right to freedom of speech guaranteed by the 1st Amendment and applicable to the states by the due process clause of the 14th Amendment. In reply, the California attorneys claimed that the law was within the state's constitutional power to maintain public order and safety. Hughes's opinion relied on the incorporation doctrine, which made 1st Amendment protections of free speech applicable to state governments through the due process clause of the 14th Amendment.

The appellant was convicted in the Superior Court of San Bernardino County, California, for violation of section 403-a of the Penal Code of that State. That section provides: "Any person who displays a red flag, banner or badge or any flag, badge, banner, or device of any color or form whatever in any public place or in

The Socialist Party leader and Presidential candidate Eugene V. Debs was convicted for publicly speaking against the federal government's recruitment of soldiers during World War I. The U.S. Supreme Court upheld his conviction under the 1917 Espionage Act in Debs v. United States (1919).

any meeting place or public assembly, or from or on any house, building or window as a sign, symbol or emblem of opposition to organized government or as an invitation or stimulus to anarchistic action or as an aid to propaganda that is of a seditious character is guilty of a felony." . . .

We are thus brought to the question whether . . . [it] is . . . repugnant to the Federal Constitution, so that it could not constitute a lawful foundation for a criminal prosecution. The principles to be applied have been clearly set forth in our former decisions. It has been determined that the conception of liberty under the due process clause of the Fourteenth Amendment embraces the right of free speech. . . . The right is not an absolute one, and the State, in the exercise of its police power, may punish the abuse of this freedom. There is no question but that the State may thus provide for the punishment of those who indulge in utterances which incite to violence and crime and threaten the overthrow of organized government by unlawful means. There is no constitutional immunity for such conduct abhorrent to our institutions. . . .

[However], the maintenance of the opportunity for free political discussion to the end that government may be responsive to the will of the people and that changes may be obtained by lawful means, an opportunity essential to the security of the Republic, is a fundamental principle of our constitutional system. A statute which, upon its face and as authoritatively construed, is so vague and indefinite as to permit the punishment of the fair use of this opportunity is repugnant to the guaranty of liberty contained in the Fourteenth Amendment.

The First Amendment does not speak equivocally. It prohibits any law "abridging the freedom of speech, or of the press." It must be taken as a command of the broadest scope that explicit language, read in the context of a liberty-loving society, will allow.
—Justice Hugo L. Black,
Bridges v. *California* (1941)

In a close decision in the case of *Near* v. *Minnesota* (1931), the Supreme Court decided by a 5-to-4 vote that the Minnesota Public Nuisance Abatement Law—used to convict Jay Near for attacking state officials in his *Saturday Press*—was a prior restraint on the press. Thus, it was an unconstitutional violation of the Constitution's 1st Amendment guarantee of the right to freedom of the press, a right that was applicable to the state of Minnesota through its incorporation under the 14th Amendment.

Four members of the Court, led by Justice Pierce Butler, dissented. They argued that the Court should not use the incorporation doctrine to limit the authority of a state government. Butler claimed that the Supreme Court had imposed upon a state government "a federal restriction that is without precedents." Further, he said it was a violation of the

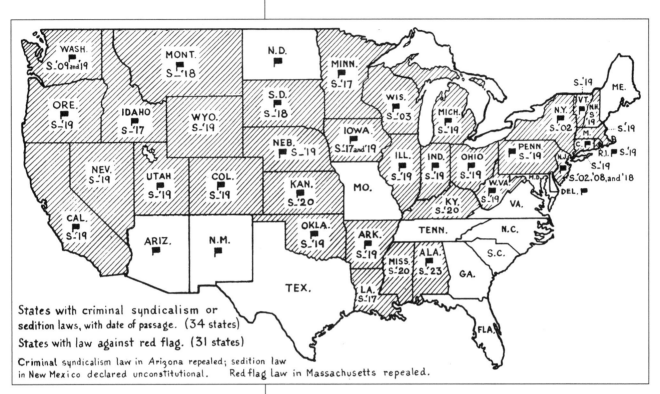

States with criminal syndicalism or sedition laws, with date of passage. (34 states)

States with law against red flag. (31 states)

Criminal syndicalism law in Arizona repealed; sedition law in New Mexico declared unconstitutional.   Red flag law in Massachusetts repealed.

This map shows the extent to which criminal syndicalism (sedition) and anti–red flag laws were enacted throughout the United States during and after World War I. These state laws were passed to control or limit public protests against the government and the established social order and they were used by state and local law-enforcement officers to break up meetings of radical political organizations like the Communist Party.

principle of federalism, whereby certain powers and rights were supposed to be reserved under the U.S. Constitution to the state governments.

Butler and the other dissenters were the voice of the past. The Court's decision, by contrast, pointed to a future in which the incorporation doctrine would be used repeatedly to expand protections of the Bill of Rights throughout the United States. Chief Justice Hughes wrote the majority decision.

This statute, for the suppression as a public nuisance of a newspaper or periodical, is unusual, if not unique, and raises questions of grave importance transcending the local interests involved in the particular action. It is no longer open to doubt that the liberty of the press, and of speech, is within the liberty safeguarded by the due process clause of the Fourteenth Amendment from invasion by state action. . . .

In maintaining this guaranty, the authority of the State to enact laws to promote the health, safety, morals and general welfare of its people is necessarily admitted. The limits of this sovereign power must always be determined with appropriate regard to the particular subject of its exercise. . . . Liberty of speech, and of the press, is also not an absolute right, and the State may punish its abuse. . . .

If we cut through mere details of procedure, the operation and effect of the statute in substance is that public authorities may bring the owner or publisher of a newspaper or periodical before a judge upon a charge of conducting a business of publishing scandalous and defamatory matter—in particular that the matter consists of charges against public officers of official dereliction—and unless the owner or publisher is able and disposed to bring competent evidence to satisfy the judge that the charges are true and are published with good motives and for justifiable ends, his newspaper or periodical is suppressed and further publication is made punishable as a contempt. This is of the essence of censorship.

The question is whether a statute authorizing such proceedings in restraint of publication is consistent with the conception of the liberty of the press as historically conceived and guaranteed. In determining the extent of the constitutional protection, it has been generally, if not universally, considered that it is the chief purpose of the guaranty to prevent previous restraints upon publication. . . .

[L]iberty of the press historically considered and taken up by the Federal Constitution, has meant, principally although not exclusively, immunity from previous restraints or censorship. The conception of the liberty of the press in this country had broadened with the exigencies of the colonial period and with the efforts to secure freedom from oppressive administration. That liberty was especially cherished for the immunity it afforded from previous restraint of the publication of censure of public officers and charges of official misconduct. . . .

The fact that the liberty of the press, may be abused by miscreant purveyors of scandal does not make any the less necessary the immunity of the press from previous restraint in dealing with official misconduct. Subsequent punishment for such abuses as may exist is the appropriate remedy, consistent with constitutional privilege.

The statute in question cannot be justified by reason of the fact that the publisher is permitted to show, before injunction issues, that the matter published is true and is published with good motives and for justifiable ends. If such a statute, authorizing suppressions and injunction on such a basis, is constitutionally valid, it would be equally permissible for the legislature to provide that at any time the publisher of any newspaper could be brought before a court, or even an administrative officer (as the constitutional protection may not be regarded as resting on mere procedural details) and required to produce proof of the truth of his publication, or of what he intended to publish, and of his motives, or stand enjoined.

Above all else, the First Amendment means that government has no power to restrict expression because of its message, its ideas, its subject matter, or its content.
—Justice Thurgood Marshall, *Police Department v. Mosley* (1972)

The October 15, 1927, front page of the Saturday Press includes an attack against the Minneapolis, Minnesota, police chief, who wanted to prohibit the newspaper from publishing scandalous articles. Conflict between the newspaper's publisher, Jay Near, and the local government led to a landmark Supreme Court decision in Near v. Minnesota (1931), which declared "prior restraint" of a publication to be a violation of the 1st Amendment right to freedom of the press.

The Saturday Press

Vol. 1, No. 4   Minneapolis, Minn., Oct. 15, 1927   Price 5 Cents

A Direct Challenge to Police Chief Brunskill

The Chief, in Banning This Paper from News Stands, Definitely Aligns Himself With Gangland, Violates the Law He Is Sworn to Uphold, When He Tries to Suppress This Publication. The Only Paper in the City That Dares Expose the Gang's Deadly Grip on Minneapolis. A Plain Statement of Facts and a Warning of Legal Action.

Possibly, there are moments when "a soft answer turneth away wrath" but as against such short periods there are long hours when the English language becomes woefully deficient in expressive words, and I find that deficiency painfully evident right now.

On September 24th, the first issue of the Saturday Press made its appearance. It launched no attack against the police department nor against Chief of Police Frank Brunskill. Its pages prove the truth of this statement.

We (Mr. Guilford and myself) attacked a gambling syndicate that has operated brazenly in this city for more than four years. We attacked that blackmailing rag, the Twin City Reporter and the men who own and publish it. We minced no words. We knew our oolong!

When it had become a matter of common knowledge that we were to expose these, we were offered a weekly "envelope" if we would "lay off" and when we spurned this bribe we were coolly informed that we would be given a "receipt" (killed) if we persisted. But I am not going to rehash that story. I'm going to rip the seams and see what is inside the rotten garment.

We made no attempt to place that first issue on the

news stands FOR WE HAD BEEN TOLD BY THE GAMBLING SYNDICATE THAT CHIEF OF POLICE BRUNSKILL WAS THE "WEAK SISTER" OF THE SYNDICATE. Think of it—the Chief of Police on whom every citizen must rely for protection of life and property, a member, by the gang's admission, OF THE GAMBLING SYNDICATE! Do you wonder that we made no attempt to place the Saturday Press on the news stands of Minneapolis where they would be at the mercy of an alleged gang member?

Moe Barnett, "Big Moe," acknowledged gunman, gang leader, the man who has boasted that he intended recruiting an army of gunmen that would rival Chicago's machinegun corps, is the man who declared that Chief Brunskill was the "weak sister" of the gambling syndicate—not "Dame Rumor" but Mose Barnett.

The Saturday Press was first published on September 24 or rather dated as of that date and actually off the press on the 22nd. On Monday, September 26th, Mr. Guilford was shot down by gunmen as he drove from his home in Robbinsdale to the office in Minneapolis. Mose Barnett had threatened Guilford with a "receipt" less than one week

(Continued on page 7)

Respectfully Submitted

There seems to be an impression among gentlemen of peculiar bent that the suppression of our street sales has rendered abortive our attempt to cleanse this city of gang rule. These gents are intellectual single-trackers; twenty - two caliber saps rattling around in a four hundred thousand city. Lest they become too hilarious, I beg to call their attention to the following letter, the original of which was mailed to the Hennepin County Grand Jury on Wednesday of this week.

Read it carefully, "me brave buckos" and see if you can discern a flutter of a white flag. We've just begun to fight!

Minneapolis, Minnesota, October 12, 1927.
To the Hennepin County Grand Jury—
Gentlemen:
Permit me to call the attention of your honorable body to the October 1st and October 8th issue of the Saturday Press in which issues both Mr. Howard A. Guilford and myself have exposed conditions that actually exist in this city or did at the time (and long prior to) of our expose.

I especially wish to call your attention to the article, written by myself, in the October 8th issue under the caption of:

"A Few of the Unsolved Minneapolis Mysteries."

In that article I gave the name of one of the numerous victims of Minneapolis gangsters, Mr. Samuel Shapiro of 2615 East Franklin Avenue, and I am positive that were Mr. Shapiro given a chance to

testify before your body he would be more than glad to give you sufficient evidence upon which to base an indictment of the acknowledged gang-leader, Mose Barnett—the man who threatened Mr. Shapiro just a comparatively few days before the assault upon his person and property was made by four gunmen.

The article as published, stands unchallenged by either Mose Barnett or any other gangster in the city. I have not been sued for libel nor has any such action been intimated, therefore it stands that I published the truth.

Gentlemen, gang rule of this city can end only with your approval and by your action. Mose Barnett, gangster, who boasts that he has shot one man (Roy Rogers) and escaped even arrest for that act, today walks the streets of the city a free man, a menace to lives and property.

I trust you will not consider me too presumptuous if I again suggest that you subpoena Mr. Samuel Shapiro and thus give that gentleman the opportunity, heretofore denied him, of telling his own story of HIS experience with Mose Barnett and the latter's hired thugs.

I am, sirs,
Very truly yours,
J. M. NEAR,
Editor, The Saturday Press
240 S. 4th Street
Minneapolis, Minn.

And further, I might add for the edification of the "unpinched gang" that I have mailed, each week, two copies of this paper to each member of the Grand Jury. I shall continue

(Continued on page 3)

If this can be done, the legislature may provide machinery for determining in the complete exercise of its discretion what are justifiable ends and restrain publication accordingly. And it would be but a step to a complete system of censorship. The recognition of authority to impose previous restraint upon publication in order to protect the community against the circulation of charges of misconduct, and especially of official misconduct, necessarily would carry with it the admission of the authority of the censor against which the constitutional barrier was erected. The preliminary freedom, by virtue of the very reason for its existence, does not depend, as this Court has said, on proof of truth. . . .

Equally unavailing is the insistence that the statute is designed to prevent the circulation of scandal which tends to disturb the public peace and to provoke assaults and the commission of crime. Charges of reprehensible conduct, and in particular of official malfeasance, unquestionably create a public scandal, but the theory of the constitutional guaranty is that even a more serious public evil would be caused by authority to prevent publication. . . .

For these reasons we hold the statute . . . to be an infringement of the liberty of the press guaranteed by the Fourteenth Amendment. We should add that this decision rests upon the operation and effect of the statute, without regard to the question of the truth of the charges contained in the particular periodical.

Dirk DeJonge distributed handbills throughout the city of Portland, Oregon, to advertise a meeting to protest certain actions of the city government. Nearly 200 people attended the meeting, where the Communist Party's newspaper, *The Daily Worker,* was sold. The local police raided the meeting and arrested DeJonge for violating the Criminal Syndicalism Act, because the Communist Party called for the violent overthrow of governments that opposed it. DeJonge's meeting was peaceful, and no violent or otherwise unlawful acts were advocated. But his association with the Communist Party was sufficient to convict and sentence him to jail.

In the case of *DeJonge* v. *Oregon* (1937), the Supreme Court held that a state law prohibiting members of the Communist Party from assembling and discussing political issues was in violation of the 1st Amendment's guarantee of peaceable assembly and of the due process clause of the 14th Amendment. The Court ruled in favor of Communist Party member DeJonge.

His [DeJonge's] sole offense as charged, and for which he was convicted and sentenced to imprisonment for seven years, was that he had assisted in the conduct of a public meeting, albeit otherwise lawful, which was held under the auspices of the Communist Party. . . .

However innocuous the object of the meeting, however lawful the subjects and tenor of the address, however reasonable and timely the discussion, all those assisting in the conduct of the meeting would be subject to imprisonment as felons if the meeting were held by the Communist Party. . . . Thus if the Communist Party had called a public meeting in Portland to discuss the tariff, or the foreign policy of the Government, or taxation, or relief,

Dirk DeJonge was an active member of the Communist Party in Portland, Oregon. He was arrested and convicted under an Oregon law that made it a crime to conduct a meeting of the Communist Party or otherwise promoting the party's agenda. DeJonge spent 18 months in jail while American Civil Liberties Union lawyers appealed his conviction all the way to the Supreme Court.

or candidacies for the offices of President, members of Congress, Governor, or state legislators, every speaker who assisted in the conduct of the meeting would be equally guilty with the defendant in this case, upon the charge as here defined and sustained. The list of illustrations might be indefinitely extended to every variety of meetings under the auspices of the Communist Party although held for the discussion of political issues or to adopt protests and pass resolutions of an entirely innocent and proper character.

While the States are entitled to protect themselves from the abuse of the privileges of our institutions through an attempted substitution of force and violence in the place of peaceful political action in order to effect revolutionary changes in government, none of our decisions go to the length of sustaining such a curtailment of the right of free speech and assembly as the Oregon statute demands in its present application. . . .

Freedom of speech and of the press are fundamental rights which are safeguarded by the due process clause of the Fourteenth Amendment of the Federal Constitution. . . . The right of peaceable assembly is a right cognate to those of free speech and free press and is equally fundamental. . . . The First Amendment of the Federal Constitution expressly guarantees that right against abridgment by Congress. But explicit mention there does not argue exclusion elsewhere. For the right is one that cannot be denied without violating those fundamental principles of liberty and justice which lie at the base of all civil and political institutions—principles which the Fourteenth Amendment embodies in the general terms of its due process clause. . . .

These rights may be abused by using speech or press or assembly in order to incite to violence and crime. The people through their legislatures may protect themselves against that abuse. But the legislative intervention can find constitutional justification only by dealing with the abuse. The rights themselves must not be curtailed. The greater the importance of safeguarding the community from incitements to the overthrow of our institutions by force and violence, the more imperative is the need to preserve inviolate the constitutional rights of free speech, free press and free assembly in order to maintain the opportunity for free political discussion, to the end that government may be responsive to the will of the people and that changes, if desired, may be obtained by peaceful means. Therein lies the security of the Republic, the very foundation of constitutional government.

It follows from these considerations that, consistently with the Federal Constitution, peaceable assembly for lawful discussion cannot be made a crime. The holding of meetings for peaceable political action cannot be proscribed. Those who assist in the conduct of such meetings cannot be branded as criminals on that score. The question, if the rights of free speech and peaceable assembly are to be preserved, is not as to the auspices under which the meeting is held but as to its purpose; not as to the relations of the speakers, but whether their utterances transcend the bounds of the freedom of speech which the Constitution protects. . . .

We are not called upon to review the findings of the state court as to the objectives of the Communist Party. Notwithstanding those objectives, the defendant still enjoyed his personal right of free speech and to take part in a peaceable assembly having a lawful purpose, although called by that Party. The defendant was none the less entitled to discuss the public issues of the day and thus in a lawful manner, without incitement to violence or crime, to seek redress of alleged grievances. That was of the essence of his guaranteed personal liberty.

We hold that the Oregon statute as applied to the particular charge as defined by the state court is repugnant to the due process clause of the Fourteenth Amendment.

The Preferred Freedoms Doctrine was put forth by Justice Harlan F. Stone in a footnote to his opinion in the 1938 case of *United States* v. *Carolene Products*, which pertained to the federal government's prohibition of a certain kind of milk product. The first paragraph affirms the incorporation doctrine and the fundamental importance of individual rights relative to laws that would limit those rights. The second paragraph suggests that the judicial branch of government has a special responsibility to protect rights necessary to political freedom, such as those in the Constitution's 1st Amendment. The third paragraph suggests that religious, national, or racial minorities have a special need for protection by the Court against laws that deny or unfairly restrict their constitutional rights.

There may be narrower scope for operation of the presumption of constitutionality when legislation appears on its face to be within a specific prohibition of the Constitution, such as those of the first ten Amendments, which are deemed equally specific when held to be embraced within the Fourteenth.

It is unnecessary to consider now whether legislation which restricts those political processes which can ordinarily be expected to bring about repeal of undesirable legislation, is to be subjected to more exacting judicial scrutiny under the general prohibitions of the Fourteenth Amendment than are most other types of legislation. . . .

Nor need we enquire whether similar considerations enter into the review of statutes directed at particular religious . . . or national . . . or racial minorities; whether prejudice against discrete and insular minorities may be a special condition, which tends seriously to curtail the operation of those political processes ordinarily to be relied upon to protect minorities, and which may call for a correspondingly more searching judicial inquiry.

Issues of Freedom during World War II

In the 1943 case of *West Virginia State Board of Education* v. *Barnette*, the Court reversed its earlier decision in the case of *Minersville School District* v. *Gobitis* (1940). In the *Barnette* case the Court decided that the rights to freedom of speech and free exercise of religion must be respected among those for whom compliance with the flag salute would be a serious violation of religious belief, such as those of the Jehovah's Witnesses involved in the case.

The opinion of the Court in the *Barnette* case, written by Justice Robert H. Jackson, is an often quoted, highly respected statement on individual rights. Jackson emphasized the American tradition rooted in the Declaration of Independence, which holds certain rights to be inviolable, even against majority vote. Like Thomas Jefferson, James Madison, and other founders of the United States, the Court in the *Barnette* case upheld constitutional limitations on majority rule in order to protect minority rights.

The freedom asserted by these appellees does not bring them into collision with rights asserted by any other individual. . . . The sole conflict is between authority and rights of the individual. The state asserts power to condition access to public education on making a prescribed sign and profession and at the same time to coerce attendance by punishing both parent and child. The latter stand on a right of self-determination in matters that touch individual opinion and personal attitude. . . .

In this photograph taken for the Office of War Information, New York City public school students pledge allegiance to the flag of the United States in January 1943. Later that year, the U.S. Supreme Court ruled in West Virginia Board of Education v. Barnette *that a state or local government could not constitutionally require by law that students salute the flag or pledge allegiance to it against their will.*

The Fourteenth Amendment, as now applied to the states, protects the citizen against the state itself and all of its creatures—boards of education not excepted. These have, of course, important, delicate, and highly discretionary functions, but none that they may not perform within the limits of the Bill of Rights. . . .

The very purpose of a Bill of Rights was to withdraw certain subjects from the vicissitudes of political controversy, to place them beyond the reach of majorities and officials, and to establish them as legal principles to be applied by the courts. One's right to life, liberty, and property, to free speech, a free press, freedom of worship and assembly, and other fundamental rights may not be submitted to vote; they depend on the outcome of no elections. . . . They are susceptible of restriction only to prevent grave and immediate danger to interests which the state may lawfully protect. . . .

If there is any fixed star in our constitutional constellation, it is that no official, high or petty, can prescribe what shall be orthodox in politics, nationalism, religion, or other matters of opinion,

A Grave Injustice

In 1980, Congress created the Commission on Wartime Relocation and Internment of Civilians to investigate the treatment of Japanese Americans during World War II. The commission issued a report on February 25, 1983, that concluded: "A grave injustice was done to American citizens and resident aliens of Japanese ancestry who, without individual review or any probative evidence against them, were excluded, removed, and detained by the United States during World War II."

In 1988, Congress, based on the 1983 report, offered payments of $20,000 as compensation to each person still living who had been detained in a relocation center.

or force citizens to confess by word or act their faith therein. If there are any circumstances which permit an exception, they do not now occur to us.

In two cases from 1943 and 1944, *Hirabayashi* v. *United States* and *Korematsu* v. *United States,* Japanese Americans claimed that they had been deprived of their constitutional rights when they were interned in camps during World War II. In both cases, the Supreme Court ruled that the needs of national security justified curtailing individual rights. In the Hirabayashi case, Chief Justice Stone wrote the majority opinion.

The challenged orders were defense measures for the avowed purpose of safeguarding the military area in question, at a time of threatened air raids and invasion by the Japanese forces, from the danger of sabotage and espionage. . . .

But appellant insists that the exercise of the power is inappropriate and unconstitutional because it discriminates against citizens of Japanese ancestry. . . .

Distinctions between citizens solely because of their ancestry are by their very nature odious to a free people whose institutions are founded upon the doctrine of equality. For that reason, legislative classification or discrimination based on race alone has often been held to be a denial of equal protection. . . .

We may assume that these considerations would be controlling here were it not for the fact that the danger of espionage and sabotage, in time of war and of threatened invasion, calls upon the military authorities to scrutinize every relevant fact bearing on the loyalty of populations in the danger areas. Because racial discriminations are in most circumstances irrelevant and therefore prohibited, it by no means follows that, in dealing with the perils of war, Congress and the Executive are wholly precluded from taking into account those facts and circumstances which are relevant to measures for our national defense and for the successful prosecution of the war, and which may in fact place citizens of one ancestry in a different category from others. . . . The adoption by Government, in the crisis of war and of threatened invasion, of measures for the public safety, based upon the recognition of facts and circumstances which indicate that a group of one national extraction may menace that safety more than others, is not wholly beyond the limits of the Constitution and is not to be condemned merely because in other and in most circumstances racial distinctions are irrelevant.

During World War II, more than 100,000 Americans of Japanese ancestry were moved from their homes on the West Coast to internment camps in the interior of the country. In Korematsu v. United States *(1944), the U.S. Supreme Court upheld this policy as a wartime necessity resulting from the Japanese attack against Pearl Harbor, Hawaii, on December 7, 1941.*

Justice Frank Murphy expressed a reluctant concurring opinion in the *Hirabayashi* case.

Distinctions based on color and ancestry are utterly inconsistent with our traditions and ideals. They are at variance with the principles for which we are now waging war. . . . Nothing is written more firmly into our law than the compact of the Plymouth voyagers to have just and equal laws. To say that any group cannot be assimilated is to admit that the great American experiment has failed, that our way of life has failed when confronted with the normal attachment of certain groups to the lands of their forefathers. As a nation we embrace many groups, some of them among the oldest settlements in our midst, which have isolated themselves for religious and cultural reasons.

Today is the first time, so far as I am aware, that we have sustained a substantial restriction of the personal liberty of citizens of the United States based upon the accident of race of ancestry. Under the curfew order here challenged no less than 70,000 American citizens have been placed under a special ban and deprived of their liberty because of their particular racial inheritance. . . . In my opinion this goes to the very brink of constitutional power.

The next year, in the *Korematsu* case, the Court again upheld the decision that the right of national security outweighed

The renowned landscape photographer Ansel Adams took a series of photographs at the Manzanar War Relocation Center in California, including this image of Roy Takeno reading a newspaper in front of the Free Press office. Adams said he took this series of photographs to depict how the Japanese Americans "suffering under a great injustice, and loss of property, businesses and professions, had overcome the sense of defeat and despair by building for themselves a vital community."

the individual rights of the interned Japanese Americans. Justice Hugo Black wrote the Court's opinion.

. . . We uphold the exclusion order as of the time it was made and when the petitioner violated it. . . . In doing so, we are not unmindful of the hardships imposed by it upon a large group of American citizens. . . . But hardships are part of war, and war is an aggregation of hardships. All citizens alike, both in and out of uniform, feel the impact of war in greater or lesser measure. Citizenship has its responsibilities as well as its privileges, and in time of war the burden is always heavier. Compulsory exclusion of large groups of citizens from their homes, except under circumstances of direst emergency and peril, is inconsistent with our basic governmental institutions. But when under conditions of modern warfare our shores are threatened by hostile forces, the power to protect must be commensurate with the threatened danger. . . .

Korematsu was not excluded from the Military Area because of hostility to him or his race. He *was* excluded because we are at war with the Japanese Empire, because the properly constituted military authorities feared an invasion of our West Coast and felt constrained to take proper security measures, because they decided that the military urgency of the situation demanded that all citizens of Japanese ancestry be segregated from the West Coast temporarily, and finally, because Congress, reposing its confidence in this time of war in our military leaders—as inevitably it must—determined that they should have the power to do just this. . . .

This time, Justice Murphy wrote a ringing dissent.

. . . The judicial test of whether the Government, on a plea of military necessity, can validly deprive an individual of any of his constitutional rights is whether the deprivation is reasonably related to a public danger that is so "immediate, imminent, and impending" as not to admit of delay and not to permit the intervention of ordinary constitutional processes to alleviate the danger. . . . Civilian Exclusion Order No. 34, banishing from a prescribed area of the Pacific Coast "all persons of Japanese ancestry, both alien and non-alien," clearly does not meet that test. Being an obvious racial discrimination, the order deprives all those within its scope of the equal protection of the laws as guaranteed by the Fifth Amendment. It further deprives these individuals of their constitutional rights to live and work where they will, to establish a home where they choose and to move about freely. In excommunicating them without benefit of hearings, this order also deprives them of all their constitutional rights to procedural due process. Yet no reasonable relation to an "immediate, imminent, and impending" public danger is evident to support this racial restriction which is one of the most sweeping and complete deprivations of constitutional rights in the history of this nation in the absence of martial law. . . .

I dissent, therefore, from this legislation of racism. Racial discrimination in any form and in any degree has no justifiable part whatever in our democratic way of life. It is unattractive in any setting but it is utterly revolting among a free people who have embraced the principles set forth in the Constitution of the United States. All residents of this nation . . . are primarily and necessarily a part of the new and distinct civilization of the United States. They must accordingly be treated at all times as the heirs of the American experiment and as entitled to all the rights and freedoms guaranteed by the Constitution.

Chapter Seven

National- ization of the Bill of Rights

At its birth, the Bill of Rights was a set of restrictions on the powers of the federal government, but not the states. Constitutional guarantees of rights against the power of state government varied from state to state. After the Civil War, however, with the passage of the 14th Amendment, states were prohibited from abridging the privileges and immunities of citizens of the United States; depriving any person of life, liberty, or property without due process of law; and denying to any person equal protection of the laws.

These limitations on state governments, in order to protect individual rights, changed the U.S. Constitution fundamentally. But civic and political life in the United States did not change until the third decade of the 20th century. Only then did the federal government begin to enforce the 14th Amendment comprehensively.

During the 1930s and 1940s, the Court developed its doctrine of incorporation and its preferred freedoms doctrine, thereby using the 14th Amendment to apply provisions of the Constitution's 1st Amendment to the states, in order to protect the rights of free speech, press, assembly, petition, and religion. These 1st Amendment freedoms were nationalized; that is, a single national standard for protection superseded the various state standards. The right to free speech or press would now mean the same thing in Alabama or Georgia as it did in New York or New Jersey.

The next question facing the Court was whether the other rights in the Bill of Rights were also applicable to the states. One response to this question, selective incorporation, would apply provisions of the Bill of Rights to the states on a case-by-case basis. An alternative response, total incorporation, would immediately apply to the states all provisions of the Bill of Rights.

In *Palko* v. *Connecticut* (1937), Justice Benjamin Cardozo set a standard for selective incorporation. The issue in the *Palko* case was whether or not the defendant had been unconstitutionally subjected to double jeopardy—being tried twice for the same crime. The Constitution's 5th Amendment says, "nor shall any person be subject for the same offense to be twice put in jeopardy of life or limb." Frank Palko, in a second trial for the same offense, was convicted of first-degree murder by the state of Connecticut and sentenced to death. Palko claimed that the U.S. Constitution's 5th Amendment protection against double jeopardy could be applied to the state government through the due process clause of the 14th Amendment.

The Supreme Court rejected Palko's appeal. But Justice Cardozo also proposed a new test, the "fundamental rights" standard, to determine which rights of the Bill of Rights should be selected for incorporation under the due process clause. According to this test, in order for a right to be incorporated, it must be deeply rooted in the history and tradition of the United States, an implication of the idea of ordered liberty, or an essential element of fundamental fairness implied by the idea of justice.

The Court uses the fundamental rights standard in decisions about substantive due process. The 14th Amendment says, for example, that a state shall not "deprive any person of life, liberty, or property without due process of law." This clause, on its face, requires procedural due process; that is, the way laws are carried out must be fair. By contrast, substantive due process means that the *content* of the laws must be fair, not merely the procedures for executing them.

Using substantive due process, the Court decides whether or not the substance of a law satisfies the fundamental rights standard. If not, then the law is an unconstitutional violation of the 14th Amendment's due process clause, even if it has been carried out according to fair procedures. Substantive due process guarantees that no person shall be arbitrarily or unreasonably deprived of rights to life, liberty, or property.

Ten years after the *Palko* case, Justice Hugo Black set forth an alternative to the fundamental rights standard for selective incorporation of the Bill of Rights. Black argued for total incorporation in his dissenting opinion in *Adamson* v. *California* and claimed this was consistent with the intentions of the authors of the 14th Amendment. His position never won a majority of the Court, which continued to incorporate more provisions of the Bill of Rights on a case-by-case basis

In 1947, for example, another significant provision was incorporated when the Supreme Court nationalized the establishment clause of the 1st Amendment, which states, "Congress shall make no law respecting an establishment of religion." In *Everson* v. *Board of Education of Ewing Township*, the Court for the first time held that the establishment clause could be at issue in a case involving a state or local government.

As the 14th Amendment and the Bill of Rights were applied in tandem against state governments during the 20th century, one result was that the civil rights movement gained momentum. The expansion of 1st Amendment rights to freedom of speech, press, assembly, and petition allowed activists to publicly express their grievances and protest unjust laws and practices of state and local governments throughout the country. These two developments—the revival of 14th Amendment protections of rights and the civil rights movement—worked in concert to overcome, or at least minimize, serious inequities in the treatment of African Americans and other minority groups.

During the 1930s and 1940s, the National Association for the Advancement of Colored People (NAACP) was at the forefront of the civil rights movement. Charles Hamilton Houston, dean of

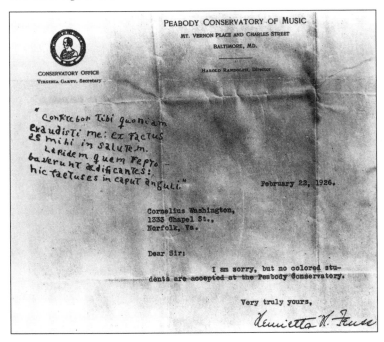

This letter dated February 22, 1926, on official stationery of the Peabody Conservatory of Music in Baltimore, Maryland, informs an applicant that "no colored students are accepted." This was one among many examples of racial discrimination against African Americans in the United States, which denied to them the rights and opportunities available to white people.

the law school at Howard University, became a prominent leader of this movement. His strategy was to challenge unfair state laws in federal courts as violations of the Constitution's 14th Amendment. His primary targets were racial segregation laws in states that prevented blacks from having educational opportunities equal to those enjoyed by whites. Houston was determined to use the law, rooted in the Constitution and Bill of Rights, to overcome unfair treatment of black Americans. The outcome he sought was equal protection of the laws for the rights of all Americans regardless of race, religion, gender, or national origin.

After the formation in 1939 of the NAACP's Legal Defense Fund, directed by Houston's former student Thurgood Marshall, the NAACP had a steady and significant impact on federal court rulings to protect and expand the civil rights of African Americans. In *Smith* v. *Allwright* (1944), the Supreme Court decided that a political party (the Democrats, in this case) could not exclude African Americans from voting in a primary election to nominate candidates for a subsequent general election. In *Sweatt* v. *Painter* (1950), the Court ruled that a state government may not deny admission of a qualified African American to a state law school on the grounds that a separate law school is available for African Americans.

The biggest legal victory for the NAACP and its chief lawyer, Thurgood Marshall, came in *Brown* v. *Board of Education* (1954), which declared racial segregation in public schools to be unconstitutional. With this decision, the "separate but equal" doctrine of the 1896 *Plessy* case was overturned. And the 14th Amendment's clause on "equal protection of the laws" became a practical extension of the Bill of Rights.

After the *Brown* decision, the NAACP and other civil rights organizations acted to influence enforcement of equal rights for African Americans. Further, they demanded new federal laws on civil rights. The Reverend Martin Luther King Jr. and the Southern Christian Leadership Conference (SCLC), which he led, advanced to the forefront of the civil rights movement.

King led a mass protest, the 1963 March on Washington, to inform Congress and the American people of the immediate need to enact a federal civil rights law to guarantee equal opportunity for all persons regardless of racial or ethnic identity. More than 200,000 Americans, blacks and whites together, attended the demonstration. King stood at the Lincoln Memorial and stirringly spoke about the great principles of the Declaration of Independence and the Bill of Rights. He implored his fellow

Thurgood Marshall, chief lawyer of the National Association for the Advancement of Colored People (NAACP), sits in the lawyer's lounge of the U.S. Supreme Court building during the Little Rock, Arkansas, school integration case, Cooper v. Aaron *(1958). The Court favored Marshall's arguments in this case by ruling unanimously against the state government's attempts to impede racial integration of the state's public schools. Behind Marshall is a portrait of Louis Brandeis, an associate justice of the Supreme Court from 1916 to 1939 and a strong defender of individual rights in the Constitution.*

Americans to live up to the ideals of equality and liberty, the immutable rights of humankind, set forth in these documents.

Less than a year later, Congress responded by passing the Civil Rights Act of 1964. Based on the 14th Amendment, this law protects individuals from unfair discrimination based on race, color, religion, national origin, or sexual identity. It also requires desegregation of public schools and facilities. It bans discrimination in places of public accommodation, such as hotels and restaurants, and in employment. All agencies receiving federal funds must provide evidence to government regulators that they are complying with the 1964 Civil Rights Act.

The Supreme Court upheld the Civil Rights Act in a landmark decision, *Heart of Atlanta Hotel* v. *United States* (1964), and established beyond challenge that no person can be excluded, because of race or color, from any facility that is open to the general public. Further, the Court in various cases has upheld Title 7 of the Civil Rights Act, which prohibits discrimination in employment.

As the civil rights movement continued, the Supreme Court acted to nationalize more of the Bill of Rights. Americans generally have favored the protection of rights of the accused, which are found in the 4th, 5th, and 6th amendments. There has often been bitter controversy, however, about the strict judicial enforcement of due process rights when it appears to allow a guilty person to escape punishment. Much of this controversy has focused on the Supreme Court's interpretation of the 4th Amendment, which says: "The right of the people to be secure in their persons, houses, papers, and effects, against unreasonable searches and seizures, shall not be violated, and no warrants shall issue, but upon probable cause, supported by oath or affirmation, and particularly describing the place to be searched, and the persons or things to be seized." The Court's "exclusionary rule" associated with the 4th Amendment provides that evidence improperly obtained by police will likely be excluded from a court of law and not used against the defendant.

The Supreme Court put forth the exclusionary rule in an earlier case, *Weeks* v. *United States* (1914): "If letters and private documents can be seized [illegally] and used in evidence against a citizen accused of an offense, the protection of the Fourth Amendment . . . is of no value, and . . . might as well be stricken from the Constitution." In *Mapp* v. *Ohio* (1961), the Court used the exclusionary rule in its incorporation of the 4th Amendment.

The 5th Amendment protects legal and procedural rights of individuals and, for example, prohibits the government from:

Earl Warren, chief justice from 1953 to 1969, presided over the Court during a period of great controversy and change. Under his leadership the Court decided landmark cases on the rights of the accused, equal protection of the laws, freedom of expression, and representation in government. His greatest opinion was written in the 1954 Brown v. Board of Education *case, which struck down state laws that required racial segregation in schools.*

- Holding an individual to answer for a serious crime unless the prosecution presents appropriate evidence to a grand jury that indicates the likely guilt of the individual;

- Trying an individual more than once for the same offense;

- Forcing an individual to act as a witness against himself in a criminal case;

- Depriving an individual of life, liberty, or property without due process of law (fair and proper legal proceedings);

- Depriving an individual of his or her private property for public use without proper compensation.

By 1969, the only part of the 5th Amendment that had not been incorporated was the provision requiring grand juries to consider evidence about a suspect's likely guilt.

During the 1960s, the Supreme Court incorporated all the rights of an accused person that the 6th Amendment guarantees to individuals, including:

- The right to a speedy public trial before an unbiased jury picked from the community in which the crime was committed;

- The right to receive information about what the accusation is and why it has been made;

- The right to face, in court, witnesses offering testimony;

- The right to subpoena witnesses to testify for the defendant in court;

- The right to help from a lawyer.

In *Gideon* v. *Wainwright* (1963), the Court used its doctrine of selective incorporation with regard to the 6th Amendment right to legal counsel for a person too poor to pay the costs of a lawyer. In *Pointer* v. *Texas* (1964), the Court nationalized a person's right to confront witnesses testifying against him in a criminal proceeding. In *Parker* v. *Gladden* (1966), the Court nationalized the right to an impartial jury; in *Klopfer* v. *North Carolina* (1967), the right to a speedy trial; and in *Duncan* v. *Louisiana* (1968), the right to a jury trial in criminal cases.

By 1971, most of the rights in the Bill of Rights were nationalized and had become effective limitations on state governments. Among amendments 1 through 8, the only parts not incorporated were:

DEVELOPMENT OF THE INCORPORATION DOCTRINE IN THE 20th CENTURY

The cases listed below established the incorporation of particular rights in the Bill of Rights into the due process clause of the 14th Amendment. Thus these rights were extended to the states.

YEAR	CASE	AMENDMENT	RIGHT
1925	*Gitlow* v. *New York*	1st	freedom of speech
1931	*Stromberg* v. *California*	1st	freedom of speech
1931	*Near* v. *Minnesota*	1st	freedom of press
1937	*DeJonge* v. *Oregon*	1st	right to assembly
1939	*Hague* v. *Congress of Industrial Organizations*	1st	right to petition
1940	*Cantwell* v. *Connecticut*	1st	free exercise of religion
1947	*Everson* v. *Board of Education of Ewing Township*	1st	no establishment of religion
1948	*Cole* v. *Arkansas*	6th	notice of accusation
1948	*In re Oliver*	6th	right to public trial
1949	*Wolf* v. *Colorado*	4th	no unreasonable searches and seizures
1961	*Mapp* v. *Ohio*	4th	exclusion from trials of illegally seized evidence
1962	*Robinson* v. *California*	8th	no cruel and unusual punishment
1963	*Gideon* v. *Wainwright*	6th	right to counsel
1964	*Malloy* v. *Hogan*	5th	no self-incrimination
1965	*Pointer* v. *Texas*	6th	right to confront witnesses
1966	*Parker* v. *Gladden*	6th	right to impartial jury
1967	*Klopfer* v. *North Carolina*	6th	right to speedy trial
1967	*Washington* v. *Texas*	6th	right to compulsory process for obtaining witnesses
1968	*Duncan* v. *Louisiana*	6th	right to jury trial in criminal prosecutions
1969	*Benton* v. *Maryland*	5th	no double jeopardy

- The 2nd Amendment right to bear arms;
- The 3rd Amendment freedom from quartering of troops in peacetime;
- The 5th Amendment grand jury clause;
- The 7th Amendment right to jury trial in civil cases;
- The 8th Amendment ban on excessive fines and bail.

Different states may variously exceed the national standards on rights, but no state may fall below them. The nationalization of the Bill of Rights has brought the country closer to fulfilling the ideals of the 1776 Declaration of Independence, which proclaims: "That to secure these Rights, Governments are instituted Among Men."

Standards for Using the Incorporation Doctrine

In *Palko* v. *Connecticut* (1937), Justice Benjamin Cardozo proposed a new standard—the fundamental rights test—for determining which provisions of the Bill of Rights should be incorporated under the 14th Amendment and applied to the states. Writing for the Court, Cardozo held that the 5th Amendment's right to protection against double jeopardy did not meet this standard, that this protection was not one of the "fundamental principles of liberty and justice." So it could not be incorporated by the due process clause of the 14th Amendment. Frank Palko, who had been tried twice by the state of Connecticut for murder and convicted of a more serious charge the second time, lost his appeal.

Other provisions in the federal Bill of Rights, however, such as 1st Amendment freedoms, had met this test. And other rights at issue in future cases might also meet the fundamental rights standard. But as Cardozo says in his opinion, not every right listed in the Bill of Rights should automatically be applied to the states.

It is possible that some of the personal rights safeguarded by the first eight Amendments against National action may also be safeguarded against state action, because a denial of them would be a denial of due process of law.

—Justice William H. Moody, *Twining* v. *New Jersey* (1908)

We have said that in appellant's view the Fourteenth Amendment is to be taken as embodying the prohibitions of the Fifth. His thesis is even broader. Whatever would be a violation of the original Bill of Rights (Amendments I to VIII) if done by the federal government is now equally unlawful by force of the Fourteenth Amendment if done by a state. There is no such general rule. . . .

On the other hand, the due process clause of the Fourteenth Amendment may make it unlawful for a state to abridge by its statutes the freedom of speech which the First Amendment safeguards against encroachment by the Congress. . . .

In these and other situations immunities that are valid as against the federal government by force of the specific pledges of particular amendments have been found to be implicit in the concept of ordered liberty, and thus, through the Fourteenth Amendment, become valid as against the states. . . .

There emerges the perception of a rationalizing principle which gives to discrete instances a proper order and coherence. The right to trial by jury and the immunity from prosecution except as the result of an indictment may have value and importance. Even so, they are not of the very essence of a scheme of ordered liberty. To abolish them is not to violate a "principle of justice so rooted in the traditions and conscience of our people as to be ranked as fundamental. . . ."

We reach a different plane of social and moral values when we pass to the privileges and immunities that have been taken over from the earlier articles of the federal bill of rights and brought within the Fourteenth Amendment by a process of absorption. These in their origin were effective against the federal government alone. If the Fourteenth Amendment has absorbed them, the process of absorption has had its source in the belief that neither liberty nor justice would exist if they were sacrificed. . . . This is true, for illustration, of freedom of thought, and speech. Of that freedom one may say that it is the matrix, the indispensable condition, of nearly every other form of freedom. With rare aberrations a pervasive recognition of that truth can be traced in our history, political and legal. So it has come about that the domain of liberty, withdrawn by the Fourteenth Amendment from encroachment by the states, has been enlarged by latter-day judgments to include liberty of the mind as well as liberty of action. . . .

On which side of the line the case made out by the appellant has appropriate location must be the next inquiry and the final one. Is that kind of double jeopardy to which the statute has subjected him a hardship so acute and shocking that our polity will not endure it? Does it violate those "fundamental principles of liberty and justice which lie at the base of all our civil and political institutions?. . . The answer surely must be "no."

As a generalization, it can be said that due process embodies the differing rules of fair play, which through the years have become associated with differing types of proceedings.
—Chief Justice Earl Warren,
Hannah v. *Larche* (1960)

Justice Hugo Black set forth an alternative to the fundamental rights standard for selective incorporation of the Bill of Rights when he argued for total incorporation in his dissenting opinion in *Adamson* v. *California* (1947). In this case, Adamson claimed that the state of California had deprived him of his 5th Amendment right not to "be compelled in any criminal case to be a witness against himself." The Supreme Court decided this particular right did not meet the fundamental rights standard and should not be incorporated by the 14th Amendment. The Court ruled against Adamson by a 5-to-4 vote.

Hugo L. Black, associate justice of the U.S. Supreme Court 1937–71 advocated strict adherence to constitutional protections of individual rights, especially freedom of speech and press. Although from 1923 to 1925 Black had been a member of the Ku Klux Klan, on the Court he was a strong advocate for the rights of African Americans. In 1962, Black wrote the order that mandated the admission of an African American student, James Meredith, to the University of Mississippi.

In his dissent, Black argued for total incorporation as consistent with the intentions of the authors of the 14th Amendment. He wanted to apply all provisions of the Bill of Rights to the state governments just as they always have been applied to the national government. His position won four votes in the *Adamson* case. But it has never won a majority of the Court, and the selective incorporation position has, thus far, prevailed.

Since 1947, however, more provisions of the Bill of Rights have been incorporated on a case-by-case basis, including the 5th Amendment rights to protection against compulsory self-incrimination (incorporated by *Malloy* v. *Hogan* in 1964) and against double jeopardy (incorporated by *Benton* v. *Maryland* in 1969). The *Malloy* ruling overturned the *Adamson* decision, and the *Benton* decision overturned the *Palko* v. *Connecticut* ruling in which Justice Benjamin Cardozo stated his doctrine of selective incorporation. So Black achieved a measure of vindication by these decisions.

My study of the historical events that culminated in the Fourteenth Amendment, and the expressions of those who sponsored and favored, as well as those who opposed its submission and passage, persuades me that one of the chief objects that the provisions of the amendment . . . were intended to accomplish was to make the Bill of Rights applicable to the states. With full knowledge of the import of the Barron decision, the framers and backers of the Fourteenth Amendment proclaimed its purpose to be to overturn the constitutional rule that case had announced.

. . . In my judgment . . . history conclusively demonstrates that the language of the first section of the Fourteenth Amendment . . . was thought by those responsible for its submission . . . sufficiently explicit to guarantee that thereafter no state could deprive its citizens of the privileges and protections of the Bill of Rights . . . . [T]he "natural law" formula which the court uses to reach its conclusion in this case should be abandoned as an incongruous excrescence on our Constitution. I believe that formula to be itself a violation of our Constitution, in that it subtly conveys to courts, at the expense of legislatures, ultimate power over public policies in field where no specific provision of the Constitution limits legislative power. . . .

In my judgment the people of no nation can lose their liberty so long as a Bill of Rights like ours survives and its basic purposes are conscientiously interpreted, enforced and respected so as to afford continuous protection against old, as well as new, devices and practices which might thwart those purposes. I fear to see the consequences of the Court's practice of substituting its own concepts of decency and fundamental justice for the language of the Bill of Rights as its point of departure in interpreting and enforcing that Bill of Rights. . . .

I would therefore hold in this case that the full protection of the Fifth Amendment's prescription against compelled testimony must be afforded by California. This I would do because of reliance upon the original purpose of the Fourteenth Amendment. . . .

[But] to pass upon the constitutionality of statutes by looking to particular standards enumerated in the Bill of Rights and other parts of the Constitution is one thing; to invalidate statutes because of application of "natural law" deemed to be above and undefined by the Constitution is another. In the one instance, courts proceeding within clearly marked constitutional boundaries seek to execute policies written into the Constitution; in the other they roam at will in the limitless area of their own beliefs as to reasonableness and actually select policies, a responsibility which the Constitution entrusts to the legislative representatives of the people.

In the case of *Everson* v. *Board of Education of Ewing Township* (1947), a New Jersey law was challenged as a violation of the 1st Amendment's establishment clause, which states, "Congress shall make no law respecting an establishment of religion." The law permitted local boards of education to pay the costs of school bus transportation for students in public and Catholic schools. Arch Everson, a resident of the school district governed by the Ewing Township Board of Education, claimed that this state law violated the 1st Amendment's prohibition against a state establishment of religion. He argued that it was unfair and unconstitutional for the state government to use money from taxpayers to pay for transportation to private religious schools.

Everson claimed that the establishment clause, which only refers to the U.S. Congress, could also be applied to state governments. The Court agreed with him and selectively incorporated this provision of the Bill of Rights. Everson also argued that the New Jersey law involved the state government with religious schools in a way that violated the

The constitutional prohibition against law respecting an establishment of religion must at least mean that in this country it is no part of the business of government to compose official prayers for any group of the American people to recite as a part of a religious program carried out by government.

—Justice Hugo L. Black,
Engel v. *Vitale* (1962)

This 1943 high school class in Penasco, New Mexico, is being taught by a nun of the Catholic Church, which administered this state-supported school. Four years later, the U.S. Supreme Court used its doctrine of selective incorporation to rule that the establishment clause of the Bill of Rights prohibits a state from using public funds to directly support any religious activities or institutions.

establishment clause. The Court disagreed with Everson on this point. The Court held that the law was intended to benefit individual students and their parents and that it served the public good by safely transporting children to and from school. It only indirectly benefited private religious schools. So this law was not a violation of the establishment clause.

The Court's opinion, written by Justice Hugo Black, stated standards for deciding whether or not a particular action by the government violates the 1st Amendment's establishment clause. These landmark standards have guided the Court's decisions on establishment clause cases up to the present. They have been used, for example, to overturn state laws requiring recitation of nondenominational prayers in public schools (*Engel* v. *Vitale,* 1962, and *Abington School District* v. *Schempp,* 1963).

What the Framers meant to foreclose, and what our decisions under the Establishment Clause have forbidden, are those involvements of religion with secular institutions which (a) serve the essentially religious activities of religious institutions; (b) employ the organs of government for essentially religious purposes; or (c) use essentially religious means to serve governmental ends, where secular means would suffice.

—Justice William J. Brennan, *Abington School District* v. *Schempp* (1963)

The New Jersey statute is challenged as a "law respecting an establishment of religion." The First Amendment, as made applicable to the states by the Fourteenth . . . commands that a state "shall make no law respecting an establishment of religion, or prohibiting the free exercise thereof.". . .

The "establishment of religion" clause of the First Amendment means at least this: Neither a state nor the Federal Government can set up a church. Neither can pass laws which aid one religion, aid all religions, or prefer one religion over another. Neither can force nor influence a person to go or to remain away from church against his will or force him to profess a belief or disbelief in any religion. No person can be punished for entertaining or professing religious beliefs or disbeliefs, for church attendance or non-attendance. No tax in any amount, large or small, can be levied to support any religious activities or institutions, whatever they may be called, or whatever form they may adopt to teach or practice religion. Neither a state nor the Federal Government can, openly or secretly, participate in the affairs of any religious organizations or groups and *vice versa*. In the words of Jefferson, the clause against establishment of religion by law was intended to erect "a wall of separation between church and State."

We must consider the New Jersey statute in accordance with the foregoing limitations imposed by the First Amendment. But we must not strike that state statute down if it is within the State's constitutional power even though it approaches the verge of that power. . . .

[The First] Amendment requires the state to be a neutral in its relations with groups of religious believers and nonbelievers; it does not require the state to be their adversary. State power is no more to be used so as to handicap religions than it is to favor them.

This Court has said that parents may, in the discharge of their duty under state compulsory education laws, send their children to a religious, rather than a public school, if the school meets the secular educational requirements which the state has power to impose. . . . It appears that these parochial schools meet New Jersey's requirements. The State contributes no money to the schools. It does not support them. Its legislation, as applied, does no more than provide a general program to help parents get their children, regardless of their religion, safely and expeditiously to and from accredited schools.

The First Amendment has erected a wall between church and state. That wall must be kept high and impregnable. We could not approve the slightest breach. New Jersey has not breached it here.

Equal Protection of the Laws

In *Brown* v. *Board of Education* (1954), the Supreme Court unanimously decided that state laws requiring racial segregation in schools were unconstitutional. Such laws violated the "equal protection" clause of the Constitution's 14th

Amendment. Thus, the Court's "separate but equal" doctrine—established by _Plessy_ v. _Ferguson_ (1896)—was overturned. Chief Justice Warren wrote the unanimous opinion.

Today, education is perhaps the most important function of state and local governments. Compulsory school attendance laws and the great expenditures for education both demonstrate our recognition of the importance of education to our democratic society. It is required in the performance of our most basic public responsibilities, even service in the armed forces. It is the very foundation of good citizenship. Today it is a principal instrument in awakening the child to cultural values, in preparing him for later professional training, and in helping him to adjust normally to his environment. In these days, it is doubtful that any child may reasonably be expected to succeed in life if he is denied the opportunity of an education. Such an opportunity, where the state has undertaken to provide it, is a right which must be made available to all on equal terms.

We come then to the question presented: Does segregation of children in public schools solely on the basis of race, even though

A 1948 U.S. Supreme Court decision ruled that the University of Oklahoma Law School could not deny admission to G. W. McLaurin, an African American, based solely on his race. Although he was admitted to the school he was seated outside the classroom to signify less-than-full acceptance of his membership in the class.

the physical facilities and other "tangible" factors may be equal, deprive the children of the minority group of equal educational opportunities? We believe that it does. . . .

We conclude that in the field of public education the doctrine of "separate but equal" has no place. Separate educational facilities are inherently unequal. Therefore, we hold that the plaintiffs and others similarly situated for whom the actions have been brought are, by reason of the segregation complained of, deprived of the equal protection of the laws guaranteed by the Fourteenth Amendment. This disposition makes unnecessary any discussion whether such segregation also violates the Due Process Clause of the Fourteenth Amendment.

Among other provisions, the Civil Rights Act of 1964 restored legal protections of the Civil Rights Act of 1875, which had prohibited discrimination in public accommodations, and which the Supreme Court had overturned as unconstitutional in the *Civil Rights Cases* of 1883. The new act also prohibited employment discrimination and was welcomed by women as well as blacks.

Civil Rights Act of 1964
Title II.
. . . All persons shall be entitled to the full and equal enjoyment of the goods, services, facilities, privileges, advantages, and accommodations of any place of public accommodation, as defined in this section, without discrimination or segregation on the ground of race, color, religion, or national origin. . . .
Title VII.
. . . It shall be an unlawful practice for an employer . . . to limit, segregate, or classify his employees or applicants for employment in any way which would deprive or tend to deprive any individual of employment opportunities or otherwise adversely affect his status as an employee, because of such individual's race, color, religion, sex, or national origin.

National Standards on Rights of the Accused

In *Mapp v. Ohio* (1961), the Supreme Court used the exclusionary rule—the prohibition against using illegally obtained evidence in a court of law—in its incorporation of the 4th

Thurgood Marshall: Mr. Civil Rights

A great-grandson of a slave, Thurgood Marshall, was the first African-American justice of the Supreme Court, where he served from 1967 until his retirement in 1991. At his death in 1993, Americans hailed him a great champion of the fundamental rights for which the United States of America had been founded.

Thurgood Marshall was determined to use the law to force governmental compliance with the high purpose for government in the Declaration of Independence—to equally secure for all individuals their rights under the Constitution. After earning his law degree from Howard University, Marshall worked with his former teacher Charles Houston for the National Association for the Advancement of Colored People (NAACP). In 1938, Marshall succeeded Houston as NAACP special counsel, and in 1939 he helped to create and then led the NAACP's Legal Defense and Education Fund. In this position, Thurgood Marshall provided free legal help to black people in cases against unjust laws by which their rights were denied to them. In a series of cases before the Supreme Court, Marshall led a legal battle that overturned racial segregation laws as unconstitutional violations of the Constitution's 14th Amendment. Marshall won 29 of the 32 cases that he argued before the U.S. Supreme Court, a stunning record of success.

Thurgood Marshall's biggest legal victory came in the landmark case, *Brown* v. *Board of Education* in 1954, which overturned state laws requiring racial segregation in public schools. This was the beginning of the eventual ending of state government laws that denied equal rights to black Americans.

The choice is not between order and liberty. It is between liberty with order and anarchy without either.
—Justice Robert H. Jackson,
Terminiello v. *Chicago* (1949)

Amendment, which states: "The right of the people to be secure in their persons, houses, papers, and effects, against unreasonable searches and seizures, shall not be violated, and no warrants shall issue, but upon probable cause, supported by oath or affirmation, and particularly describing the place to be searched, and the persons or things to be seized." For the first time, the exclusionary rule was used in a case involving a state or local government. The Court had originally incorporated the 4th Amendment in *Wolf v. Colorado* in 1949. In *Mapp*, the Court expanded 4th Amendment protections to the 50 state governments by ruling that evidence illegally obtained through a search would be excluded from a trial. Justice Tom Clark's opinion nationalized both the 4th Amendment and the exclusionary rule.

Appellant stands convicted of knowingly having had in her possession and under her control certain lewd and lascivious books, pictures, and photographs in violation [of Ohio law]. . . . The Supreme Court of Ohio found that her conviction was valid though "based primarily upon the introduction in evidence of lewd and lascivious books and pictures unlawfully seized during an unlawful search of defendant's home." . . .

We hold that all evidence obtained by searches and seizures in violation of the Constitution is, by that same authority, inadmissible in a state court. . . .

Since the Fourth Amendment's right of privacy has been declared enforceable against the States through the Due Process Clause of the Fourteenth, it is enforceable against them by the same sanction of exclusion as is used against the Federal Government. . . .

This Court has not hesitated to enforce as strictly against the States as it does against the Federal Government the rights of free speech and of a free press, the rights to notice and to a fair, public trial, including, as it does, the right not to be convicted by use of a coerced confession, however logically relevant it be, and without regard to its reliability. . . . Why should not the same rule apply to what is tantamount to coerced testimony by way of unconstitutional seizure of goods, papers, effects, documents, etc.? We find that as to the Federal Government, the Fourth and Fifth Amendments and, as to the States, the freedom from unconscionable invasions of privacy and the freedom from convictions based upon coerced confessions do enjoy an "intimate relation" in their perpetuation of "principles of humanity and civil liberty [secured] . . . only after years of struggle." . . . The very least that together they assure in either sphere is that no man is to be convicted on unconstitutional evidence.

The 5th Amendment protection against self-incrimination was nationalized in the case of *Malloy* v. *Hogan* (1964). The Supreme Court, in the opinion delivered by Justice Brennan, emphasized the importance of national standards on the rights of the accused so that individuals would have the same guarantee of fair legal procedures everywhere in the United States.

We hold that the Fourteenth Amendment guaranteed the petitioner the protection of the Fifth Amendment's privilege against self-incrimination, and that under the applicable federal standard, the Connecticut Supreme Court of Errors erred in holding that the privilege was not properly invoked. . . .

This conclusion is fortified by our recent decision in *Mapp* v. *Ohio*, . . . overruling *Wolf* v. *Colorado*, . . . which had held "that in a prosecution in a State court for a State crime the Fourteenth

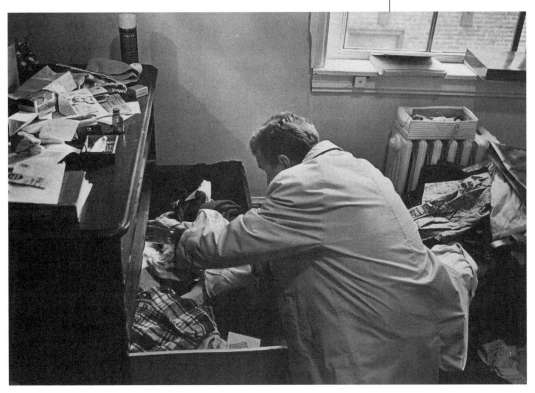

A federal government agent, Jan Larsen, searches a bedroom during a raid on an illegal narcotics laboratory in New York City, 1968. In accord with the 4th Amendment, federal law-enforcement officials have to obtain a search warrant based "upon probable cause" of criminal activity involving "the place to be searched, and the persons or things to be seized."

Chief Justice Warren and the Due Process Revolution

Earl Warren, the 14th Chief Justice of the United States, had a strong influence on the range and reach of the Bill of Rights in the lives of Americans. During his tenure of office from 1953 to 1969, the "Warren Court" greatly expanded the nationalization of rights in the Bill of Rights. Under his leadership, due process rights of a person accused of crime, in the 4th, 5th, and 6th amendments, were nationalized.

In an interview with the *New York Times Magazine,* Chief Justice Warren argued for strict limitation on the power of government to protect the rights of accused individuals: "The prosecutor under our system is not paid to convict people [but to] protect the rights of people . . . and to see that when there is a violation of the law, it is vindicated by trial and prosecution under fair judicial standards." Justice Byron White, by contrast, warned, "In some unknown number of cases, the Court's rule will return a killer, a rapist or other criminal to the streets . . . to repeat his crime whenever it pleases him." (*Miranda* v. *Arizona,* 1966). And so the argument has continued about the proper balance between the rights of criminal suspects and the public's need for safety and security against crime.

Amendment does not forbid the admission of evidence obtained by an unreasonable search and seizure," . . . *Mapp* held that the Fifth Amendment privilege against self-incrimination implemented the Fourth Amendment in such cases, and that the two guarantees of personal security conjoined in the Fourteenth Amendment to make the exclusionary rule obligatory upon the States. . . .

The respondent Sheriff concedes in his brief that under our decisions, particularly those involving coerced confessions, "the accusatorial system has become a fundamental part of the fabric of our society and, hence, is enforceable against the States." The State urges . . . that the availability of the federal privilege to a witness in a state inquiry is to be determined according to a less stringent standard than is applicable in a federal proceeding. We disagree. We have held that the guarantees of the First Amendment, . . . the prohibition of unreasonable searches and seizures of the Fourth Amendment, . . . and the right to counsel guaranteed by the Sixth Amendment, . . . are all to be enforced against the States under the Fourteenth Amendment according to the same standards that protect those personal rights against federal encroachment. In the coerced confession cases, involving the policies of the privilege itself, there has been no suggestion that a confession might be considered coerced if used in a federal but not a state tribunal. The Court thus has rejected the notion that the Fourteenth Amendment applies to the States only a "watered-down, subjective version of the individual guarantees of the Bill of Rights," . . . What is accorded is a privilege of refusing to incriminate one's self, and the feared prosecution may be by either federal or state authorities. . . . It would be incongruous to have different standards determine the validity of a claim of privilege based on the same feared prosecution, depending on whether the claim was asserted in a state or federal court. Therefore, the same standards must determine whether an accused's silence in either a federal or state proceeding is justified.

In its opinion in the 1968 case of *Duncan* v. *Louisiana,* the Supreme Court incorporated the 6th Amendment right to a jury trial in criminal cases. Some Americans have hotly denounced the Court's strict protection of criminal suspects, because they fear that some guilty individuals will be permitted to escape punishment. Others have countered with their belief in an old Anglo-American legal tradition: "It is better for 100 guilty persons to go free than to permit even

one innocent person to be punished." Writing for the Court, Justice Byron White also took this opportunity to review the Court's past use of the 14th Amendment's due process clause to incorporate selected provisions of the Bill of Rights and to nationalize them.

The Fourteenth Amendment denies the States the power to "deprive any person of life, liberty, or property, without due process of law." In resolving conflicting claims concerning the meaning of this spacious language, the Court has looked increasingly to the Bill of Rights for guidance; many of the rights guaranteed by the first eight Amendments to the Constitution have been held to be protected against state action by the Due Process Clause of the Fourteenth Amendment. That clause now protects the right to compensation for property taken by the State; the rights of speech, press, and religion covered by the First Amendment; the Fourth Amendment rights to be free from unreasonable searches and seizures and to have excluded from criminal trials any evidence illegally seized; the right guaranteed by the Fifth Amendment to be free of compelled self-incrimination; and the Sixth Amendment rights to counsel, to a speedy and public trial, to confrontation of opposing witnesses, and a compulsory process for obtaining witnesses.

The test for determining whether a right extended by the Fifth and Sixth Amendments with respect to federal criminal proceedings is also protected against state action by the Fourteenth Amendment has been phrased in a variety of ways in the opinions of this Court. The question has been asked whether a right is among those "fundamental principles of liberty and justice which lie at the base of all our civil and political institutions," . . . whether it is "basic in our system of jurisprudence," . . . and whether it is "a fundamental right, essential to a fair trial". . . . The claim before us is that the right to trial by jury guaranteed by the Sixth Amendment meets these tests.

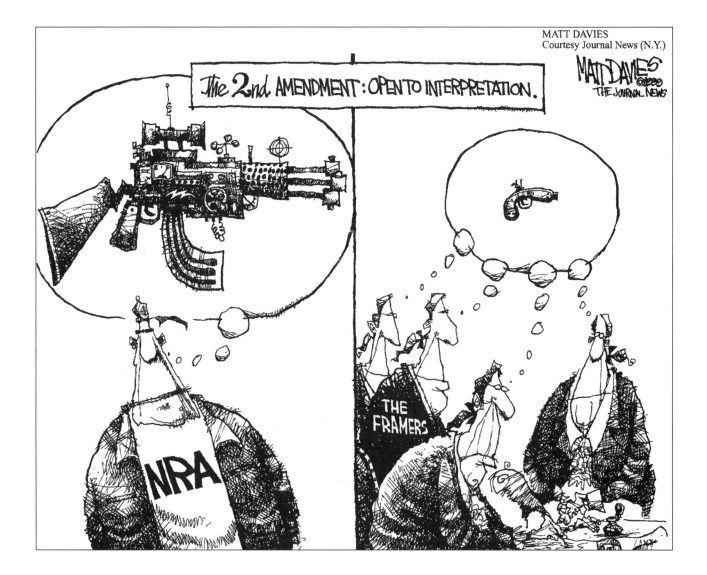

Chapter Eight: Picture Essay

Political Cartoons on the Right to Bear Arms

This political cartoon from 2000 emphasizes the unresolved arguments in U.S. constitutional history about what the 2nd Amendment means and how to apply it. The cartoon shows a member of the National Rifle Association, who thinks that the 2nd Amendment protects his right to "keep and bear arms," including high-powered automatic weapons. The cartoonist also depicts the framers of the U.S. Constitution, who appear to have a more limited view of the right to own and use guns.

The 2nd Amendment of the U.S. Constitution states: "A well regulated Militia being necessary to the security of a free state, the right of the people to keep and bear arms shall not be infringed." This part of the Bill of Rights has been an object of continuing controversy. Thus it has been a favored subject of political cartoons.

On one side of the argument are advocates of strict gun control laws who stress the militia clause in the opening segment of the 2nd Amendment. To them, the right to "keep and bear arms" is inseparable from service in a state militia, today, the National Guard. It is a collective and public right of the people for their self-defense. In their view, the 2nd Amendment prohibits the federal government from disarming the National Guard units of the states. But it does not prevent the government from regulating, on behalf of the public good, private gun use by individuals.

On the other side of this issue are opponents of stricter gun control laws. They emphasize the second clause of the 2nd Amendment and argue that "the people" refers to practically everyone in the United States. To them, there is an unequivocal individual and private right "to keep and bear arms," which the government cannot prohibit. They accept the purpose of maintaining a "well regulated militia," but they recognize individual self-defense as an equivalent purpose that should not be subordinated.

The U.S. Supreme Courts interpretation of the 2nd Amendment has been limited. In *Presser* v. *Illinois* (1886), the Court decided that the 2nd Amendment only pertained to the federal government and did not prohibit state governments from regulating an individual's ownership and use of weapons. In 1983, the Court reaffirmed the *Presser* ruling by letting stand the decision of the Seventh Circuit Court of Appeals in *Quilici* v. *Village of Morton Grove*, which exempts state and local laws from 2nd Amendment restrictions. Thus, the 2nd Amendment remains one of the few parts of the Bill of Rights that is not incorporated under the due process clause of the 14th Amendment and applied to state governments.

The last time the U.S. Supreme Court decided a case on the meaning of the 2nd Amendment was in the 1939 case *United States* v. *Miller*. The Court upheld a federal gun control law, the National Firearms Act of 1934, which required taxation and registration of sawed-off shotguns and automatic weapons. The defendant in this case, Jack Miller, had been charged with possession of an unregistered sawed-off shotgun. In his opinion for the Court, Justice James C. McReynolds wrote:

> In the absence of any evidence tending to show that possession or use of a "shotgun having a barrel of less than eighteen inches in length at this time has some reasonable relationship to the preservation or efficiency of a well regulated militia, we cannot say that the Second Amendment guarantees the right to keep and bear such an instrument. Certainly it is not within judicial notice that this weapon is any part of the ordinary military equipment or that its use could contribute to the common defense.

Furthermore, Justice McReynolds said, "Most if not all of the States have adopted provisions touching the right to keep and bear arms. Differences in the language employed in these have naturally led to somewhat variant conclusions concerning the scope of the right guaranteed."

Since the *Miller* decision, lower-level courts have upheld various gun control laws. Sometimes they have justified their rulings with the collective rights interpretation of the 2nd Amendment, emphasizing the state militia clause. Usually they have pointed to the "nonincorporation" of the 2nd Amendment through the 14th Amendment's due process clause. On this ground, state governments are not prohibited by the 2nd Amendment from enacting gun control laws, and legal issues about these laws have been left to the state legislatures and state court to decide.

Most existing state laws limit the types of guns or other weapons that can be bought or sold, require a waiting period before the weapons can be purchased, or regulate the sale of weapons to persons with records of criminal behavior or mental illness. Some see these laws as necessary for public safety and permitted by a 2nd Amendment, which in their view pertains primarily to a collective right "to keep and bear arms" for use in a state militia. By contrast, others see many gun control laws as an infringement of an individual and private right to self-defense against predators and tyrants, which is guaranteed by the 2nd Amendment. This ongoing public controversy about the "right to keep and bear arms" is not likely to be resolved soon.

One means of mass communication about 2nd Amendment issues is the political cartoon, a distinctive and often humorous drawing about current events. Political cartoons can be very entertaining, but they usually have the serious purpose of influencing public opinion about government officials, candidates for election to public office, pressing social problems, and political and constitutional issues, such as gun control and the right to bear arms.

Political cartoons have been an important part of political affairs throughout American history, from the founding era until the present. They typically appear in daily newspapers, usually on the editorial pages where various political opinions are expressed. Political cartoons, such as those on gun control, can also be found in magazines, books, and the Internet.

The 1st Amendment of the U.S. Constitution protects the right of political cartoonists to freely express opinions, including criticisms about controversial topics and prominent persons or groups.

A Long History

The controversy about gun control and the meaning of the 2nd Amendment right to keep and bear arms has been going on for a long time. This cartoon was published in San Francisco, California, in 1878. The cartoon makes the argument that continues to be made by some modern cartoonists that the restriction of guns would leave citizens vulnerable to criminals. The caption is a criticism of local government officials who favor strict gun control laws.

DAVID HITCH
Courtesy Worcester Telegram & Gazette

Why Wait?

This 1992 cartoon from the *Worcester Telegraph & Gazette* critically depicts a member of the National Rifle Association (NRA), the leading interest group that opposes strict or extensive gun control laws. The cartoonist satirizes the NRAs opposition to the Brady Bill, named for President Reagan's press secretary, Jim Brady, who was shot and seriously wounded during the attempted assasination of the President. This proposed federal law that required a "waiting period" to allow for background checks of individuals wanting to make purchases at gun shows. The last frame of the cartoon includes a comic adaptation of the NRA slogan "Guns don't kill people. People do." Congress passed the Brady Gun Act in 1993 despite the objections of the NRA.

Second Thoughts

To attract the reader's attention, political cartoonists often use caricature to depict people, places, or events in an exaggerated form that highlights some aspect of a person or a thing. This cartoon published in the *Gainesville Sun* in 2000 caricatures a member of the NRA, who gleefully points his high-powered weapon at three framers of the Bill of Rights, who are having second thoughts about the 2nd Amendment. At the sight of the gun-bearing NRA member, they express a desire to "white out" or erase the 2nd Amendment's phrase about the right to bear arms, which appears in handwritten script at the top of the cartoon.

Self-defense

The effectiveness of guns as a means of crime prevention is part of the ongoing debate about the issue of gun control. Organizations such as the NRA claim that restriction of gun ownership would leave an unarmed population at the mercy of armed criminals. Whereas, gun control advocates assert that guns in the home are just as likely to be the cause of tragic accidents or to be used against the homeowner by a criminal than to effectively protect the home from crime.

"SEE HOW DANGEROUS IT IS TO ALLOW PEOPLE TO HAVE EASY ACCESS TO GUNS?"

Political cartoonists often use sarcasm to make a point. This cartoonist shows two burglars fleeing from a house protected by a gun-wielding homeowner. In his caption, the cartoonist mocks a typical argument of gun control advocates, who claim that widespread possession of guns is dangerous. The cartoon published in the Tampa Tribune in 1994 expresses the contrary opinion that guns can be used as protection against criminals.

This cartoonist appears to agree that the individual's private right to keep and bear arms can provide protection against dangerous criminals. In this cartoon published in 2000 in the Colorado Springs Gazette-Telegraph, *the cartoonist uses his caption and three thought bubbles labeled A, B, and C to express the opinion that in a threatening situation most people would wish they had a gun, and not stricter gun control.*

PATRICK RICE
Courtesy Jupiter Courier

Word Play

This 1999 cartoon from the *Jupiter Courier* mocks the NRA arguments against gun control laws. The cartoonist creates a dialogue between two characters, an NRA representative and a U.S. senator, whom the NRA is trying to influence. The senator raises the series of school shootings such as the April 20, 1999, mass killing at Columbine High School in Littleton, Colorado, to suggest that a bill to control guns would be prudent. The NRA representative responds to the senator with glib repudiations of any attempt to restrict guns. At the end of the cartoon, the NRA representative gets trapped in his own play on words.

Defending the Home

Many Americans support the NRA, which is the main point of this 1999 political cartoon from the *Tampa Tribune.* The cartoonist shows a man taking a poll about opinions for and against gun control. The guns in the hands of the respondents clearly indicate their opposition to gun control laws and their belief that guns are necessary to defend their home. According to the NRA, 45 percent of American households have guns.

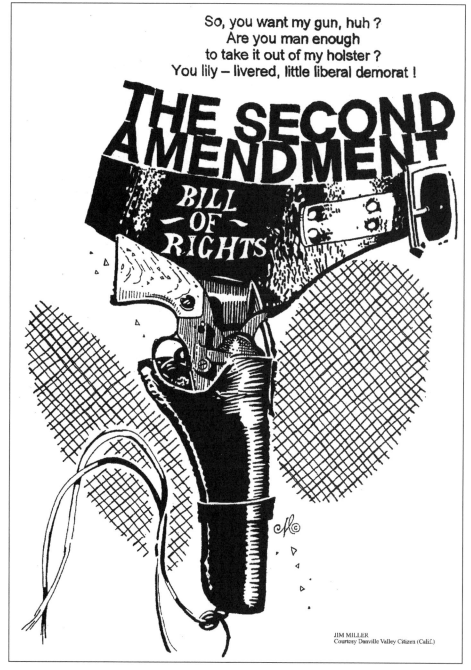

So, you want my gun, huh ?
Are you man enough
to take it out of my holster ?
You lily – livered, little liberal demorat !

THE SECOND AMENDMENT

BILL OF RIGHTS

JIM MILLER
Courtesy Danville Valley Citizen (Calif.)

Gunslingers

This cartoonist uses his sarcastic caption and an attention-getting drawing
to ridicule the opponents of gun control laws in this cartoon published in
the *Danville Valley Citizen* in 2000. He derisively suggests that the pro-gun
groups act tough in their denunciations of gun control. The gunslinger in
the cartoon whose holster bears the title Bill of Rights uses language that
has the flavor of the Old West. He refers to Democratic Party leaders, who
have often supported gun control laws, as "demorats."

LIFE,   LIBERTY   ...AND THE PURSUIT OF HAPPINESS.

Life, Liberty, and the Pursuit of Happiness

A famous phrase from the 1776 Declaration of Independence is the organizing feature of this caricature of those who favor an unlimited right to possess weapons. In the cartoonist's opinion, as presented in this 1999 cartoon from the *Green Bay Press-Gazette*, widespread possession of guns threatens ones right to life and liberty. And it is a negative or perverse use of the right to pursuit of happiness.

Guns and Patriots

This cartoonist, in a cartoon published in the *Indianapolis News* in 2000, depicts George Washington and his soldiers armed with clubs and slingshots as they cross the Delaware River to attack British troops during the American War of Independence. His message is that patriots in possession of guns were needed to defeat the British and to found the United States of America. The cartoonist seems to suggest that gun control contradicts the very founding principles of the nation.

JERRY BARNETT
Courtesy Indianapolis News

Chapter Nine

Consensus and Controversy

rom 1989 to 1991, Americans celebrated the bicentennial of their Bill of Rights, whose protection of fundamental rights finally applied to all Americans in every part of the nation.

Americans have generally agreed on the value of minimal national standards for rights, but these standards have evolved as a consequence of Supreme Court decisions, congressional enactments, Presidential policies, political activities of citizens' organizations and civil rights movements, and public opinion.

Consensus on nationwide application of most provisions of the Bill of Rights has often been accompanied by fierce controversy, usually peaceful, about the meaning of particular rights in certain circumstances. By the later years of the 20th century, for example, nearly all Americans agreed that the 1st Amendment freedoms of religion, speech, press, assembly, and petition are fundamentally important and should be protected against abridgment by the federal or state governments. Since the 1970s, however, Americans have argued vigorously about how extensive the latitude or limitations of these freedoms should be. During the Vietnam War, there was ongoing debate about the government's need to limit constitutional rights in order to maintain national security. This controversy peaked in 1971, when the federal government restricted the publication of military documents in privately owned newspapers.

Since the Sedition Act controversy of 1798, citizens have argued about whether the government has the authority to limit individual rights during a national crisis. Should national security concerns ever outweigh the rights guaranteed in the Bill of Rights? A landmark

The American Civil Liberties Union (ACLU) promotes education of the public about constitutional rights through posters such as "The ACLU Illustrated Guide to the Bill of Rights."

The first edition of the June 30, 1971, Washington Post comes off the printing press after the Supreme Court's ruling against federal government restrictions on publication of the Pentagon Papers. Newspapers throughout the country resumed printing of the series following the Court's decision.

victory for freedom of expression came in the 1971 case of *New York Times Company* v. *United States*, known as the Pentagon Papers Case. The Supreme Court rejected the federal government's attempt to restrain the press and concluded that the government had failed to show that publication of material from the Pentagon Papers—top-secret government documents—would cause harm serious enough to outweigh the value of free expression of information.

Issues about national security versus constitutional rights have emerged again in the aftermath of the terrorist attacks against the United States on September 11, 2001. The deliberate destruction of the World Trade Center in New York City and the Pentagon in Washington, D.C., which killed nearly 3,000 people, was an act of war against the United States. In response to this crisis, President George W. Bush issued on November 3, 2001, a military order for the detention of noncitizens accused of international terrorism.

This executive order empowers the secretary of defense to establish military tribunals to conduct trials of persons accused of terrorist acts or of aiding terrorists. Persons accused and tried in a military tribunal, however, may not have all the constitutional rights that are usually guaranteed to criminal defendants. Thus, Bill of Rights issues may be raised during the U.S. war against terrorism as government officials try to simultaneously provide for national security and guarantees of civil liberties.

In a constitutional, democratic government, the majority rules. At the same time, legal limits are placed on the power of the majority in order to protect the rights of those in the minority. And every person of the polity may at some moment, in response to some issue, be in the minority and against the majority will. The Bill of Rights and the Constitution were designed to limit the power of the people's representatives in government and thereby to protect the rights of everyone, even those who might be unpopular or despised by a momentary or prevailing majority.

The relationship between majorities and minorities poses a never-ending question for the citizens of a constitutional democracy. At what point, and under what circumstances, should the power of the democratic majority be limited by the supreme law of the Constitution to secure the rights of individuals, including those in the minority? And conversely, at what point, and under what conditions, should the rights of individuals or minorities be limited in order to support and maintain majority rule? Alternative responses to these basic questions have raised critical constitutional controversies throughout the history of the United States. The people, if they are to take responsibility for their Bill of Rights, must never stop responding to such controversies.

If the people's rights are to be secure, then their government must have sufficient power to protect and maintain them. But if the government's power to enforce law and order is too strong, then it might use this power to deny or abuse the people's rights. When should the power of government be limited to protect the rights of individuals? And when should the rights of individuals be limited by the compelling public need for order and safety?

Debate continues about the interpretation and application of the Bill of Rights. One prominent controversy pertains to the presumption of an individual's right to privacy, which is not stated explicitly in the Bill of Rights or in any other part of the Constitution. Nonetheless, the Constitution requires limitations on the power of government. And limited government implies restrictions on its capacity to reach into the private domain of life. So an individual's general right to privacy is inherent in the very idea of a constitutionally limited government.

Supreme Court Justice Louis Brandeis emphasized the importance of a right to privacy in a dissenting opinion in the case of *Olmstead* v. *United States* (1928). He wrote: "The right to be let alone . . . [is] the most comprehensive of rights and the right most valued by civilized men. To protect that right, every unjustified intrusion of the government upon the privacy of the individual, whatever the means employed, must be deemed a [constitutional] violation." Not until 1965, in *Griswold* v. *Connecticut*, did the Supreme Court agree with Brandeis and recognize a constitutional right to privacy.

The *Griswold* case concerned a Connecticut law that limited the use of birth control devices and made it a criminal offense for a person to provide information or instruction about the use of such devices. Estelle Griswold, executive director of the Planned Parenthood League, was convicted of giving birth control information to married people. After the Connecticut Supreme Court affirmed her conviction, Griswold appealed to the U.S. Supreme Court. The Court decided in favor of Griswold, overturned the Connecticut law as unconstitutional, and established a right to privacy in American constitutional law. The decision remains controversial, but it also continues to be invoked by Americans seeking the benefit of a right to privacy against intrusion by government.

In 1973, this right to privacy was used by the Supreme Court to justify its decision in *Roe* v. *Wade*, a landmark case about the right

A movie industry group—including actors Tim Robbins and Susan Sarandon—joins a 1989 demonstration in Washington, D.C., to protest proposed limitations on a woman's right to choose an abortion, established by the U.S. Supreme Court's decision in Roe v. Wade *(1973).*

to choose an abortion. A Texas law made it a crime to have an abortion unless the operation was necessary to save the mother's life. This law was typical of those in most states. An unmarried Texas woman, known by the pseudonym of Jane Roe to protect her anonymity, filed suit against Henry Wade, district attorney of Dallas County, to challenge the state's anti-abortion law as unconstitutional. She requested an injunction from a federal court to stop Wade from enforcing this law. Her case went on appeal to the Supreme Court. The Court ruled in favor of Jane Roe and based its decision on a right to privacy inherent within the Bill of Rights and the 14th Amendment. Together, the *Griswold* and *Roe* decisions set forth minimal national standards on the right to privacy and the freedom to choose an abortion.

Since the 1970s, Americans have continued to argue about various constitutional issues. Although there is certainly a consensus about the value of 1st Amendment freedoms of expression, especially political expression, controversy erupts from time to time about what limits the government should impose on this freedom in particular cases. During the 1990s, for example, Americans argued vigorously about whether or not the federal government should be able to ban pornographic messages on the Internet.

In 1996, Congress, with the strong support of President Bill Clinton, passed the Communications Decency Act (CDA) to limit transmission of indecent or pornographic material on the Internet. The law prohibited anyone from sending indecent messages to those under 18 years old. It also banned displays of pornographic material in a manner accessible to anyone younger than 18. Violators of the law could be fined up to $25,000 and sent to prison for up to two years.

Supporters of the CDA argued that its limitations on free speech served a compelling public interest—the common good of protecting the moral development of preadults. Opponents disagreed and denounced it as unconstitutional. The CDA was challenged by the American Civil Liberties Union (ACLU) and others as a violation of 1st Amendment freedoms, and a three-judge panel of a federal district court decided that the new federal law was unconstitutional. The U.S. Supreme Court affirmed the lower court's ruling, but this did not end the controversy. The executive director of the Center for Democracy and Technology spoke for many Americans when he said, "The Supreme Court has written the Bill of Rights for the twenty-first century." Many others, however, sided with Senator Dan Coats of Indiana, who regretted that "the Court was telling families to fend for themselves in an Internet of raw indecency."

There have also been heated public debates about the 1st Amendment's prohibition of an establishment of religion. Everyone agrees that the establishment clause prohibits the federal government from imposing religious beliefs or practices upon individuals, but arguments continue about the extent to which there should be separation between government and religion.

Most Supreme Court decisions on the 1st Amendment's establishment clause maintain some kind of separation of government and religion. The 1992 decision in *Lee* v. *Weisman*, for example, prohibited prayers led by a rabbi at a public school graduation ceremony. This decision was consistent with a long line of 20th-century cases in which formal or official prayers or religious ceremonies have been prohibited in public schools (*Engel* v. *Vitale*, 1962; *Abington School District* v. *Schempp*, 1963; and *Wallace* v. *Jaffree*, 1985).

In the wake of these rulings, many students and parents complained that their constitutional rights to free exercise of religion had been abused. Others, by contrast, claimed that the Court had protected their rights to be free from government-sponsored religious ceremonies. The controversy continued into 2000, when the Supreme Court ruled, in a split decision, against recitation of a nonsectarian and nonproselytizing prayer before a public high school football game (*Santa Fe Independent School District* v. *Doe*).

Although the Court has ruled that the government may not establish an official religion, may not favor one religion over others, and may not provide support for all religions equally, it has also ruled that there may in certain circumstances be an accommodation of government to religion. In *Agostini* v. *Felton* (1997), the Court ruled that it is constitutional for remedial instruction to be provided through a federal government program to needy students in private religious schools. Further, in *Mitchell* v. *Helms* (2000), the Court decided in favor of a federal government program that provided computers, software, and other instructional media materials to religiously affiliated schools. In both cases, the Court's guiding principle was that government aid to a private religious school is constitutional if it goes directly to students in need of particular

Students of Clear Lake High School, near Houston, Texas, gather around the flagpole on school grounds for a voluntary prayer session before the beginning of the school day. These students are using their 1st Amendment right to free exercise of religion by choosing to participate in an extra-curricular program not sponsored by the public school.

assistance and not to the general support of the school.

In several recent cases, the Supreme Court has decided that government aid to a private religious school is constitutional if it goes directly to benefit particular students and not for general support of the school and its religious mission. This principle was followed by the Supreme Court in ruling for an Ohio school voucher program in *Zelman* v. *Simmons-Harris* (2002). Because the publicly-funded vouchers were provided to parents—who freely and privately chose how to use them in selecting a school for their children to attend—the Court held that there was no official endorsement of religion and no violation of the 1st Amendment clause prohibiting an establishment of religion. Writing for the Court, Chief Justice William Rehnquist said: "The Ohio program is entirely neutral with respect to religion. It provides benefits directly to a wide spectrum of individuals, defined only by financial need and residence in a particular school district. It permits such individuals to exercise genuine choice among options public and private, secular and religious. The program is therefore a program of true private choice." The Court's controversial 5-4 decision in the Ohio school voucher case is part of the ongoing public debate on the meaning and application of the 1st Amendment clauses on the relationship between government and religion.

Another question is whether a public school violates the establishment clause when it provides religious groups with equal access to school facilities on the same terms as other student groups. Many public school districts argue that it is a violation to provide religious groups with access, but many students and parents disagree with that policy. They complained to their representatives in Congress.

In response, Congress passed the 1984 Equal Access Act, which requires public schools to provide religious groups with equal access to school facilities for meetings. If a public school receives federal funds and permits other student groups not related to the curriculum, such as the chess club, to use school facilities for meetings, then it could not deny the same privileges for religious

The right to be let alone is indeed the beginning of all freedom.
—Justice William O. Douglas,
Public Utilities Commission
v. *Pollak* (1952)

groups. According to the law, schools cannot deny access "on the basis of religious, political, philosophical, or other content of the speech at such meetings."

The Supreme Court ruled in *Westside Community Board of Education v. Mergens* (1990) that the Equal Access Act is a constitutional accommodation of government to religion. And in *Good News Club v. Milford Central School* (2001), in which public school officials barred a religious group from after-school use of facilities, the Court decided in favor of the Good News Club, again supporting a particular kind of accommodation of the government to religion.

Although Americans continue to argue about such cases, they also continue to agree about the enduring worth of their Bill of Rights. That document belongs to the people, and it is their right and responsibility to participate vigorously in decisions about its interpretation and application to political and civic life.

The Rights to Privacy and Abortion

In the case of *Griswold* v. *Connecticut* (1965), the Supreme Court overturned as unconstitutional a Connecticut law that limited the use of birth control devices and made it a crime to provide information about these products. Writing for the Court, Justice William O. Douglas said that the 1st, 4th, 5th, and 9th amendments collectively imply "a general right to privacy" and that the law at issue had violated that right. And he claimed that the 14th Amendment's due process clause allows these provisions of the Bill of Rights to limit a state government.

We are met with a wide range of questions that implicate the Due Process Clause of the Fourteenth Amendment. . . .

[Previous] cases suggest that specific guarantees in the Bill of Rights . . . create zones of privacy. The right of association [implied by] the First Amendment is one. . . . The Third Amendment in its prohibition against the quartering of soldiers "in any house" in time of peace without the consent of the owner is another facet of that privacy. The Fourth Amendment explicitly affirms the "right of the people to be secure in their persons, houses, papers, and effects, against unreasonable searches and seizures." The Fifth Amendment in its Self-Incrimination Clause enables the citizen to create a zone of privacy which government may not force him to surrender to his detriment. The Ninth

We are rapidly entering the age of no privacy, where everyone is open to surveillance at all times; where there are no secrets from government.
—Justice William O. Douglas, *Osborn v. United States* (1966)

C. Lee Buxton, the medical director of a Planned Parenthood Clinic, and Estelle Griswold, director of the Planned Parenthood League of Connecticut, were honored with an award for their roles in the landmark Supreme Court decision in Griswold v. Connecticut (1965). As a consequence of the Griswold decision, the Court recognized an individual's constitutional right to privacy, and the decision has been used to support the right to an abortion against restrictive state laws.

Our cases long have recognized that the Constitution embodies a promise that a certain private sphere of individual liberty will be kept largely beyond the reach of government.

—Justice Harry A. Blackmun, *Thornburgh* v. *American College of Obstetricians & Gynecologists* (1986)

Amendment provides: "The enumeration in the Constitution, of certain rights, shall not be construed to deny or disparage others retained by the people. . . .

The Fourth and Fifth Amendments were described in *Boyd* v. *United States* (1886) . . . as protection against all governmental invasions "of the sanctity of a man's home and the privacies of life." We recently referred in *Mapp* v. *Ohio* [1961] . . . to the Fourth Amendment as creating a "right to privacy, no less important than any other right carefully and particularly reserved to the people." . . . These cases bear witness that the right to privacy which presses for recognition here is a legitimate one.

The present case, then, concerns a relationship lying within the zone of privacy created by several fundamental constitutional guarantees. And it concerns a law which, in forbidding the *use* of contraceptives rather than regulating their manufacture or sale, seeks to achieve its goals by means having a maximum destructive impact upon that relationship. Such a law cannot stand. . . . Would we allow the police to search the sacred precincts of marital bedrooms for telltale signs of the use of contraceptives? The very idea is repulsive to the notions of privacy surrounding the marriage relationship.

In his concurring opinion, Justice Arthur Goldberg emphasized the Constitution's 9th Amendment: "The enumeration in the Constitution of certain rights shall not be construed to deny or disparage others retained by the people." He claimed that a right to privacy was one of the "others retained by the people." Justice Goldberg was joined in concurring by the Chief Justice and Justice Brennan. The justices turned to the 14th Amendment and substantive due process to argue that a right to privacy is applicable to the states.

The Court stated many years ago that the Due Process Clause protects those liberties that are "so rooted in the traditions and conscience of our people as to be ranked as fundamental." . . . This Court, in a series of decisions, has held that the Fourteenth Amendment absorbs and applies to the States those specifics of the first eight amendments which express fundamental personal rights. The language and history of the Ninth Amendment reveal that the Framers of the Constitution believed that there are additional fundamental rights, protected from governmental infringement, which exist alongside those fundamental rights specifically mentioned in the first eight constitutional amendments. . . .

In sum, I believe that the right of privacy in the marital relation is fundamental and basic—a personal right "retained by the people" within the meaning of the Ninth Amendment. Connecticut cannot constitutionally abridge this fundamental right, which is protected by the Fourteenth Amendment from infringement by the States. I agree with the Court that petitioners' convictions must therefore be reversed.

In their dissent, justices Hugo Black and Potter Stewart strongly objected to the Court's claims that the Bill of Rights in combination with the 14th Amendment guarantees a right to privacy. They argued that since there is no specific statement in the Constitution about such a right, it is not available to individuals under the Constitution's authority.

Since 1879 Connecticut has had on its books a law which forbids the use of contraceptives by anyone. I think this is an uncommonly silly law. As a practical matter, the law is obviously unenforceable, except in the oblique context of the present case. . . . [W]e are not asked in this case to say whether we think this law is unwise, or

The task of this Court to maintain a balance between liberty and authority is never done, because new conditions today upset the balance of yesterday. The seesaw between freedom and power makes up most of the history of government. . . . The Court's day-to-day task is to reject as false, claims in the name of civil liberty which, if granted, would paralyze or impair authority to defend existence of our society, and to reject as false, claims in the name of security which would undermine our freedoms and open the way to oppression.

—Justice Robert H. Jackson, *American Communications Association* v. *Douds* (1980)

Justice Harry A. Blackmun explained his position about a woman's right to choose an abortion in a memorandum to his colleagues on the U.S. Supreme Court regarding the case Roe *v.* Wade *(1973). Following oral arguments on a case, the justices exchange ideas through such memoranda as this one.*

Supreme Court of the United States
Washington, D. C. 20543

CHAMBERS OF
JUSTICE HARRY A. BLACKMUN

December 21, 1972

MEMORANDUM TO THE CONFERENCE

Re: Abortion Cases

Herewith are revised drafts of the Texas and Georgia memoranda.

I have endeavored to accommodate the various views expressed to me orally or by letter. The principal change in the Texas memorandum is at page 47 et seq. Here I have tried to recognize the dual state interests of protecting the mother's health and of protecting potential life. This, I believe, is a better approach than that contained in the initial memorandum. I have tried to follow the lines suggested by Bill Brennan and Thurgood.

The Chief has expressed concern about the rights of the father. I have mentioned these in footnote 67. This will not be very satisfying, but I am somewhat reluctant to try to cover the point in cases where the father's rights, if any, are not at issue. I suspect there will be other aspects of abortion that will have to be dealt with at a future time.

Sincerely,

H. A. B.

even asinine. We are asked to hold that it violated the United States Constitution. And that I cannot do.

In the course of its opinion the Court refers to no less than six Amendments to the Constitution: the First, the Third, the Fourth, and Fifth, and Ninth, and the Fourteenth. But the Court does not say which of these Amendments, if any, it thinks is infringed by this Connecticut law. . . .

The Court also quotes the Ninth Amendment, and my Brother GOLDBERG's concurring opinion relies heavily upon it. But to say that the Ninth Amendment has anything to do with this case is to turn somersaults with history. . . .

What provision of the Constitution, then, does make this state law invalid? The Court says it is the right of privacy "created by several fundamental constitutional guarantees." With all deference, I can find no such general right of privacy in the Bill of Rights, in any other part of the Constitution, or in any case ever before decided by this Court.

The Supreme Court ruled in the case of *Roe* v. *Wade* (1973) that a Texas law prohibiting abortion was unconstitutional. Writing for the Court, Justice Harry Blackmun recognized that a woman's freedom to choose an abortion was not unlimited, however. It could be restricted by "a compelling state interest" to protect her health or life. Blackmun concluded that a state government might regulate the right to choose an abortion during the second trimester of a woman's pregnancy. And the state might absolutely prohibit abortion during the third trimester. But during the first trimester, the woman has the freedom to choose an abortion.

The principal thrust of appellant's attack on the Texas statutes is that they improperly invade a right, said to be possessed by the pregnant woman, to choose to terminate her pregnancy. Appellant would discover this right in the concept of personal "liberty" embodied in the Fourteenth Amendment's Due Process Clause; or in personal, marital, familial, and sexual privacy said to be protected by the Bill of Rights . . . or among those rights reserved to the people by the Ninth Amendment. . . .

The Constitution does not explicitly mention any right of privacy. In a line of decisions, however. . . . the Court has recognized that a right of personal privacy, or a guarantee of certain areas or zones of privacy, does exist under the Constitution.

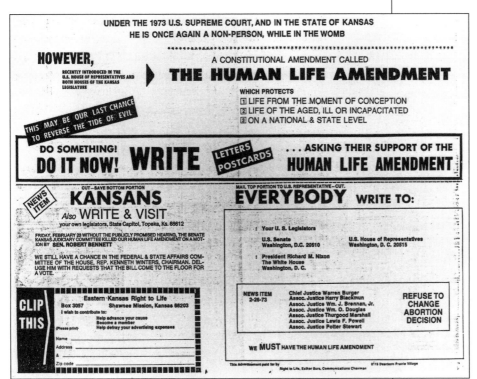

A pro-life organization in Kansas promoted a "human life" amendment to the U.S. Constitution to overturn the Supreme Court's decision in Roe v. Wade (1973) that established a woman's right to choose an abortion. The 11th, 13th, 14th, 16th, and 26th Amendments to the Constitution were enacted to overturn unpopular decisions of the Supreme Court.

This right of privacy, whether it be founded in the Fourteenth Amendment's concept of personal liberty and restrictions upon state action, as we feel it is, or, as the District Court determined, in the Ninth Amendment's reservation of rights to the people, is broad enough to encompass a woman's decision whether or not to terminate her pregnancy. . . .

The Court's decisions recognizing a right of privacy also acknowledge that some state regulation in areas protected by that right is appropriate. . . . [A] State may properly assert important interests in safeguarding health, in maintaining medical standards, and in protecting potential life. At some point in pregnancy, these respective interests become sufficiently compelling to sustain regulation of the factors that govern the abortion decision. The privacy right involved, therefore, cannot be said to be absolute. . . .

We, therefore, conclude that the right of personal privacy includes the abortion decision, but that this right is not unqualified and must be considered against important state interests in regulation. . . .

Measured against these standards, Art. 1196 of the Texas Penal Code, in restricting legal abortions to those "procured or attempted by medical advice for the purpose of saving the life of the mother," sweeps too broadly. The statute makes no distinction between abortions performed early in pregnancy and those performed later, and it limits to a single reason, "saving" the mother's life, the legal justification for the procedure. The statute, therefore, cannot survive the constitutional attack made upon it here.

Justices William Rehnquist and Byron White strongly dissented from the Court's opinion. They claimed that the 14th Amendment does not guarantee a right to privacy that prohibits states from regulating the practice of abortion during the first three months of a pregnancy. White remarked that the freedom to choose an abortion is an issue about which "reasonable men may easily and heatedly differ." And thus it has been since 1973, when the Court decided the *Roe* case.

MR. JUSTICE REHNQUIST, dissenting.

. . . I have difficulty in concluding, as the Court does, that the right of "privacy" is involved in this case. Texas, by the statute here challenged, bars the performance of a medical abortion by a licensed physician on a plaintiff such as Roe. A transaction resulting in an operation such as this is not "private" in the ordinary usage of that word. Nor is the "privacy" that the Court finds here even a distant relative of the freedom from searches and seizures protected by the Fourth Amendment to the Constitution, which the Court has referred to an embodying a right to privacy. . . .

The decision here to break pregnancy into three distinct terms and to outline the permissible restrictions the State may impose in each one . . . partakes more of judicial legislation than it does of a determination of the intent of the drafters of the Fourteenth Amendment.

Limits to Freedom of Expression

In June 1971, *the New York Times* and the *Washington Post* started to publish a series of articles based on U.S. government documents that became known as the Pentagon Papers. These documents included information about U.S. military involvement in Vietnam and federal government policies on the war that was classified "top secret." Federal officials did not want the Pentagon Papers released to the public and printed only 15 copies. Daniel Ellsberg, a researcher involved in compiling and editing the documents, made a photocopy and gave most of them to Neil Sheehan of the *New York Times*. A team of *Times* reporters wrote a series

The Flag-Burning Controversy

An especially sharp controversy about the 1st Amendment right to freedom of expression erupted in 1989 when protesters, including Gregory Johnson, were arrested and convicted in Dallas, Texas, for violating a state law against desecration of the national flag.

Johnson said that his act of flag burning was a public expression of opposition to federal government policies of President Ronald Reagan's administration. It was "symbolic speech" protected by the 1st and 14th amendments against repression by the state of Texas. Not so, responded the Texas Supreme Court, which upheld Johnson's conviction. The case went on appeal to the U.S. Supreme Court, which reversed the Texas court's decision and declared the Texas law against flag burning to be an unconstitutional violation of a person's right to free speech. The Court's decision in *Texas v. Johnson* (1989) was very controversial. Public opinion polls showed that more than 80 percent of Americans opposed the Court's decision in the *Johnson* case and wanted a constitutional amendment or a federal law to override it.

In response to the public outrage, Congress passed the Flag Protection Act of 1989, which specified penalties of one year in jail and a $1,000 fine for desecration of the American flag. This federal law was declared unconstitutional in 1990 in *United States* v. *Eichman, Blalock, and Tyler*.

of articles based on information in the Pentagon Papers. A short time later, Ellsberg also provided materials from the Pentagon Papers to the *Washington Post,* and articles based on these documents began to appear in that paper, too.

The federal government objected to the publication in daily newspapers of information it classified as top secret and brought legal action against the *New York Times* and the *Washington Post* to stop them, and other newspapers, from publishing articles about the Pentagon Papers. Representatives of the *New York Times* said the federal government's attempt to stop publication was an example of prior restraint—when the government restricts a publisher in advance from publishing certain information—and a violation of freedom of the press guaranteed in the 1st Amendment. The federal government argued that publication of this information would put soldiers in danger and give assistance during wartime to enemies of the United States. Ruling in the case of *New York Times Company* v. *United States,* the Supreme Court rejected the federal government's arguments for prior restraint and concluded that the government had failed to show that publication of this information would cause enough damage to national security to outweigh the value of free expression of information. Justice Hugo Black delivered the opinion of the Court.

Now, for the first time in the 182 years since the founding of the Republic, the federal courts are asked to hold that the First Amendment does not mean what it says, but rather means that the Government can halt the publication of current news of vital importance to the people of this country. . . .

In the First Amendment the Founding Fathers gave the free press the protection it must have to fulfill its essential role in our democracy. The press was to serve the governed, not the governors. The Government's power to censor the press was abolished so that the press would remain forever free to censure the Government. The press was protected so that it could bare the secrets of government and inform the people. Only a free and unrestrained press can effectively expose deception in government. And paramount among the responsibilities of a free press is the duty to prevent any part of the government from deceiving the people and sending them off to distant lands to die of foreign fevers and foreign shot and shell. In my view, far from deserving condemnation for their courageous reporting, the *New York Times,*

We can imagine . . . no better way to counter a flag-burner's message than by saluting the flag that he burns. . . . We do not consecrate the flag by punishing its desecration, for in doing so we dilute the freedom that this cherished emblem represents.

—Justice William J. Brennan, *Texas* v. *Johnson* (1989)

The government is simply recognizing as a fact the profound regard for the American flag created by [United States] history when it enacts statutes prohibiting the disrespectful burning of the flag.

—Chief Justice William Rehnquist, in dissent, *Texas* v. *Johnson* (1989) the *Washington Post,* and other newspapers should be commended for serving the purpose that the Founding Fathers saw so clearly. In revealing the workings of government that led to the Vietnam war, the newspapers nobly did precisely that which the Founders hoped and trusted they would do. . . .

The word "security" is a broad, vague generality whose contours should not be invoked to abrogate the fundamental law embodied in the First Amendment. The guarding of military and diplomatic secrets at the expense of informed representative government provides no real security for our Republic. The Framers of the First Amendment, fully aware of both the need to defend a new nation and the abuses of the English and Colonial governments, sought to give this new society strength and security by providing that freedom of speech, press, religion, and assembly should not be abridged.

The Court decided unanimously in *Reno* v. *American Civil Liberties Union* (1997) to strike down a federal statute that limited freedom of expression over the Internet in order to protect children from exposure to pornography. Justice Stevens's opinion declared the Communications Decency Act to be an unconstitutional violation of 1st Amendment freedoms of speech and press.

At issue is the constitutionality of two statutory provisions enacted to protect minors from "indecent" and "patently offensive" communications on the Internet. Notwithstanding the legitimacy and importance of the congressional goal of protecting children from harmful materials, we agree with the three-judge District Court that the statute abridges "the freedom of speech" protected by the First Amendment. . . .

In this Court, though not in the District Court, the Government asserts that—in addition to its interest in protecting children—its "[e]qually significant" interest in fostering the growth of the Internet provides an independent basis for upholding the constitutionality of the CDA. The Government apparently assumes that the unregulated availability of "indecent" and "patently offensive" material on the Internet is driving countless citizens away from the medium because of the risk of exposing themselves or their children to harmful material.

We find this argument singularly unpersuasive. The dramatic expansion of this new marketplace of ideas contradicts the factual basis of this contention. The record demonstrates that the growth of the Internet has been and continues to be phenomenal. As a matter of constitutional tradition, in the absence of evidence to the contrary, we presume that governmental regulation of the content of speech is more likely to interfere with the free exchange of ideas than to encourage it. The interest in encouraging freedom of expression in a democratic society outweighs any theoretical but unproven benefit of censorship.

For the foregoing reasons, the judgment of the district court is affirmed.

JUSTICE O'CONNOR, with whom THE CHIEF JUSTICE joins, concurring in the judgment in part and dissenting in part.

I write separately to explain why I view the Communications Decency Act of 1996 (CDA) as little more than an attempt by Congress to create "adult zones" on the Internet. Our precedent indicates that the creation of such zones can be constitutionally sound. Despite the soundness of its purpose, however, portions of the CDA are unconstitutional because they stray from the blueprint our prior cases have developed for constructing a "zoning" law that passes constitutional muster. . . .

Our cases make clear that a "zoning" law is valid only if adults are still able to obtain the regulated speech. If they cannot, the law does more than simply keep children away from speech they have no right to obtain—it interferes with the rights of adults to obtain constitutionally protected speech and effectively "reduce[s] the adult population . . . to reading only what is fit for children." *Butler* v. *Michigan* (1957). The First Amendment does not tolerate such interference. . . .

Thus, the constitutionality of the CDA as a zoning law hinges on the extent to which it substantially interferes with the First Amendment rights of adults. Because the rights of adults are infringed only by the "display" provision and by the "indecency transmission" and "specific person" provisions as applied to communications involving more than one adult, I would invalidate the CDA only to that extent. Insofar as the "indecency transmission" and "specific person" provisions prohibit the use of indecent speech in communications between an adult and one or more minors, however, they can and should be sustained. The Court reaches a contrary conclusion, and from that holding I respectfully dissent.

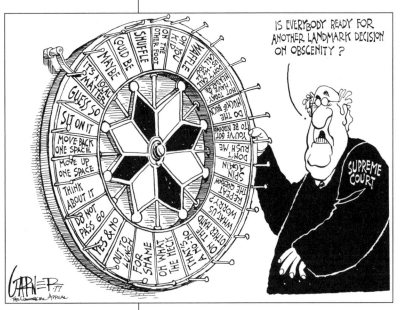

Expressions of obscenity—things that a society deems disgusting or morally unhealthy—are not necessarily protected by the 1st Amendment. However, shifting community standards have made it difficult for the Court to establish criteria by which to decide cases in which the justices must balance freedom of expression against the community's interest in preventing the communication of obscenity. This cartoon caricatures the Court's decision-making process in obscenity cases as haphazard and imprecise.

The Government and Religion

In the case of *Santa Fe Independent School District* v. *Doe* (2000), the Supreme Court ruled against recitation of a non-sectarian and nonproselytizing prayer before a public high school football game. The decision was based on the 1992 case of *Lee* v. *Weisman,* which held that an agency of government (in this case, a public school) may not force or pressure anyone to promote, participate, or otherwise be involved in a religious exercise. However, a large majority of the students had voted for particular students to say a nondenominational prayer before each football game, and they believed that the Court's decision, delivered by Justice Stevens, ignored the common good of the school community.

The first Clause in the First Amendment to the Federal Constitution provides that "Congress shall make no law respecting an establishment of religion, or prohibiting the free exercise thereof." The Fourteenth Amendment imposes those substantive limitations on the legislative power of the States and their political subdivisions. In *Lee* v. *Weisman* (1992), we held that a prayer delivered by a rabbi at a middle school graduation ceremony violated that Clause. Although this case involves student prayer at a different type of school function [a football game], our analysis is properly guided by the principles that we endorsed in Lee.

As we held in that case: "The principle that government may accommodate the free exercise of religion does not supersede the fundamental limitations imposed by the Establishment Clause. It is beyond dispute that, at a minimum, the Constitution guarantees that government may not coerce anyone to support or participate in religion or its exercise, or otherwise act in a way which establishes a [state] religion or religious faith, or tends to do so." [quoting *Lynch* v. *Donnelly* (1984)]

. . . [T]he school allows only one student, the same student for the entire season, to give the invocation. The statement or invocation, moreover, is subject to particular regulations that confine the content and topic of the student's message. . . .

Santa Fe's student election system ensures that only those messages deemed "appropriate" under the District's policy may be delivered. That is, the majoritarian process implemented by the District guarantees, by definition, that minority candidates will never prevail and that their views will be effectively silenced. . . .

[T]his student election does nothing to protect minority views but rather places the students who hold such views at the mercy of the majority. Because "fundamental rights may not be submitted to vote; they depend on the outcome of no elections," *West Virginia Bd. of Ed.* v. *Barnette* (1943), the District's elections are insufficient safeguards of diverse student speech. . . .

In *Lee*, the school district made the related argument that its policy of endorsing only "civic or nonsectarian" prayer was acceptable because it minimized the intrusion on the audience as a whole. We rejected that claim by explaining that such a majoritarian policy "does not lessen the offense or isolation to the objectors. At best it narrows their number, at worst increases their sense of isolation and affront." Similarly, while Santa Fe's majoritarian election might ensure that most of the students are represented, it does nothing to protect the minority; indeed, it likely serves to intensify their offense. . . .

The actual or perceived endorsement of the message, moreover, is established by factors beyond just the text of the policy. Once the student speaker is selected and the message composed, the invocation is then delivered to a large audience assembled as part of a regularly scheduled, school-sponsored function conducted on school property. The message is broadcast over the school's public address system, which remains subject to the control of school officials. It is fair to assume that the pregame ceremony is clothed in the traditional indicia of school sporting events, which generally include not just the team, but also cheerleaders and band members dressed in uniforms sporting the school name and mascot. The school's name is likely written in large print across the field and on banners and flags. The crowd will certainly include many who display the school colors and insignia on their school T-shirts, jackets, or hats and who may also be waving signs displaying the school name. It is in a setting such as this that "[t]he board had chosen to permit" the elected student to rise and give the "statement or invocation."

In this context the members of the listening audience must perceive the pregame message as a public expression of the views of the majority of the student body delivered with the approval of the school administration. . . .

Even if we regard every high school student's decision to attend a home football game as purely voluntary, we are nevertheless persuaded that the delivery of a pregame prayer has the improper effect of coercing those present to participate in an act of religious

Controversy about the Establishment Clause of the 1st Amendment

In 1802 Thomas Jefferson wrote about the 1st Amendment Clause prohibiting an establishment of religion. He said the clause built "a wall of separation between church and state."

In 1947, Justice Hugo L. Black agreed with Thomas Jefferson's interpretation of the establishment clause. In his opinion for the Court in Everson v. Board of Education, Black wrote, "The First Amendment has erected a wall between church and state. That wall must be kept high and impregnable. We could not approve the slightest breach."

In 1948, Justice Stanley F. Reed disagreed with Justice Black's use of Jefferson's metaphor on the separation of church and state. In *Illinois ex rel. McCollum* v. *Board of Education* Reed wrote, "A rule of law should not be drawn from a figure of speech."

In 1984, Chief Justice Warren E. Burger also criticized Jefferson's metaphor. In *Lynch* v. *Donnelly*, the chief justice wrote:

"The concept of a 'wall of separation' is . . . not a wholly accurate description of the practical aspects of the relationship that in fact exists between church and state. No significant segment of our society and no institution within it can exist in a vacuum or in total or absolute isolation from all the other parts, much less from government. . . . Nor does the Constitution require complete separation of church and state; it affirmatively mandates accommodation, not merely tolerance, of all religions, and forbids hostility toward any."

A High School Student Takes a Stand for Free Exercise of Religion

Bridget Mergens, a senior at Westside High School in Omaha, Nebraska, decided to organize a Bible club, and she wanted to use school facilities as other school clubs did. But the principal refused. He feared that a student Bible club meeting in the school would violate the 1st Amendment's establishment clause. Bridget, however, believed that her 1st Amendment rights to free speech and free exercise of religion were being denied. So she took the issue to court.

Bridget Mergens and her parents argued that the Equal Access Act, passed by Congress in 1984, gives students the right to have school approval for a Bible study group. So she brought suit against the Westside Community Schools for violating the Equal Access Act. The case reached the U.S. Supreme Court in 1990.

The Court ruled that the Equal Access Act did not violate the 1st Amendment's establishment clause and therefore was a constitutional accommodation of government and religion. Bridget Mergens won her case and received protection of her rights to free speech and to free exercise of religion. Furthermore, the outcome of her case had an impact on public schools and their policies throughout the United States.

worship. . . . The constitutional command will not permit the District "to exact religious conformity from a student as the price" of joining her classmates at a varsity football game. . . .

The Religion Clauses of the First Amendment prevent the government from making any law respecting the establishment of religion or prohibiting the free exercise thereof. By no means do these commands impose a prohibition on all religious activity in our public schools. Indeed, the common purpose of the Religion Clauses "is to secure religious liberty." *Engel* v. *Vitale* (1962) Thus, nothing in the Constitution as interpreted by this Court prohibits any public school student from voluntarily praying at any time before, during, or after the schoolday. But the religious liberty protected by the Constitution is abridged when the State affirmatively sponsors the particular religious practice of prayer.

Chief Justice William Rehnquist, in his dissent, was joined by Antonin Scalia and Clarence Thomas. They argued that the majority of students at Santa Fe High School were wrongly denied their 1st Amendment rights to free speech and free exercise of religion. The split decision in this case reflects the divided public opinion of Americans about the meaning and uses of the 1st Amendment's establishment clause.

The Court distorts existing precedent to conclude that the school district's student-message program is invalid on its face under the Establishment Clause. But even more disturbing than its holding is the tone of the Court's opinion; it bristles with hostility to all things religious in public life. Neither the holding nor the tone of the opinion is faithful to the meaning of the Establishment Clause, when it is recalled that George Washington himself, at the request of the very Congress which passed the Bill of Rights, proclaimed a day of "public thanksgiving and prayer, to be observed by acknowledging with grateful hearts the many and signal favors of Almighty God."

We do not learn until late in the Court's opinion that respondents in this case challenged the district's student-message program at football games before it had been put into practice. As the Court explained in *United States* v. *Salerno* (1987), the fact that a policy might "operate unconstitutionally under some conceivable set of circumstances is insufficient to render it wholly invalid." . . .

Although the Court apparently believes that solemnizing football games is an illegitimate purpose, the voters in the school district seem to disagree. Nothing in the Establishment Clause prevents them from making this choice.

In 1990, the Supreme Court decided in *Westside Community Board of Education* v. *Mergens* that the Equal Access Act—which requires public schools to provide religious groups with equal access to school facilities for after-hours meetings—is a constitutional accommodation of government to free exercise of religion. However, the issue was raised again in 2001 in *Good News Club* v. *Milford Central School*. In this case, public school officials barred a religious group, the Good News Club, from after-school use of facilities on equal terms with nonreligious organizations.

The club was an organization for children, ages 6 to 12, who met weekly to sing Christmas songs, study the Bible, and pray. The Court was asked to determine if the public school officials violated the free speech and free exercise of religion rights of the students in the Good News Club, and if the denial of access was permissible under the 1st Amendment's prohibition of a governmental establishment of religion. The Supreme Court decided, in an opinion delivered by Justice Clarence Thomas, in favor of the Good News Club, thereby supporting free exercise of religion and free speech.

Students of Anoka High School in Minnesota participate in a voluntary prayer session. They belong to the Teens for Christ organization, a freely formed extracurricular student group, which is not funded by the public school. Thus, the students are exercising their 1st Amendment right to freedom of religion but the school has not violated the 1st Amendment prohibition of an establishment of religion.

This case presents two questions. The first question is whether Milford Central School violated the free speech rights of the Good News Club when it excluded the Club from meeting after hours at the school. The second question is whether any such violation is justified by Milford's concern that permitting the Club's activities would violate the Establishment Clause. We conclude that Milford's restriction violates the Club's free speech rights and that no Establishment Clause concern justifies that violation. . . .

The standards that we apply to determine whether a State has unconstitutionally excluded a private speaker from use of a public forum depend on the nature of the forum. . . . If the forum is a traditional or open public forum, the State's restrictions on speech are subject to stricter scrutiny than

are restrictions in a limited public forum. . . . [W]e simply will assume that Milford operates a limited public forum.

When the State establishes a limited public forum, the State is not required to and does not allow persons to engage in every type of speech. The State may be justified "in reserving [its forum] for certain groups or for the discussion of certain topics." *Rosenberger* v. *Rector and Visitors of Univ. of Va.* (1995). . . . The State's power to restrict speech, however, is not without limits. The restriction must not discriminate against speech on the basis of viewpoint, . . . and the restriction must be "reasonable in light of the purpose served by the forum," *Cornelius* v. *NAACP Legal Defense & Ed. Fund, Inc.* (1985). . . .

[W]e first address whether the exclusion constituted viewpoint discrimination. We are guided in our analysis by two of our prior opinions, *Lamb's Chapel* [1993] and *Rosenberger* [1995]. In *Lamb's Chapel,* we held that a school district violated the Free Speech Clause of the First Amendment when it excluded a private group from presenting films at the school based solely on the films' discussions of family values from a religious perspective. Likewise, in *Rosenberger,* we held that a university's refusal to fund a student publication because the publication addressed issues from a religious perspective violated the Free Speech Clause. Concluding that Milford's exclusion of the Good News Club based on its religious nature is indistinguishable from the exclusions in these cases, we hold that the exclusion constitutes viewpoint discrimination. Because the restriction is viewpoint discriminatory, we need not decide whether it is unreasonable in light of the purposes served by the forum.

Just as there is no question that teaching morals and character development to children is a permissible purpose under Milford's policy, it is clear that the Club teaches morals and character development to children. For example, no one disputes that the Club instructs children to overcome feelings of jealousy, to treat others well . . . and to be obedient, even if it does so in a nonsecular way. Nonetheless, because Milford found the Club's activities to be religious in nature—"the equivalent of religious instruction itself," . . .—it excluded the Club from use of its facilities.

. . .[W]e find it quite clear that Milford engaged in viewpoint discrimination when it excluded the Club from the afterschool forum. . . .

[T]he Club's meetings were held after school hours, not sponsored by the school, and open to any student who obtained parental consent, not just to Club members. . . . Milford made its forum available to other organizations. . . . Thus, Milford's reliance on the Establishment Clause is unavailing.

. . . According to Milford, children will perceive that the school is endorsing the Club and will feel coercive pressure to participate, because the Club's activities take place on school grounds, even though they occur during nonschool hours. This argument is unpersuasive. . . .

When Milford denied the Good News Club access to the school's limited public forum on the ground that the Club was religious in nature, it discriminated against the Club because of its religious viewpoint in violation of the Free Speech Clause of the First Amendment. Because Milford has not raised a valid Establishment Clause claim, we do not address the question whether such a claim could excuse Milford's viewpoint discrimination.

Dissenting opinions by justices John Paul Stevens and David Souter reflected the continuing controversy about the meaning and application of the establishment clause to the lives of Americans.

JUSTICE STEVENS, dissenting.

The Milford Central School has invited the public to use its facilities for educational and recreational purposes, but not for "religious purposes." Speech for "religious purposes" may reasonably be understood to encompass three different categories. First, there is religious speech that is simply speech about a particular topic from a religious point of view. . . . Second, there is religious speech that amounts to worship, or its equivalent. . . . Third, there is an intermediate category that is aimed principally at proselytizing or inculcating belief in a particular religious faith.

. . . The novel question that this case presents concerns the constitutionality of a public school's attempt to limit the scope of a public forum it has created. More specifically, the question is whether a school can, consistently with the First Amendment, create a limited public forum that admits the first type of religious speech without allowing the other two.

Distinguishing speech from a religious viewpoint, on the one hand, from religious proselytizing, on the other, is comparable to distinguishing meetings to discuss political issues from meetings whose principal purpose is to recruit new members to join a political organization. If a school decides to authorize after school discussions of current events in its classrooms, it may not exclude people from expressing their views simply because it dislikes their

Wasn't it the best minds of your country . . . who wrote your famous Declaration of Independence, your Bill of Human Rights, and your Constitution? Those great documents inspire us despite the fact that they are over 200 years old. They inspire us to be citizens.

—Vaclav Havel, president of Czechoslovakia, address to the U.S. Congress, February 21, 1990

What do we mean when we say that first of all we seek liberty? I often wonder whether we do not rest our hopes too much upon constitutions, upon laws, and upon courts. These are false hopes; believe me, these are false hopes. Liberty lies in the hearts of men and women; when it dies there, no constitution, no law, no court can save it; no constitution, no law, no court can even do much to help it. While it lies there it needs no constitution, no law, no court to save it. And what is this liberty which must lie in the hearts of men and women? It is not the ruthless, the unbridled will; it is not freedom to do as one likes. This is the denial of liberty, and leads straight to its overthrow. A society in which men recognize no check upon their freedom soon becomes a society where freedom is the possession of only a savage few—as we have learned to our sorrow.

—Judge Learned Hand, "I Am an American Day" speech, New York City, May 21, 1944

particular political opinions. But must it therefore allow organized political groups—for example, the Democratic Party, the Libertarian Party, or the Ku Klux Klan—to hold meetings, the principal purpose of which is not to discuss the current-events topic from their own unique point of view but rather to recruit others to join their respective groups? I think not. Such recruiting meetings may introduce divisiveness and tend to separate young children into cliques that undermine the school's educational mission. . . .

School officials may reasonably believe that evangelical meetings designed to convert children to a particular religious faith pose the same risk. And, just as a school may allow meetings to discuss current events from a political perspective without also allowing organized political recruitment, so too can a school allow discussion of topics such as moral development from a religious (or nonreligious) perspective without thereby opening its forum to religious proselytizing or worship. . . .

The line between the various categories of religious speech may be difficult to draw, but I think that the distinctions are valid, and that a school, particularly an elementary school, must be permitted to draw them.

This case is undoubtedly close. Nonetheless, regardless of whether the Good News Club's activities amount to "worship," it does seem clear, based on the facts in the record, that the school district correctly classified those activities as falling within the third category of religious speech and therefore beyond the scope of the school's limited public forum. In short, I am persuaded that the school district could (and did) permissibly exclude from its limited public forum proselytizing religious speech that does not rise to the level of actual worship.

An American Heritage

In 1991, Warren E. Burger issued a proclamation to recognize the Bill of Rights during its 200th year. The former chief justice of the United States, who served on the Supreme Court from 1969 to 1986, had retired from the Supreme Court to become chairman of the Commission on the Bicentennial of the United States Constitution. In this role, he oversaw and coordinated programs to commemorate and celebrate the world's oldest Constitution still in use by a nation.

Burger's proclamation reminds Americans of the fundamental importance of rights in their political and civic

heritage. It points the way to a future in which guarantees for the rights of the people might unfailingly prevail. The primary purpose of a free government today is the same as it was on July 4, 1776, when our founders declared, "That to secure these Rights, Governments are instituted among Men, deriving their just Powers from the Consent of the Governed."

AMERICA HAS ALWAYS BEEN ABOUT RIGHTS. We were the first people in history to found a nation on the bases of individual rights—a nation governed by "we the people." We have learned, not just by studying the "old parchments," but by living out their promise. While many nations are based upon a common religion or ethnic heritage, or upon natural geographic frontiers, Americans have made individual rights the foundation of our national identity.

We the people provided for a government instituted to provide order with liberty. Our Declaration of Independence offered the promise of such a government; the men who endured great hardships and suffering from Lexington to Valley Forge and Yorktown were not thinking about the details of a new national government or separation of powers, but they were fighting for the freedoms embodied in the ringing phrases of the Declaration of 1776. The Constitution and the Bill of Rights began to fulfill these promises by providing for a new system of government which the people controlled.

For those who sought our shores from many countries and cultures, America has remained the great land of opportunity with no aristocracy except for the aristocracy of achievement. Even our failures have been measured by the rights to which we aspire. Throughout our history, we have not always been successful in balancing the interests of the minority with the wishes of the majority. The promises of the new nation were not immediately extended to native Americans who were here first, or to African-Americans brought here against their will. But the struggle to right the wrongs has continued, and as Martin Luther King exhorted us, America has risen up "to live out the true meaning of its creed."

Americans have always believed, in the words of Henry Steele Commager, "that nothing in all history . . . ever succeeded like America." As it stands today, our Constitution and the Bill of Rights express the fundamental ideal of liberty, justice, and equality which have shaped the American experience, and have also made us a beacon to other peoples seeking a better life.

This commemorative stamp was issued on July 1, 1966, by the U.S. Post Office to recognize the 175th anniversary of the Bill of Rights, which was ratified in 1791.

Timeline

1215

King John of England signs the Magna Carta, which recognizes certain rights for his barons that become precedents for the development of English legal rights.

1606

First Virginia Charter, granted to the London Company of Virginia, sets the terms for founding the English colony of Virginia in North America.

1641

The General Court of the Massachusetts Bay colony enacts The Body of Liberties, the first bill of rights in the American colonies.

1689

The Parliament of England asserts its supremacy over the monarchy by enacting the English Bill of Rights.

1776

The 13 British colonies of North America issue the Declaration of Independence to proclaim their formation of the United States of America. Virginia is a leader among American states to draft a Constitution and a Declaration of Rights, which serves as a model for the American Bill of Rights in 1791.

1780

The people of Massachusetts draft and ratify a state Constitution and Declaration of Rights.

1783

The United States of America achieves recognition of independence in the Treaty of Paris, which concludes the Revolutionary War.

1787

A Constitutional Convention meets in Philadelphia and drafts a Constitution for the United States of America, but it does not include a Bill of Rights.

1788

The 1787 Constitution is ratified by the states.

1789

The First Federal Congress meets and proposes Amendments, a Bill of Rights, for the U.S. Constitution.

1791

The first 10 Amendments of the Constitution, a Bill of Rights, are ratified by the states.

1798

The governing Federalist Party passes a Sedition Act that strictly limits free speech and press rights.

1801

After winning the national elections of 1800, President Thomas Jefferson and a majority of Republicans in Congress prohibit renewal of the Sedition Act.

1833

Chief Justice John Marshall's opinion for the U.S. Supreme Court, in *Barron* v. *Baltimore*, decides that the Bill of Rights had been enacted to limit only the federal government, not the state governments.

1848

In New York State, the women's rights movement has its organized beginnings at the Seneca Falls Convention.

1857

In *Dred Scott* v. *Sandford,* the U.S. Supreme Court categorically denies a black person the rights of citizenship.

1863

In his Gettysburg Address, President Abraham Lincoln commemorates the bravery of U.S. soldiers in the Civil War and calls for a postwar renewal of the nation's founding ideals of equal rights to liberty for all Americans.

1865

Ratification of the 13th Amendment of the Constitution, which abolishes slavery.

1868

Ratification of the 14th Amendment of the Constitution, which is designed to protect the rights of former slaves and prohibit states from denying basic rights to anyone.

1870

Ratification of the 15th Amendment of the Constitution, which prohibits the federal and state governments from denying a person's right to vote because of "race, color, or previous condition of servitude."

1920

Ratification of the 19th Amendment, which prohibits the federal and state governments from denying to women the right to vote.

1925

In *Gitlow* v. *New York,* the U.S. Supreme Court recognizes that 1st Amendment Freedoms can be applied against the states by absorption or "incorporation" under the due process clause of the 14th Amendment.

1931

The Supreme Court uses the "incorporation doctrine" asserted in *Gitlow* v. *New York* to apply against state governments the 1st Amendment right to free speech (*Stromberg* v. *California*) and free press (*Near* v. *Minnesota*).

1937

The Supreme Court, in *Palko* v. *Connecticut,* pronounces the "fundamental rights" standard by which to decide selectively on provisions of the Bill of Rights that may be incorporated by the 14th Amendment's due process clause and used to restrict state governments.

1938

The Supreme Court, in the *Carolene Products* case, pronounces the "preferred freedoms" doctrine to guide its decisions on incorporation of 1st Amendment rights in cases involving discrimination against individuals of particular racial or ethnic minority groups.

1961–69

Supreme Court decisions in several cases bring about incorporation of most provisions of the Bill of Rights under the due process clause of the 14th Amendment.

1991

Americans celebrate the bicentennial, or 200th anniversary, of their Bill of Rights.

1997

In *Reno* v. *American Civil Liberties Union,* the Supreme Court responds for the first time to an issue about 1st Amendment rights to freedom of expression via the Internet and strikes down as unconstitutional the Communication Decency Act.

2002

In *Zelman* v. *Simmons-Harris,* the Supreme Court rules for the first time that the government may provide financial aid to parents who chose to send their children to a religious private school.

Further Reading

Abraham, Henry J., and Barbara A. Perry. *Freedom and the Court: Civil Rights and Liberties in the United States.* New York: Oxford University Press, 1998.

Alderman, Ellen, and Caroline Kennedy. *In Our Defense: The Bill of Rights in Action.* New York: William Morrow, 1991.

Alderman, Ellen, and Caroline Kennedy. *The Right to Privacy.* New York: Knopf, 1995.

Amar, Akhil Reed. *The Bill of Rights: Creation and Reconstruction.* New Haven: Yale University Press, 1998.

Amar, Akhil Reed, and Alan Hirsch. *For the People: What the Constitution Really Says about Your Rights.* New York: Free Press, 1998.

Barnett, Randy E., ed. *The Rights Retained by the People: The History and Meaning of the Ninth Amendment.* Fairfax, Va.: George Mason University Press, 1989.

Bickford, Charlene Bangs, and Kenneth R. Bowling. *Birth of the Nation: The First Federal Congress, 1789–1791.* Madison, Wisc.: Madison House, 1989.

Biskupic, Joan, and Elder Witt. *The Supreme Court and Individual Rights.* Washington, D.C.: Congressional Quarterly, 1997.

Bodenhamer, David. *Fair Trial: Rights of the Accused in American History.* New York: Oxford University Press, 1992.

Bodenhamer, David J., and James W. Ely, Jr., eds. *The Bill of Rights in Modern America after 200 Years.* Bloomington: Indiana University Press, 1993.

Cogan, Neil H., ed. *The Complete Bill of Rights: The Drafts, Debates, Sources, and Origins.* New York: Oxford University Press, 1997.

Conley, Patrick T., and John P. Kaminski, eds. *The Bill of Rights and the States: The Colonial and Revolutionary Origins of American Liberties.* Madison, Wisc.: Madison House, 1992.

Curry, Thomas J. *The First Freedoms: Church and State in America to the Passage of the First Amendment.* New York: Oxford University Press, 1986.

Dinan, John J. *Keeping the People's Liberties: Legislators, Citizens, and Judges as Guardians of Rights.* Lawrence: University Press of Kansas, 1998.

Ellis, Joseph J. *What Did the Declaration Declare?* Boston: Bedford, 1999.

Fleming, Thomas. *Liberty! The American Revolution.* New York: Viking, 1997.

Glaser, Ira. *Visions of Liberty: The Bill of Rights for All Americans.* New York: Arcade, 1991.

Hall, Kermit L. ed. *By and For the People: Constitutional Rights in American History.* Arlington Heights, Ill.: Davidson, 1991.

———ed. *The Oxford Guide to United States Supreme Court Decisions.* New York: Oxford University Press, 2001.

Hentoff, Nat. *Living the Bill of Rights: How to Be an Authentic American.* Berkeley: University of California Press, 1999.

Howard, A. E. Dick. *The Road from Runnymede: Magna Carta and Constitutionalism in America.* Charlottesville: University Press of Virginia, 1998.

Irons, Peter. *The Courage of Their Convictions: Sixteen Americans Who Fought Their Way to the Supreme Court.* New York: Free Press, 1988.

———. *Justice at War: The Story of the Japanese American Internment Cases.* Berkeley: University of California Press, 1983.

Levy, Leonard W. *Emergence of a Free Press.* New York: Oxford University Press, 1985.

———. *The Establishment Clause: Religion and the First Amendment.* New York: Macmillan, 1986.

———. *Origins of the Bill of Rights.* New Haven: Yale University Press, 1999.

Lloyd, Gordon, and Margaret Lloyd, eds. *The Essential Bill of Rights: Original Arguments and Fundamental Documents.* Lanham, Md.: University Press of America, 1998.

Maier, Pauline. *American Scripture: Making the Declaration of Independence.* New York: Knopf, 1997.

Meltzer, Milton. *The Bill of Rights: How We Got It and What It Means.* New York: Crowell, 1990.

Monk, Linda. *The Bill of Rights: A User's Guide.* Alexandria, Va.: Close Up Foundation, 1995.

Nardo, Don. *The Bill of Rights.* San Diego: Greenhaven, 1998.

Nieman, Donald G. *Promises to Keep: African-Americans and the Constitutional Order.* New York: Oxford University Press, 1991.

Patrick, John J. *The Supreme Court of the United States: A Student Companion.* 2nd ed. New York: Oxford University Press, 2001.

Patrick, John J., and Gerald P. Long. *Constitutional Debates on Freedom of Religion.* Westport, Conn.: Greenwood, 1999.

Rabban, David M. *Free Speech in Its Forgotten Years.* Cambridge, England: Cambridge University Press, 1997.

Rakove, Jack N. *Declaring Rights: A Brief History with Documents.* Boston: Bedford, 1998.

Rauch, Jonathon. *Kindly Inquisitors: The New Attacks on Free Thought.* Chicago: University of Chicago Press, 1993.

Schwartz, Bernard. *The Great Rights of Mankind: A History of the American Bill of Rights.* Madison, Wisc.: Madison House, 1992.

Smith, Duane E., et al. *We the People: The Citizen and the Constitution.* Calabasas, Calif.: Center for Civic Education, 1998.

Veit, Helen E., Kenneth R. Bowling, and Charlene Bangs Bickford, eds. *Creating the Bill of Rights: The Documentary Records from the First Federal Congress.* Baltimore: Johns Hopkins University Press, 1991.

Walker, Samuel. *The Rights Revolution: Rights and Community in Modern America.* New York: Oxford University Press, 1998.

Wheeler, Marjorie Spruill, ed. *One Woman, One Vote: Rediscovering the Woman Suffrage Movement.* Troutdale, Ore.: New Sage, 1995.

Text Credits

Main Text

p.22: A. E. Dick Howard, ed., *Magna Carta: Text and Commentary* (Charlottesville: University Press of Virginia, 1964), 34, 38, 43, 45, 49, 52.

pp. 23–24: Bernard Schwartz, *The Roots of the Bill of Rights*, vol. 1 (New York: Chelsea House, 1980), 54–61.

pp. 24–25: Schwartz, ed., *The Roots of the Bill of Rights*, 19–21.

pp. 26–27: Donald S. Lutz, ed., *Colonial Origins of the American Constitution: A Documentary History* (Indianapolis: Liberty Fund, 1998), 71–79.

pp. 28–30: Schwartz, ed., *The Roots of the Bill of Rights*, 41–43.

pp. 30–31: John Locke, *Two Treatises of Government*, Peter Laslett, ed. (Cambridge, U.K.: Cambridge University Press, 1988), 268, 330–32, 350, 400–1, 415.

pp. 32–33: Lutz, ed., *Colonial Origins of the American Constitution: A Documentary History*, 291–296.

pp. 42–43: L. K. Wroth and H. B. Zobel, eds., *The Legal Papers of John Adams*, vol. 2 (Cambridge, Mass.: Harvard University Press, 1965), 123–130.

pp. 43–44: Samuel Eliot Morison, ed., *Sources and Documents Illustrating the American Revolution, 1764–1788, and the Formation of the Federal Constitution* (New York: Oxford University Press, 1965), 32–34.

p. 45: Morison, ed., *Sources and Documents Illustrating the American Revolution*, 53.

pp. 45–47: Morison, ed., *Sources and Documents Illustrating the American Revolution*, 118–121.

p. 47: Worthington C. Ford, ed., *Journal of the Continental Congress*, vol. 5 (Washington: U.S. Government Printing Office, 1904), 425.

pp. 48–50: *United States at Large*, vol. 1 (Washington: U.S. Government Printing Office, 1845), 1–4.

pp. 50–51: *Collections, Massachusetts Historical Society*, 5th series, vol. 3 (Boston, 1877), 436–37.

pp. 59–61: Morison, ed., *Sources and Documents Illustrating the American Revolution*, 149–53.

pp. 61–62: *The Journal of the Convention for Framing a Constitution of Government for the State of Massachusetts-Bay* (Boston: Massachusetts Historical Society, 1832), 222–23.

p. 62: Morison, ed., *Sources and Documents Illustrating the American Revolution*, 215–16.

p. 63: Morison, ed., *Sources and Documents Illustrating the American Revolution*, 292.

pp. 64–65: Bernard Bailyn, ed., *The Debate on the Constitution*, vol. 1 (New York: Library of America, 1993), 345–49.

pp. 65–66: Morison, ed., *Sources and Documents Illustrating the American Revolution*, 297–98, 302, 304.

pp. 67–68: Gaillard Hunt and James Brown Scott, eds., *The Debates in the Federal Convention of 1787, Reported by James Madison* (New York: Oxford University Press, 1920), 271–75.

pp. 68–71: National Archives and Records Administration, *The Bill of Rights: Milestone Documents in the National Archives* (Washington, D.C.: National Archives Trust Fund Board, 1986), 5–6.

pp. 80–81: Nicholas N. Kittrie and Eldon D. Wedlock, Jr., eds., *The Tree of Liberty: A Documentary History of Rebellion and Political Crime in America* (Baltimore: Johns Hopkins University Press, 1986), p. 88.

pp. 81–82: Kermit L. Hall, William M. Wiecek, and Paul Finkelman, eds., *American Legal History: Cases and Materials* (New York: Oxford University Press, 1991), 101.

p. 82: H. A. Washington, ed., *The Writings of Thomas Jefferson*, vol. 8 (Washington, D.C.: Taylor and Maury, 1854), 1–6.

pp. 82–83: *Marbury v. Madison*, 1 Cranch 137 (1803).

pp. 83–84: *Barron v. Baltimore*, 7 Pet. 243 (1833).

pp. 85–86: Edward Beecher, *Narratives of Riots at Alton* (New York, 1838), 121–41.

pp. 87–91: Henry Steele Commager, ed., *Documents of American History* (Englewood Cliffs, N.J.: Prentice Hall, 1973), 315–17.

pp. 92–95: *Dred Scott v. Sandford*, 19 How. (60 U.S.) 393 (1857).

pp. 102–3: Andrew Delbanco, ed., *The Portable Abraham Lincoln* (New York: Viking, 1992), 205.

pp. 104–5: Morison, ed., *Sources and Documents Illustrating the American Revolution*, 365–66.

pp. 105–6: *Slaughterhouse Cases*, 16 Wall. (83 U.S.) 36 (1873).

pp. 107–8: *Bradwell v. Illinois*, 16 Wall. 130 (1873).

pp. 108–9: Lewis Copeland and Laurence W. Lamm, eds., *The World's Great Speeches* (Mineola, N.Y.: Dover, 1973), 321–22.

p. 110: *Minor v. Happersett*, 21 Wall. 162 (1875).

pp. 110–12: *Civil Rights Cases*, 109 U.S. 3 (1883).

p. 113: Frederick Douglass, *Three Addresses on the Relations Subsisting Between the White and Colored People of the United States* (Washington, D.C., 1886), 3–23.

pp. 113–15: *Plessy v. Ferguson*, 163 U.S. 537 (1896).

pp. 123–24: *Schenck v. United States*, 249 U.S. 47 (1919).

pp. 124–25: *Abrams v. United States*, 250 U.S. 616 (1919).

pp. 125–26: *Gitlow v. New York*, 268 U.S. 652 (1925).

pp. 126–27: *Stromberg v. California*, 283 U.S. 359 (1931).

pp. 128–31: *Near v. Minnesota*, 283 U.S. 697 (1931).

pp. 131–33: *DeJonge v. Oregon*, 229 U.S. 353 (1937).

p. 133–34: *United States v. Carolene Products*, 304 (U.S.) 144 (1938).

pp. 134–36: *West Virginia Board of Education v. Barnette*, 319 U.S. 624 (1943).

pp. 136–37: *Hirabayashi v. United States*, 320 U.S. 81 (1943).

pp. 138–39: *Korematsu v. United States*, 323 U.S. 214 (1944).

pp. 148–49: *Palko v. Connecticut*, 302 U.S. 319 (1937).

pp. 150–51: *Adamson v. California*, 332 U.S. 46 (1947).

pp. 152–53: *Everson v. Board of Education of Ewing Township*, 330 U.S. 1 (1947).

pp. 154–55: *Brown v. Board of Education*, 347 U.S. 483 (1954).

p. 155: 78 U.S. Statutes at Large, Public Law 88-352, 241.

pp. 156–57: *Mapp v. Ohio*, 367 U.S. 643 (1961).

pp. 157–58: *Malloy v. Hogan*, 378 U.S. 1 (1964).

p. 159: *Duncan v. Louisiana*, 391 U.S. 145 (1968).

pp. 177–80: *Griswold v. Connecticut*, 381 U.S. 479 (1965).

pp. 180–82: *Roe v. Wade*, 410 U.S. 113 (1973).

pp. 183–84: *New York Times Company v. United States*, 403 U.S. 713 (1971).

pp. 184–85: *Janet Reno, Attorney General of the United States v. American Civil Liberties Union*, 533 U.S. 833 (1997).

pp. 186–89: *Santa Fe Independent School District v. Doe*, 530 U.S. 290 (2000).

pp. 189–92: *Good News Club v. Milford Central School*, 533 U.S. 98 (2001).

p. 193: Herbert M. Atherton and J. Jackson Barlow, eds., *The Bill of Rights and Beyond, 1791–1991* (Washington, D.C.: Commission on the Bicentennial of the United States Constitution, 1991), p. v.

Sidebars

p. 18: Algernon Sidney, *Discourses Concerning Government* (Indianapolis: Liberty Fund, 1990), xxxvi.

p. 20: Winston S. Churchill, *The Birth of Britain, 1958* (New York: Dodd, Mead 1958), 256.

p. 26: Bernard Schwartz, ed., *The Roots of the Bill of Rights* (New York: Chelsea House, 1960), 97.

p. 32: David L. Jacobson, ed., *The English Libertarian Heritage* (San Francisco: Fox & Wilkes, 1994), 38–39.

p. 42: Alpheus Thomas Mason and Gordon E. Baker, eds., *Free Government in the Making* (New York: Oxford University Press, 1985), 93.

p. 48: Thomas Paine, *Common Sense* (Middlesex, U.K.: Penguin, 1976), 100.

p. 49: Charles Francis Adams, ed., *Familiar Letters of John Adams and His Wife Abigail Adams, During the Revolution* (Boston: Houghton Mifflin, 1876), 149.

p. 58: Samuel Eliot Morison, *Sources and Documents Illustrating the American Revolution, 1764–1788, and the Formation of the Federal Constitution* (New York: Oxford University Press, 1965), 163–164.

p. 61: Gordon Lloyd and Margie Lloyd, *The Essential Bill of Rights: Original Arguments and Fundamental Documents* (Lanham, Md.: University Press of America, 1998), 219.

p. 66: Alexander Hamilton, *Independent Journal* (October 27, 1787).

p. 67: James Madison, *Daily Advertiser* (November 22, 1787).

p. 68: Merrill D. Peterson, ed., *The Portable Thomas Jefferson* (New York: Penguin, 1987), 430.

p. 69: James Madison, *Annals of Congress*, vol. 1, 1789, 457.

p. 79: William L. Andrews, ed., *Frederick Douglass: The Oxford Reader* (New York: Oxford University Press, 1996), 118–19.

p. 82: James Madison, *National Gazette*, (March 27, 1792).

p. 85: Joseph Story, *A Familiar Exposition of the Constitution of the United States*, (Regnery Gateway, Chicago: 1986), 313.

p. 87: David Brion Davis and Steven Mintz, eds., *The Boisterous Sea of Liberty: A Documentary History of America from Discovery through the Civil War* (New York: Oxford University Press, 1998), 401.

p. 89: Davis and Mintz, eds., *The Boisterous Sea of Liberty*, 403.

p. 93: Robert W. Johannsen, ed., *The Lincoln-Douglass Debates of 1858* (New York: Oxford University Press, 1965), 14.

p. 95: Johannsen, ed., *The Lincoln-Douglass Debates of 1858*, 304.

p. 102: *U.S. Statutes at Large*, vol. 7, 1268–69.

p. 103: Davis and Mintz, eds., *The Boisterous Sea of Liberty*, 524.

p. 104: Kermit Hall, ed., *Major Problems in American Constitutional History*, vol. 1 (Lexington, Mass.: D.C. Heath, 1992), 538.

p. 105: Hall, ed., *Major Problems in American Constitutional History*, 539

p. 108: Susan B. Anthony, *Arena*, (May 1897).

p. 125: U.S. Supreme Court, *Bradenburg v. Ohio*, 395 U.S. 144 (1969).

p. 127: Hugo L. Black, *Bridges v. California*, 314 U.S. 252 (1941).

p. 129: Thurgood Marshall, *Police Department v. Mosley*, 408 U.S. 92 (1972).

p. 148: William H. Moody, *Twining v. New Jersey*, 211 U.S. 78 (1908).

p. 149: Earl Warren, *Hannah v. Larche*, 363 U.S. 420 (1960).

p. 151: Hugo L. Black, *Engel v. Vitale*, 370 U.S. 421 (1962).

p. 152: William J. Brennan, *Abington School District v. Schempp*, 174 U.S. 203 (1963).

p. 156: Robert H. Jackson, *Terminello v. Chicago*, 337 U.S. 1 (1949).

p. 163 (top): William J. Brennan, *Texas v. Johnson*, 491 U.S. 397 (1989).

P. 163 (bottom): William Rehnquist, *Texas v. Johnson*, 491 U.S. 397 (1989).

p. 176: William O. Douglas, *Public Utilities Commission v. Pollack*, 1952.

p. 177: William O. Douglas, *Osborn v. United States*, 385 U.S. 323 (1966).

p. 178: Harry A. Blackmun, *Thournburgh v. American College of Obstetricians & Gynecologists*, 476 U.S. 747 (1986).

p. 179: Robert H. Jackson, *American Communications Association v. Doubs*, 339 U.S. 382 (1980).

p. 187: Warren E. Burger, *Lynch v. Donnelly*, 465 U.S. 668 (1984).

p. 191: Herbert M. Atherton and J. Jackson Barlow, eds., *The Bill of Rights and Beyond* (Washington, DC: Commission on the Bicentennial of the United States Constitution, 1991), 85.

p. 192: Irving Dilliard, ed., *The Spirit of Liberty: Papers and Addresses of Learned Hand* (New York: Knopf, 1960), 190–191.

Picture Credits

© Bob Adelman: 157; American Civil Liberties Union Archive. Public Policy Papers Division. Department of Rare Books and Special Collections. Princeton University Library: 128, (Box 1146, F.14) 181; Courtesy American Antiquarian Society: 83; American Philosophical Society: 12, 49; By permission of Chuck Asay and Creators Syndicate, Inc.: 166b; Courtesy of the Association for the Preservation of Virginia Antiquities: 17; Paul Avrich collection: 119; Jerry Barnett, courtesy *Indianapolis News*: 169b; © Bettmann/CORBIS: 172, 178; The British Library—Cotton Ms. Claudius 1D 70, fo.116: 21; British Public Records Office: 23; California History Section, California State Library: 164; Chicago Historical Society (ICHi-09585; Mosher, Photographer): 107; Matt Davies, courtesy *Journal News*: Jake Fuller, courtesy *Gainesville Sun*: Bill Garner, the *Commercial Appeal*: 185; 165b; Courtesy of Special Collections Department, Harvard Law School Library: 27; Joe Heller, courtesy *Green Bay Press-Gazette*: 169t; The Historic New Orleans Collection, accession no. 1951.41.21: 106; David Hitch, courtesy *Worcester Telegram-Gazette*: 165t;

House of Lords Record Office: 25; The Library Company of Philadelphia: 34; Library of Congress: 2, (LC-DIG-ppmsc-02748) 10, 13, (LC-USZ62-59655) 19, (LC-USZ62-121998) 24, (LC-USZ62-82852) 31, (LC-USZ62-83689) 32, (LC-USZ62-102561) 36, (LC-USZ62-45556) 41, 43, (LC-USZ62-45528) 45, (LC-USZ62-45328) 46, (LC-USZ62-22023) 51, (LC-USZ62-3992) 54, (LC-USZ62-9486) 55, (LC-USZ62-46659) 59, (LC-MSS-31021-102) 69, (LC-USZ62-1551) 80, (LC-USZ62-34049) 86, (LC-USZ62-32499) 98, (LC-MSS-30189-76) 101, 102, (LC-USZ62-128619) 111, (LC-USZC2-866) 116, (LC-MSS-78637-1) 122, (LC-USZ62-90457) 123, (LC-USZ62-29375) 124, (LC-digital: fsa 8d25792) 135, (LC-USZ62-44093) 137, (LC-A35-4M-04) 138, 143, (LC-USZ62-112130) 144, (LC-UZW3-015304-C) 152, (LC-USZ62-116927) 154, (LC-Pos. 6-U.S., no. 1391 (C Size)) 170, 179; Louisiana State Museum: 114; Courtesy of Massachusetts Archive: 14; Massachusetts Historical Society: 62; Jim Miller, courtesy of the *Valley Citizen*: 168; Minnesota Historical Society: 130; National Archives and

Records Administration, Washington, D.C.: (NAF 169) 66, (NAF 1a-b) 70, 77, (NWCTB-267-PI139E21-3230(JUDGMENT)) 93; By courtesy of the National Portrait Gallery, London: 28; National Portrait Gallery, Smithsonian Institution: 52, (Gift of Mrs. Katie Louchheim) 67, (Mr. and Mrs. Paul Mellon) 84; National Postal Museum: 193; © Collection of The New-York Historical Society (neg. 21342): 72; New York Public Library: 39, 57, 94; The Oregonian: 131; Patrick Rice, courtesy *Jupiter Courier*: 167t; Rochester Public Library, Local History Division: 109; Franklin Delano Roosevelt Presidential Library: 140; Smithsonian Institution: (S64-75) 76, (74-4829) 89; Collection of the Supreme Court of the United States: 3, 145, 150; Wayne Stayskal, courtesy *Tampa Tribune*: 166t; Tamiment Library, New York University: 126; Courtesy *Tampa Tribune*: 167b; Time Pix: cover, 174, 176, 189; Gary Tong: 29; University of Rochester Library, Rare Books & Special Collections: 88, 91; Virginia Museum of Fine Arts, Richmond. Gift of K. E. Bruce. Photo: Ron Jennings. © Virginia Museum of Fine Arts: 65.

Index

Illustrations and captions are indicated by page numbers in **bold**.

Abington School District v. *Schempp*, 152, 175
Abolitionists, 79, 84–**89**, 92–93
Abortion, **174**, **178**–82
Abrams v. *United States*, 117–18, 124–25
Accused, rights of, 29, 54, 60, 65, 71, 79, 142, 145–51, 155–59, 172
Adams, Abigail, 44, 49
Adams, Ansel, 138
Adams, John, 36, 40, 42–44, 48–49, 53–**54**, 61–**62**, 74–76, **84**
Adams, Samuel, 44, **62**
Adamson v. *California*, 142–43, 149–50
African Americans, **13**, 50–**51**, **59**, **88**, 92, 97–106, 110–15, 143–**45**, 153–55
Agostini v. *Felton*, 175
Alien Acts, 75, 81
Alton Observer, 79, 84–**86**
Amendments, constitutional. *See specific amendments*
American Civil Liberties Union, **131**, **170**–71, 174, 184–86
American Communications Association v. *Douds*, 179
American Revolution, 18, 32–51, **168**
Anoka High School, **189**
Anthony, Susan B., 92, 99, 108–**9**
Anti-Federalists, 56
Armies, standing, 29, 61, 65
Arms, right to bear, 29, 54, 70, 147, **160**–**69**
Articles of Confederation, 11, 54–55, 64, 94
Assembly, freedom of, 12, 47, 69, 120, 131–33, 141, 143, 171

Barron v. *Baltimore*, 77, 83, 103, 118, 150
Beecher, Edward, 85–86
Benton v. *Maryland*, 150

Bill of Rights: antecedents of, 15–33, 53–54; debates about, 56–58, 63–71; nationalization of, 141–59; ratification of, 11, 56–58, 65. *See also specific amendments*
Bills of attainder, 65
Bingham, John, 98, 103–4
Birth control, 173–74, 177–80
Black, Hugo L., 127, 138–39, 142–43, **150**, 149–53, 179–80, 183–84
Blackmun, Harry A., 178–82
Boston, Mass., 38–**39**
Bowdoin, James, **62**
Boyd v. *United States*, 178
Bradley, Joseph, 100, 110–11
Bradwell, Myra, 106–8
Bradwell v. *Illinois*, 106–8
Brady Gun Act, **164**
Brandeis, Louis, **144**, 173
Brandenburg v. *Ohio*, 118, 125
Brennan, William J., 152, 156–58, 178, 183
Brown, Henry, 113–14
Brown v. *Board of Education*, 144, 153–55
Burger, Warren E., 180, 192–93
Bush, George W., 172
Butler, Pierce, 127–28
Butler v. *Michigan*, 185
Buxton, C. Lee, **178**

Calvin, John, 16
Cantwell v. *Connecticut*, 121
Cardozo, Benjamin, 142, 148–50
Carolina, colonial, 22
Cartoons, political, **34**–**35**, **39**, **59**, **72**–**73**, **80**, **83**, **91**, **105**, **111**, **120**, **124**, **140**–**41**, **160**–**69**, **185**
Cato's Letters (Trenchard & Gordon), 32–33
Center for Constitutional Rights, **159**
Center for Democracy and Technology, 175
Charles I, King, 17–18, 24
Charles II, King, 18, 20

Charters, colonial, 16–18, 22–28, 32–33, 35
Checks and balances, 56–57, 64, 67
Churchill, Winston S., 20
Citizenship, U.S., 75, 91–95, 98, 104–9
Civil Rights Act, **96**–100, 110, 145, **147**, 155
Civil Rights Cases, **96**–100, 110, 115, 155
Civil rights movement, **13**, 143–45, 153–55
Civil War, 91–92, 97, 101–3
Civil War Amendments, 100, 103–15
Clark, Tom, 156
Clear Lake High School, **176**
Clinton, Bill, 174
Clymer, Hiester, **98**
Coats, Dan, 175
Coke, Edward, 17–18, **24**
Colonies, American, 15–20, 22–28, 32–51
Columbian Centinel, 76
Columbine High School, **166**
Committee of Public Safety and Inspection, 38
Common law, 17–18, **24**, 42, 48
Common Sense (Paine), 48
Communications Decency Act, 174, 184–85
Communists, 119–**20**, 126–28, 131–33
Concord, Mass., 39, 43
Congress, U.S., 47, 53–57, 62–63, 64, 68–**70**, 80
Connecticut, 18, 22
Constitution, U.S.: English roots of, 15–33; ratification of, 56–57, 65–66; writing of, **54**–57, 63–71. *See also* Bill of Rights; *specific amendments*
Constitutional Convention, 55–56, 63–**67**
Constitutions, state, 53–54, 57–**62**, 78, 84, 95
Continental Congress: First, 38, 45–47; Second, 39–40, 47–48, 54

Cooper v. *Aaron*, **144**
Cornelius v. *NAACP Legal Defense & Ed. Fund*,
  190
Criminal Anarchy Law, 118–19, 125
Criminal syndicalism laws, **128**, 131
Cromwell, Oliver, 18
Curtis, Benjamin, 91–95

Debs, Eugene V., **126**
Declaration of Independence, 40, 42,
  47–**51**, 53, 59, 87, 92, 95, 102–4, 134,
  167
Declaration of Sentiments and Resolutions,
  87–91
Declaratory Act, 38
DeJonge v. *Oregon*, 120, **131**–33
Delaware, 26
Democratic Party, 74, **98**, **167**
Dickinson, John, 43–**45**
Double jeopardy, 142, 146–50
Douglas, William O., 176–78
Douglass, Frederick, 79, **88**, 92, **101**,
  112–13
Due process, 12, 22, 25, 71, 104, 118, 123,
  125–27, 131–33, 141–42, 145–46, 148,
  155–56, 158, 177–78, 180
Duncan v. *Louisiana*, 146, 158

Edward III, King, 25
Eighth Amendment, 71, 147
Eleventh Amendment, **181**
Ellsberg, Daniel, 182–83
Emancipation Proclamation, 92, 97, 102–3
Emerson, Ralph Waldo, 39
Employment discrimination, 155
Engel v. *Vitale*, 151–52, 175, 188
England, 15–25, 28–30. *See also* Great
  Britain
Equal Access Act, 176–77, 188–89
Espionage Act, 117–18, 123–**24**, **126**

Establishment, 143, 151–53, 175–76, 180,
  186–92
Everson v. *Board of Education of Ewing Township*,
  143, 151, 180
Exclusionary rule, 145, 155–57
Ex post facto laws, 65
Expression, freedom of. *See* Press, freedom
  of the; Speech, freedom of

Federalism, 56, 128
Federalist Papers (Hamilton & Madison), **57**,
  66–67
Federalists, 56–**57**, 65–66, **72–76**, 80, **83**
Fifteenth Amendment, 97–100, 103–5
Fifth Amendment, 71, 77, 83–84, 123, 139,
  142, 145–51, 156–59, 177–78, 180
Filmer, Robert, **31**
First Amendment, 69, 79, 80, 117–34, 141,
  143, 148, 151–53, 157, 163, 171,
  174–77, 180, 182–92
Flags, U.S.: burning, 182–83; saluting,
  121–**22**, 134–**35**
Fourteenth Amendment, 64, **93**, 97–100,
  103–15, 118–22, 125–28, 131–35,
  141–45, 148–59, 162, 174, 177–82, 186
Fourth Amendment, 42, 54, 70–71, 145,
  155–58, 177–78, 180
France, 35, 74–75, **83**
Franklin, Benjamin, 48–**49**
French, Daniel Chester, 43
Freneau, Philip, 73
Fundamental rights test, 142, 148–49

Gazette of the United States, 74
Geary, John White, **98**
George III, King, 18, 40–41, **51**
Georgia, 22
Gerry, Elbridge, 63
Gettysburg Address, 101–3
Gideon v. *Wainwright*, 146

Gitlow v. *New York*, 118–19, 125
Glorious Revolution, **19**, 28–**29**, 33
Gobitis, Billy, **122**
Goldberg, Arthur, 178, 180
Good News Club v. *Milford Central School*, 177,
  189–92
Gordon, Thomas, 19, 32–33
Great Britain, 31, **34**–51, 74, **83**. *See also*
  England
Grenville, George, **34–35**
Grimké, Angelina, 87
Griswold, Estelle, 173, **178**
Griswold, Roger, 74, **80**
Griswold v. *Connecticut*, 173–74, 177–80
Gun control. See Arms, right to bear

Habeas corpus, writ of, 65
Hamilton, Alexander, 55–**57**, 66, 74
Hancock, John, 44
Hand, Learned, 192
Hannah v. *Larche*, 149
Harlan, John Marshall, 100, 111–12,
  114–15
Harrington, James, 19
Heart of Atlanta Hotel v. *United States*, 145
Henry, Patrick, 37–38
Hirabayashi v. *United States*, 123, 136–37
History of the . . . American Revolution (Warren),
  44
Holmes, Oliver Wendell, 117–**18**, 123–25
Houston, Charles Hamilton, 143–44, 155
Howard University, 144, 155
Hughes, Charles Evans, 126–28
Hume, David, 19

Illinois ex rel. McCollum v. *Board of Education*,
  180
Incorporation doctrine, 98, 105, 119–22,
  125–34, 141–43, 145–59, 162
Independence Hall, **55**

Internet, 174–75, 184–85
Internment camps, 122, 136–39
Intolerable Acts, 38

Jackson, Robert H., 134–36, 179
James II, King, 18–19, 28
Jamestown, Va., 16–17, 22
Japanese Americans, 122–23, 136–39
Jay, John, 63
Jefferson, Thomas, 37–38, 40, 48–49,
  67–68, 72–76, 81–83, 85, 104, 153, 180
Jehovah's Witnesses, 121–22, 134
Jim Crow laws, 114
John, King, 15–16, 21–22
Johnson, Gregory, 182
Judicial review, 75, 77, 79, 82
Judiciary Act, 82

Kentucky Resolution, 75–76, 81–82
King, Martin Luther, Jr., 144–45, 193
Klopfer v. *North Carolina*, 146
Korematsu v. *United States*, 123, 136–39
Ku Klux Klan, 111, 145

Lamb's Chapel, 190
Lechmere's case, 41
Lee, Richard Henry, 47, 53
Lee v. *Weisman*, 175, 186–87
Lerner, Max, 116–17
"Letters from a Farmer in Pennsylvania"
  (Dickinson), 44–45
Lexington, Mass., 39, 40, 43
Liberty Bell, 50, 109
Lincoln, Abraham, 92–93, 95, 97, 99,
  101–3
Lincoln Cathedral, 22
Little Rock, Ark., 144
Livingston, Robert, 48
Locke, John, 18–20, 30–32, 36, 48, 59, 82,
  104

Louisiana, 100–101, 105, 113–15
Lovejoy, Elijah, 79, 84–86
Lynch v. *Donnelly*, 180, 186
Lyon, Matthew, 74–75, 80–81

Madison, James, 55–58, 67–69, 73–79,
  81–83, 103
Magna Carta, 14–17, 20–25, 42, 45
Maine, Henry Summer, 117
Malloy v. *Hogan*, 150, 156–58
Mapp v. *Ohio*, 145, 155–57, 178
Marbury v. *Madison*, 77, 79, 82
Marshall, John, 76–77, 82–84
Marshall, Thurgood, 129, 144, 155
Martial law, 24–25
Mary, Queen, 19, 28–29
Maryland, 22, 77
Mason, George, 56, 58, 63–65
Massachusetts, 14–18, 22, 25–28, 38–41,
  50–51, 61–62
Mayflower Compact, 16
McLaurin, G. W., 154
McLean, John, 91
McReynolds, James C., 162
Meredith, James, 145
Mergens, Bridget, 188
Military tribunals, 172
Militias, 38, 43, 61, 70, 161–63
Miller, Jack, 162
Miller, Samuel, 105–8
Minersville School District v. *Gobitis*, 121–22,
  134
Minor, Virginia, 99, 109–10
Minority rights, 85, 133–39, 143, 147, 172
Minor v. *Happersett*, 109–10
Minutemen, 38, 43
Missouri, 79, 91, 109–10
Missouri Compromise, 79, 91, 95
Mitchell v. *Helms*, 175
Monarchy, English, 15–25, 28–31, 41–42

Moody, William H., 148
Morris, Gouverneur, 63
Mott, Lucretia, 87
Murphy, Frank, 137, 139

Nast, Thomas, 111
National American Woman Suffrage
  Association, 108
National Association for the Advancement
  of Colored People, 143–44, 155, 190
National Firearms Act, 162
National Gazette, 73–74, 82
National Rifle Association, 160–61,
  164–66
National security, 117–18, 122–24,
  136–39, 171–72, 179, 182–84
National Woman Suffrage Association, 92,
  108
Naturalization Law, 75
Natural rights, 19–22, 30–33, 36, 42, 48,
  50–51, 54, 58–59, 61, 67, 73, 104, 108
Near, Jay, 120, 127, 130
Near v. *Minnesota*, 120, 122, 127–31
New Hampshire, 18, 94
New Jersey, 26, 94
New York, 18, 51, 94, 135
New York Times v. *United States*, 172, 182–84
Nineteenth Amendment, 108
Ninth Amendment, 71, 177–81
North Carolina, 94
North Star, 88
Northwest Ordinance, 64

Obscenity, 174–75, 184–85
O'Connor, Sandra Day, 185
Olmstead v. *United States*, 173
Osborn v. *United States*, 177
Otis, James, 36–37, 41–42

Paine, Thomas, 48, 72–73

Palko, Frank, 142, 148
Palko v. *Connecticut*, 142, 148–50
Parker v. *Gladden*, 146
Parliament, British, 15–19, 21–22, 24–25, 28–**30**, **34**–38, 42–46
Paterson, Thomas, 80–81
Peabody Conservatory of Music, **143**
Penn, William, 20, **32**–33
Pennsylvania, 18, 20, 26, 32–33, 54, 58
Pentagon Papers, **172**, 182–84
Petition, freedom of, 69, 141, 143, 171
Petition of Right, 15, 18, 24–25, 42
Philadelphia, Pa., 39, 45–**46**, 50, **55**, 73
Pilgrims, 16
Planned Parenthood, 173, **178**
Pledge of Allegiance, 121–**22**, **135**
Plessy v. *Ferguson* 100–101, 113–15, 144
Pointer v. *Gladden*, 146
Police Department v. *Mosley*, 129
Prayers, 151–52, 175–**76**, 186–89
Preferred freedoms, 120–21, 123, 133, 141
Press, freedom of the, 60, 65, 69, 74, 79–80, 82, 84–86, 119–20, 124–32, 141, 143, 171–72, 182–86
Presser v. *Illinois*, 162
Preston, Levi, 40
Prior restraint, 120, 127–31, 183
Privacy, right to, 173–74, 177–82
Probable cause, **157**
Property, right to, 19–22, 30–33, 45, 54, 77, 82
Public Utilities Commission v. *Pollak*, 176
Puritans, 20

Quakers, 20, **32**
Quilici v. *Village of Morton Grove*, 162

Randolph, Peyton, **46**
Reagan, Ronald, 182
Reed, Stanley F., 180
Rehnquist, William, 176, 182–83, 188–89

Religion, freedom of, 12, 16, 20, 26, 32–33, 58, 61, 66, 69, 121–23, 133–34, 141, 171, 175–76, 188–92. *See also* Establishment
Relocation centers, 136–39
Reno v. *ACLU*, 184–86
Republican Party, 74–**76**, **83**, **98**
Rhode Island, 18, 20, 22, 26
Rights of the British Colonies Asserted and Proved. (Otis), 36, 42
Robbins, Tim, **174**
Roe v. *Wade*, **174**, 179–82
Roosevelt, Theodore, 124
Rosenberger v. *Rector & Visitors of Univ. of Va.*, 190

Sanford, Edward Terry, 125–26
San Francisco, Calif., **168–69**
Santa Fe Independent School District v. *Doe*, 175, 186–89
Saradon, Susan, **174**
Saturday Press, 120, 127, **130**
Scalia, Antonin, 188
Schenck v. *United States*, 117, 123–24
School: prayer in, 121–22, 134–35, 151–52, 175–77, 186–92; religious, 151–53, 175–76, 180; segregation in, 114, **144–45**, 153–55; voucher programs, 176
Scott, Dred, 79, 91–95
Scott v. *Sandford*, 79, 91–95
Searches and seizures, unwarranted, 36–38, 41–43, 60, 70–71, 145, 155–58
Second Amendment, 54, 70, 147, **160–69**
Sedition, 75–**78**, 80–82, 117–18, **128**, 171
Segregation, 100–101, 113–15, 144–45, 153–55
Selective incorporation, 142, 146, 149–51
Seneca Falls convention, 87–91
"Separate but equal," 101, 113–15, 144, 153
Separation of powers, 47, 53–**54**, 56–57, 60, 67

Seventh Amendment, 71, 147
Sheehan, Neil, 183
Sherman, Roger, 48, 63–**64**, 68–69
Sidney, Algernon, 18–19, 30, 32, 36
Sixteenth Amendment, **181**
Sixth Amendment, 54, 71, 145–46, 157–59
Slaughterhouse Cases, 98–99, 105–7
Slavery, 12, 40, 50–51, 54, 58–**59**, 64, 79, 91–95, 97–98, 104
Smith v. *Allwright*, 144
Soldiers, quartering of, 24–25, 70, 147
Sons of Liberty, 44
Souter, David, 191
Speech, freedom of, 12, 29, 32, 54, 69, 74–75, **78**–82, 84–86, 117–28, 132–34, 141, 143, 148, 171, 174, 182–92
Stamp Act, **34**–35, 37–38, **41**, 43–44, 48
Stanton, Elizabeth Cady, 87, 89, 92
Stevens, John Paul, 184–88, 191–92
Stevens, Thaddeus, 105
Stewart, Potter, 179–80
Stone, Harlan F., 133, 136
Story, Joseph, 85
Stromberg v. *California*, 119–20, 122, 126–27
Sweatt v. *Painter*, 144

Taney, Roger B., 79, 91–**93**
Taxation, 22, 24–25, 29, 35–37, **41**, 43–46
Teens for Christ, **189**
Tenth Amendment, 71
Terrorism, 172
Texas v. *Johnson*, 182–83
Third Amendment, 70, 147, 180
Thirteenth Amendment, 64, **93**, 97–98, 100–101, 103–4, **106**, 111–12, **181**
Thomas, Clarence, 188–91
Thornburgh v. *American College of Obstetricians & Gynecologists*, 178
Thoughts on Government (Adams), 53
Trenchard, John, 19, 32–33
Twenty-sixth Amendment, **181**

Twining v. *New Jersey*, 148
Two Treatises of Government (Locke), 19,
  30–32, 48, 82

United States v. *Carolene Products*, 120, 133–34
United States v. *Eichman, Blalock, and Tyler,*
  182
United States v. *Miller,* 162
United States v. *Salerno,* 188
United States v. *Schwimmer,* **118**, 124
University of Mississippi, **145**
University of Oklahoma, **154**

Vietnam War, 171, 182–84
Virginia, 16–**17**, 22–24, 37, 38, 54, 56,
  58–61, 68, 75–76, **78**, 81
Voting rights, **30,** 87, 92, **98**–100, 104–**5,**
  108–10, 144

Wade, Henry, 174
Waite, Morrisson R., 110
Wallace v. *Jaffreye,* 175
Warren, Earl, **145,** 149, 153–55, 158
Warren, James, 44
Warren, Joseph, 44
Warren, Mercy Otis, 44
Washington, George, **52–53,** 55, 57,
  62–63, **66, 72**–74, **168,** 188
Washington Post, **172,** 182–84
Weeks v. *United States,* 145
West, Richard, 15
Westside Community Board of Education v.
  Mergens, 177, 188–89
West Virginia Board of Education v. *Barnette,*
  121–22, 134–36, 187
White, Byron, 158–59, 182
White League, **111**

William III, King, 28–**29**
Williams, Roger, 26
Wolf v. *Colorado,* 155, 157
Women's rights, 49, 87–92, 99, 106–10.
  See also Voting rights
World Anti-Slavery Convention, 87
World Trade Center, 172
World War I, 117, 123–**24, 126, 128**
World War II, 122–23, 134–39
Writs of assistance, 36–38, 41–43

Zelman v. *Simmons-Harris,* 176

Acknowledgments

I thank my editors at Oxford University Press, Nancy Toff, Karen Fein, and Brigit Dermott, for their assistance in developing this book. I am especially grateful to Nancy Toff for inviting me to do this project and helping me to improve early drafts of this work.

I greatly appreciate the ongoing encouragement and support given to me by my wife, Patricia, and my daughters, Rebecca and Barbara, and my granddaughters, Rachel and Abigail. So I dedicate this book to them.

About the Author

John J. Patrick is a professor of education, director of the Social Studies Development Center, and director of the ERIC Clearing House for Social Studies/Social Science Education at Indiana University, Bloomington. He is the author or co-author of many publications in history, civic education, and government. Among his recent publications are *Founding the Republic* (1995), *Constituional Debates on Freedom of Religion: A Documentary History* (1999), *The Oxford Guide to the U.S. Government* (2001), and *The Supreme Court of the United States: A Student Companion* (2001).

Since 1991 Professor Patrick has served as a consultant, lecturer, and seminar leader on topics pertaining to civic education for democracy to several post-communist countries in Central and Eastern Europe. He has served in a similar capacity to local school districts, state departments of education, and university centers in the United States. Since 1995, he has directed the International Civic Education Project with the Republic of Latvia, and since 1998 he has also directed this project with Lithuania and Estonia. In 1999 Patrick was awarded a U.S. Speaker and Specialist grant by USIA to serve as a visiting professor at the University of Sarajevo in Bosnia-Herzegovina.

Professor Patrick was a member of the planning committee for the 1994 and 2001 National Assessments of Educational Progress (NAEP) in U.S. history and in 1998 he was a member of the planning committee for the NAEP in civics. In 2002 he received Indiana University's John W. Ryan award for distinguished achievement in international programs.